Chairman Mao's Children

In the 1960s and 1970s, around 17 million Chinese youths were mobilized or forced by the state to migrate to rural villages and China's frontiers. Bin Xu tells the story of how this "sent-down" generation have come to terms with their difficult past. Exploring representations of memory including personal life stories, literature, museum exhibits, and acts of commemoration, he argues that these representations are defined by a struggle to reconcile worthiness with the political upheavals of the Mao years. These memories, however, are used by the state to construct an official narrative that weaves this generation's experiences into an upbeat story of the "China dream." This marginalizes those still suffering and obscures voices of self-reflection on their moral-political responsibility for their actions. Xu provides careful analysis of this generation of "Chairman Mao's children," caught between the political and the personal, past and present, nostalgia and regret, and pride and trauma.

Bin Xu is Associate Professor at Emory University, and the author of *The Politics of Compassion: The Sichuan Earthquake and Civic Engagement in China* (2017), which won the 2018 Mary Douglas Best Book Prize for Cultural Sociology and Honorable Mention for Asia from the American Sociological Association.

Chairman Mao's Children

Generation and the Politics of Memory in China

Bin Xu

Emory University

CAMBRIDGE
UNIVERSITY PRESS

University Printing House, Cambridge CB2 8BS, United Kingdom

One Liberty Plaza, 20th Floor, New York, NY 10006, USA

477 Williamstown Road, Port Melbourne, VIC 3207, Australia

314–321, 3rd Floor, Plot 3, Splendor Forum, Jasola District Centre, New Delhi – 110025, India

79 Anson Road, #06–04/06, Singapore 079906

Cambridge University Press is part of the University of Cambridge.

It furthers the University's mission by disseminating knowledge in the pursuit of education, learning, and research at the highest international levels of excellence.

www.cambridge.org
Information on this title: www.cambridge.org/9781108844253
DOI: 10.1017/9781108934114

First published 2021

A catalogue record for this publication is available from the British Library.

ISBN 978-1-108-84425-3 Hardback

For my mother, Zhang Siwei, a former zhiqing who went down to Subei.

Contents

Figures

Tables

Acknowledgments

Without the help and support of many institutions and people, this book would not have been possible. Institutional support is essential for this decade-long, multi-stage project. I particularly thank the International Center for Studies of Chinese Civilization at Fudan University and Professor Jin Guangyao for inviting me to reside at Fudan as a visiting scholar in Fall 2013. It was during my stay at Fudan that I officially started this project. I also thank Professors He Xuesong and Wang Hua at the East China University of Science and Technology, who provided me with an office for research interviews during my fieldwork. The American Sociological Association and the National Science Foundation awarded me a grant from the "Fund for the Advancement of the Discipline," which facilitated the initial stage of the research. In the academic year of 2017–2018, I was fortunate enough to receive the "Luce/ACLS China Studies Postdoctoral Fellowship" (now the "Luce/ACLS China Studies Early Career Fellowship") from the American Council on Learned Societies and the Henry Luce Foundation, which allowed me to finish most of the book manuscript. The final stage of writing and revising was made possible by Emory University's Chronos Faculty Fellowship, which was generously provided by the Abraham J. & Phyllis Katz Foundation.

My mentors, colleagues, and friends read parts of the manuscripts and gave me valuable feedback: Weihua An, Deborah Davis, Tim Dowd, Tom DeGloma, Gary Alan Fine, Wendy Griswold, Denise Ho, Frank Lechner, Christina Simko, Pengfei Zhao, among others. I also thank a number of scholars for inviting me to give talks on this project at their institutions: Wendy Griswold at Northwestern, Deborah Davis at Yale, Ruth Rogaski at Vanderbilt, Mary Gallagher at Michigan, Ka Zeng at University of Arkansas, Ruijie Peng at UT-Austin, Ya-Wen Lei at Harvard, Denise Ho at Yale, Dylan Riley at Berkeley, and Jack Zinda at Cornell. I also gave multiple talks on this project at my home institution, Emory, as part of the China's colloquia series. I am grateful to the audiences who attended my various talks for their valuable feedback and comments. Special thanks go to my friend Dr. Dong Guoli and his student Ren Jiping, who collaborated with me in the pilot stage of this project. Lucy Rhymer, Michael Watson, and Emily Sharp at Cambridge University Press professionally and patiently navigated me through the reviewing and publishing process. Without their help, this book would have been simply impossible. My wife, Yao Li, carefully transcribed many of the interviews and did meticulous fact checking. Last but not least, I am indebted to those people whom I met in the fieldwork and who shared with me their life stories, views, feelings, and memories. Some interviews lasted as long as six hours; some activities lasted a few days. My biggest regret is that this book – or any book – does not have enough space for their intriguing stories.

Introduction

My coming of age and growth started in the seven years I spent in
Northern Shaanxi. Two things I learned were of utmost importance.
First, I learned to be down-to-earth, seek truth from facts, and know the
lives of the masses. ... Second, I learned to become confident. As the
saying goes, a knife is sharpened on a stone, and a person is built in
difficulties. Suffering and hardship can strengthen one's willpower. The
tough life of the seven years of going "Up to the Mountains and
Down to the Villages" built my character.   Xi Jinping (President of
                                China), *I Am a Son of the Yellow Soil* (Xi 2012)

The send-down program caused a lot of damages to us. It changed
my whole life. If I had had the opportunity to go to college, I would
have been better off. How would I be like this if I hadn't gone down
to the countryside? It was said that people could make an effort and
change their lives. But in reality, not everyone could get what they
wanted. ... If I couldn't pass the exam, that would be my problem.
But they didn't allow you to apply! That ruined my career. Now the
zhiqing experience still haunts my life. I hate Lao Mao [the Old Mao,
Mao Zedong]!   Gu Huifang (a retiree in Shanghai)[1]

The words above come from two people who seem to have nothing in
common: one, the president of China, the other, a struggling Shanghai
retiree. But they belong to the same generation. Both were born in the
early 1950s. Both were among the 17 million urban youths who were
mobilized or forced by the state to settle in villages, semi-military corps,
and state farms. They were participants of the "Up to the Mountains and
Down to the Villages Campaign" (*shangshan xiaxiang yundong,* or the
"send-down program," for short), a large-scale forcible migration program in the 1960s and 1970s (Bernstein 1977; Ding 2009; Liu 2009;
Bonnin 2013). They were called the "educated youths" (*zhishiqingnian,*
or "zhiqing" for short, as used in this book) or the "sent-down youths."
They spent most of their adolescence and early adulthood years – seven
years for Xi and eight for Gu – in the countryside. The program was

---

[1] Pseudonyms are used in this book to protect research subjects' identities.

Figure I.1 *Xi Jinping's Seven Years as a Zhiqing* (the two piles in the middle) displayed in a bookstore in China. Photo taken by the author in 2018

designed to achieve several practical and political goals, including alleviating the grave unemployment problem in major cities, sending the youth to the countryside to be "re-educated" by the poor but supposedly more revolutionary peasants, demobilizing the Red Guards who caused a mess in the Cultural Revolution, and so on. The program, however, failed to achieve most of these goals and ended in the late 1970s and early 1980s, when most zhiqing returned to their hometowns.

Nevertheless, Xi and Gu tell dramatically different life stories. Xi Jinping's zhiqing experience has been made into *Xi Jinping's Seven Years as a Zhiqing* (2017), a 452-page book based on interviews with his peer zhiqing, local peasants, and various other people (Figure I.1). The book was published by the Central Party School Press and is clearly endorsed by the Party and Xi himself. It contains a narrative of resilience, perseverance, and success: Xi Jinping voluntarily went down to Shaanxi to escape the horrifying chaos in Beijing, especially his family's ordeal due to the purge of his father, Xi Zhongxun, a high-ranking official. In his sent-down village, Xi performed so superbly that, despite his father's political problems, the local people recommended him to become a "worker-peasant-soldier college student" (*gongnongbing xueyuan*) at Tsinghua University.[2]

In this narrative, Xi's past difficulties in the countryside are "assets" that contribute to his tremendously successful career and help perfect his "man-of-the-people" leadership style. He thanks the zhiqing years for building his tough character in dire circumstances and forming close relationships with ordinary people. A prudent observer, however, may notice some political subtleties in this official story. It quietly responds to a widely held opinion that Xi is the epitome of the "princelings" – children of high-ranking officials – whose careers or businesses benefit from their family backgrounds. The official narrative also keeps silent on evaluations of the send-down program. It is a story of a resilient, self-made leader with a common touch, against an ambiguous historical background.

Gu Huifang's life story is the opposite of Xi's. In Heilongjiang, where she was sent down, Gu performed well in work and political activities but was not given opportunities for returning, especially for a recommendation for college, mostly due to her problematic *chushen* (family class background). To seek comfort in despair, Gu dated and later married a local zhiqing and moved to Harbin, the capital of Heilongjiang, in 1977. Two years later, when many other zhiqing were allowed to leave, her marriage and *hukou* (household registration) as an urban resident in Harbin, however, disqualified her from returning to Shanghai.

In 1990, Gu and her husband left Harbin for Shanghai to take care of their son, who returned to Shanghai for high school according to a new policy. Thirty years after she left Shanghai, Gu had finally returned, but only to find misery for a family with no hukou, no high-school education, no money, no jobs. They had to stay first in a makeshift house, then an attic. They did odd jobs, for example, they worked as unlicensed street vendors, but they often had to dodge the street administrators who tried to arrest them. Adding to her misery, her husband died of cancer. When Gu was interviewed in 2007, she lived off her pensions from her Harbin *danwei* (work unit), 570 yuan a month, while Shanghai's average wage was more than 1,000.

---

[2] College admission in the Cultural Revolution mostly, if not entirely, relied on recommendations from the local authorities.

No one has made Gu's story into a book, not even an online post. Nor did Gu herself want to talk about it. She still met regularly with her zhiqing friends, but they rarely recounted their sent-down experience, which would only bring pain and regret. For the same reason, Gu also did not watch TV series or read novels about zhiqing. Her youth remained a liability rather than an "asset." In contrast to Xi's political ambiguity, Gu expressed unambiguous resentment toward the send-down program, the political class system of chushen, and capricious policies under the leadership of "Lao Mao," an expression that would have sent her to prison in the years when she was growing up.

Same generation, different memories.

The state media now focus on people like Xi rather than people like Gu, especially after the 18th Party Congress in November 2012, when Xi became China's highest leader. A search in the the newspaper database at the China National Knowledge Infrastructure (CNKI) shows that from the 18th Congress to October 2018, there have been 428 reports with "zhiqing" as their subjects and with "Xi Jinping" in their full texts, compared to only two from the 17th and 18th Congresses. Major foreign media also speculated about how Xi's zhiqing experience had shaped his mindset and whether his coming-of-age experience under Mao contributed to the recent revival of a Mao-style personality cult of Xi (Buckley 2017). Despite their different political stances, both the state and Western media share an almost exclusive focus on President Xi.

One man's apotheosis, however, overshadows the memories of 17 million.

What rarely makes it to the mainstream media is a boom of memory of the zhiqing generation. Since the end of the send-down program, the former zhiqing have been telling their life stories in numerous ways – in novels, TV series, memoirs, exhibits, and museums. This memory boom has lasted for more than four decades and never subsided. Since the new millennium, it has culminated in frequent self-organized commemorative activities, from as small as a reunion dinner party of tens of people to as big as a week-long trip with hundreds of participants. A Beijing scholar, a former zhiqing, jokes, "If you see a big crowd of elderlies singing old songs and dancing like crazy in a restaurant, I am 80% to 90% sure that they are zhiqing!" Hardly any other group or generation in the history of the People's Republic of China (PRC) has generated so much memory, in so many forms, for so long.

On the one hand, this memory boom is unsurprising. Remembering youth is a universal psychological phenomenon. We all yearn for our youthful passions, energetic bodies, simple lives, and romantic love. "The symbolic prominence of the adolescent years for later nostalgic experience persists despite the recoil many feel from their own adolescence" (Davis 1979, 62–63). Even if our adult lives do not treat us well, remembering is a way to figure out where our present convoluted mess started.

Remembering individuals' youth is often intertwined with remembering a generation's collective past. People in approximately the same age cohort who experience the same series of historical happenings constitute a "generation" (Mannheim 1952 [1923]). Members of the same generation tend to name the events they collectively experience in their adolescence and early adulthood as the most important ones (Schuman and Scott 1989). Thus, it is natural for the zhiqing generation to remember their collective experience of the send-down program, which happened in their formative years and altered the courses of their lives.

On the other hand, "memory," in the sociological sense, is a complex social, political, and symbolic process rather than merely a cognitive function of individual psychology (Olick, Vinitzky-Seroussi, and Levy 2011). The zhiqing memory boom is more than natural nostalgia. It is something to be explained instead of something to be taken for granted.

Like other beautiful things in society, nostalgia is unevenly distributed. While zhiqing like President Xi tell stories of "suffering to success," numerous zhiqing like Gu believe suffering begets suffering. Historian Michel Bonnin uses "lost generation" to describe the zhiqing's difficulties re-joining normal social life upon their return to cities (Bonnin 2013). Sociologists have shown that the send-down program has caused lower education levels, delayed life stages, led to less satisfying jobs, and other negative impacts as long-term, accumulative effects of their long stay in the countryside (Qian and Hodson 2011). Many in this generation believe that their suffering in the present was caused by the state's forcible migration forty years ago as well as by the policies that are designed to deal with the aftermath of the program. Even today, some zhiqing are still protesting to demand that the government solve problems with their pensions and healthcare, which they believe resulted from the program.

Another source of the difficulties in remembering this generation's past is the overlapping of the send-down program, especially its "big-wave" period (1968–1980) (Liu 2009), with the Cultural Revolution (1966–1976). Many in this generation were former "Red Guards," but others were not: they were too young, unqualified, or simply uninterested. Despite these variations and their reluctance, the Red Guards label has been firmly attached to the zhiqing. In today's China, the popular stereotype of the Red Guards portrays a generation of poorly educated fanatics associated with foolish and violent activities such as beating teachers, humiliating classmates, singing Mao songs, doing "loyalty dances," and so forth. Now, as some claim, the aging Red Guards have become angry old men with no sense of decorum and the "square-dancing mamas," who recklessly play loud, annoying music to accompany their collective dancing in public spaces. The zhiqing, therefore, carefully, sometimes unconsciously, choose their identity label. Most of them now are eager to talk about their youthful passions, recount the hardship they experienced in the countryside, and call themselves "zhiqing," making the "Red Guard," their unsavory political face, slip into oblivion.

Red Guards or not, the zhiqing were "Chairman Mao's children" (Chan 1985), the first generation who grew up after 1949 and carried the hope of the Party to be successors of Communism. Chairman Mao told them that they were like the "morning sun" at eight or nine o'clock, "full of vigour and vitality." Therefore, "the world is yours!" (Mao 1966, 288). They were indoctrinated into a Manichean, bellicose political culture. Forty-something years later, they are still struggling to reconcile "Mao's legacies" in their minds and dispositions with the rapidly changing society and politics in post-Mao China.

The Chinese state has been tiptoeing around two difficult issues related to the zhiqing generation: first, how to evaluate the controversial send-down program; second, how to deal with its aftermaths. After briefly acknowledging the failure of the program in the late 1970s and early 1980s, the state became ambiguous in its official statements about the program. State leaders avoided commenting on the program. Even the carefully crafted official narrative about Xi's zhiqing experience highlights only himself but makes no explicit comments on the program. Meanwhile, the state attempts to salvage some useful political-moral values from the relics of the policy havoc, including adherence to the Communist ideal, integration of intellectuals with the peasants, patriotism, diligence, perseverance, and so on.

In short, the send-down program is uncomfortably situated in China's national memory. It is a "difficult past": "The event is swallowed, as it were, but never assimilated" (Wagner-Pacifici and Schwartz 1991, 380). It poses three types of problems for the society, the state, and the zhiqing themselves: first, the political problem of how to evaluate the controversial program against the backdrop of the Cultural Revolution and other upheavals in the Mao years; second, the social problem related to impacts of the event on the zhiqing's life course and present living conditions; and, third, the cultural problem of how the zhiqing generation remembers their youth and the event that altered their youth and subsequent lives. The three problems are intertwined, but the cultural problem – the difficult memories of this generation – is the focus of this book.

Three Goals of This Book

I intend to achieve three goals in this book, one empirical, another theoretical, and the other normative.

The empirical goal is to understand how the zhiqing generation comes to terms with their difficult personal and collective past and what can explain the variations in their memories. This topic has received only sporadic scholarly attention even if the memory of this important generation has been booming for decades. A comprehensive, in-depth study of this generation of "Chairman Mao's children" can help us understand the "red legacies" of the Mao years in today's China, not only in relics like Mao badges but also in people's mentalities and dispositions (Li and Zhang 2016).

The second goal of this book, more general and theoretical, is to contribute to our sociological understanding of memory, particularly generation and memory (Corning and Schuman 2015). Social changes in human societies can be imagined as a continuous biological and social transition from older to younger generations (Mannheim 1952 [1923]). Members of a generation remember and understand their personal pasts by locating themselves in their temporal position in history, mostly in the significant historical event that has defined their collective experience, such as a war, an economic recession, or a political incident. Such memory also varies across their different social positions in the past and present. Through examining generation and memory, we can understand the intersections between personal biography and history, an essential theme in sociology, and achieve the "sociological imagination," the ability to "understand the larger historical scene in terms of its meaning for the inner life and the external career of a variety of individuals" (Mills 1959, 5).

The third goal of this book is to use the empirical and theoretical analysis to contemplate some ethical and political issues, including social inequality and historical responsibility. At the heart of the "sociological imagination," Mills argues, is the distinction between "personal troubles of milieu" and "the public issues of social structure." For instance, a person's unemployment might be his or her personal trouble, but, if the society's unemployment rate is exceedingly high, it is also part of a public issue (Mills 1959, 10). From this perspective, the zhiqing generation's difficulties are not individuals' personal troubles but a public issue as a result of structural failures, including the state's forcible migration policy that ended as a fiasco, the rigid political class system in the Mao years that deprived many in this generation of education and job opportunities, and the post-Mao state's inability to respond to the legacies of the program.

Nevertheless, looking beyond oneself is hard; self-enlightening is rare; emancipatory thinking like the sociological imagination is politically dangerous. "Winners" in this generation, such as President Xi, attribute their successes and other people's troubles to personal effort instead of public issues. Those who once enthusiastically participated in the radical political activities in the Cultural Revolution now rarely reflect on their responsibility for their wrongdoing and fanaticism. Also, questions about "public issues" threaten the state because the sociological imagination can be easily enacted in actions that demand the state to be accountable for a generation's suffering and loss. These ethical–political issues have been topics of public debates in China for decades. But most debates are divided along pre-held stances. This book, on the contrary, will address these issues by drawing on a solid empirical and theoretical analysis rather than mere opinions. In other words, the normative message of this book is based on rather than dictates the empirical analysis.

I pursue these three interrelated goals in a decade-long (2007–2018), multi-stage, mixed-method project. In writing the book, the main product of this project, I draw on extensive data collected from 124 in-depth interviews about the zhiqing's life history and other issues, 61 ethnographic observations that lasted from several hours to a week, thousands of press reports, numerous archival materials, personal texts, and literary works (see the Appendix for technical details about data and methods). I describe, analyze, and explain memories of the zhiqing generation, in several time periods, at different levels, and in various forms, including their life stories, literature, exhibits, museums, and commemorative activities. With this mountain of data and, more importantly, my longtime, on-the-ground interactions with the zhiqing, I attempt to offer a vivid picture of their passions, struggles, and dilemmas.

In the rest of this introduction, I first provide a brief account of the history of the send-down program. Readers interested in a more thorough historical narrative can consult the important historical works to which I am greatly indebted (Bernstein 1977; Ding 2009; Liu 2009; Bonnin 2013; Honig and Zhao 2019). Then I provide a snapshot of the diverse memories of this generation, which is followed by a discussion about how I dialog with the existing literature on the memory of the Mao years and the theoretical scholarship on generation and memory. Finally, I present a theoretical framework on which my analysis relies and a preview of the chapters and arguments before I share with readers some of my methodological reflections.

"Up to the Mountains and Down to the Villages": China's Difficult Past

According to the most common definition in historical studies, the "send-down" program started in the first half of the 1960s, when the ad hoc practice of sending youths to the countryside became a long-term policy. The program reached its peak stage from 1968 to 1979.[3] About 17 million zhiqing went down from cities, and most of them returned to their hometowns in the late 1970s or early 1980s (Ding 2009; Gu 2009a; Liu 2009).[4] Their sent-down places included villages (this form of send-down was called *chadui*, meaning "being inserted into production teams"), farms, and the Production and Construction Corps (the Corps or *bingtuan*), a semi-military form of reclamation farm.

The send-down program was designed to achieve several ideological and practical goals. The main ideological goal was to "re-educate" the youths who were believed to have been contaminated by the "bour-geoisie-dominated" education system. Going to the countryside and being re-educated by poor but revolutionary peasants, as the leadership believed, could effectively eliminate the bad influences. The youths were expected to "temper" (*duanlian*, a metallurgical term used in the political vocabulary, meaning "building character") themselves in the "revolutionary crucible" through strenuous manual labor and a stoic life (Cheng 2009; Bonnin 2013, 3–18). The zhiqing were also expected to pioneer the grand plan of overcoming the three great divides (industry and agriculture, rural and urban areas, and mental and manual labor). A slogan, derived from Mao's 1955 "directive," summarized these lofty goals: "[the zhiqing] should go to the vast universe of the countryside, where they can make a huge difference!" (*guangkuo tiandi dayou zuowei*).

---

[3] This definition does not include two populations who were often referred to as "zhiqing" but did not share with the zhiqing of this inquiry the same generational experience: those who voluntarily went down in the 1950s, before the program started as a state policy; and those "returning zhiqing" (*huixiang zhiqing*), rural youths who studied in towns and cities and returned home after graduation (Liu 2009). In terms of memory, some models of the early zhiqing in the 1950s, such as Xing Yanzi and Hou Jun, were incorporated into the political propaganda used in the mobilization in the 1960s and still appear in many exhibits and narratives today. Thus, they are included in the public memory (Chapter 4). The huixiang zhiqing, however, have been marginal, if not nonexistent, in the zhiqing memory, and thus are not included in this book. Needless to say, this analytical decision based on the purpose of the book – inquiry about memory rather than history – by no means dismisses their historical importance.

[4] Some, like Gu Huifang, returned in the 1990s when they accompanied their children for school, allowed by a new policy in Shanghai and other source cities. A small percentage returned after they retired.

The ideological terms, however, cloaked the state's practical purposes. The most important practical goal was to solve the grave problem of urban youths' unemployment in the 1960s. This generation was equivalent to America's "baby boomers," born after WWII or the Chinese Civil War (1945–1949). The rigid command economy could not absorb the youths into the labor force, and colleges did not have the capacity to admit so many secondary school graduates (Bernstein 1977; Ding 2009; Liu 2009). The problem was aggravated by the turmoil in the early years of the Cultural Revolution, when schools were shut down, and the youths idled their time away in political activities or at home or on the streets.

Another practical objective was to use the zhiqing as the major labor force to develop the rural areas and the frontiers. In the frontiers, the send-down program was a continuation of the reclamation migration, which started long before the zhiqing's arrival and was intended to solve the labor shortage problem there. In Yunnan, Xinjiang, and Heilongjiang, there had been the practice of migration and settlement of outside peasants, demobilized soldiers, and the "rightists" (Ding 2009; Bin Yang 2009; Wang 2017). The reclamation also had its political purposes – for example, to send many Han Chinese to settle in the ethnic regions like Xinjiang to maintain the stability in the frontiers. In the Heilongjiang Corps, youths were occasionally used as military reserve forces for the conflict with the Soviet Union. However, many zhiqing went to villages (chadui), where there often was a surplus of labor (Bonnin 2013, 30–32). In those chadui cases, the practical goal of dispersing an unemployed urban population made more sense than meeting the labor shortage.

On December 22, 1968, *The People's Daily* published Mao's famous directive (Bonnin 2013, 4):

It is absolutely necessary for educated young people to go to the countryside to be re-educated by the poor and lower-middle peasants. Cadres and other city people should be persuaded to send their sons and daughters to the countryside when they have finished junior or senior high school, college, or university. Let's mobilize. Comrades throughout the countryside should welcome them.

Accompanying Mao's directive on the front page was a report on the urban youths in a Gansu town going to settle in villages. The title of the report subtly alluded to the urban unemployment problem: "We also have two hands and will not idle in cities!"

This amalgam of ideological and practical goals significantly shaped the zhiqing's personal experience. Some zhiqing went down with political enthusiasm, sometimes even before the program became a forcible migration plan at the end of 1968. Historical works have recorded well-known cases like that of Qu Zhe (Liu 2009, 67–76). Among my interviewees, there were some less famous but equally idealistic youths. For example, in August 1968, Mr. Zhu, together with other student activists, decided to send themselves down to Jinggangshan, a mecca of the Chinese Communist revolution.[5] The zhiqing who went to the Heilongjiang Corps also had a high level of revolutionary fervor for good reason: the Corps was at the front of China-Soviet military conflicts, and the selected zhiqing, many of whom had good chushen, believed they were fulfilling their honorary responsibility to defend and protect the frontier.

Many zhiqing and their parents, however, were reluctant. They were concerned with the poor living conditions in the countryside and uncertain career and life prospects. Those practical concerns often silently overrode ideological enthusiasm. Resistance existed, even after the program became compulsory. For example, in 1969–1971, all secondary school graduates in Shanghai were mobilized to go down, with very few exceptions, to achieve the "all red" goal (yipianhong). Even urban working-class families, probably emboldened by their red chushen, sometimes defied the government's order because, despite their straitened circumstances in Shanghai, they dreaded going to the more impoverished places (Honig and Zhao 2019, 32–38). The state used its pervasive and coercive apparatuses at the local level – schools, street administrations, and danwei – to put pressure on those reluctant zhiqing and their parents. One of the mechanisms was the "study workshop" (xuexiban), an ironically scholarly term, which in reality meant parents were forced to be on leave and subject to "thought work" – repeated interrogation and persuasion. Another mechanism, as my interviewees described, was more theatrical and even comedic. The street administration sent a small band to the resister's house to play brass instruments and drums and put up a red-paper poster on their door to "celebrate" their child's being selected as a zhiqing. The purpose was certainly not to celebrate but to put the resister to shame.

Even those who voluntarily signed up did not always do so out of a singular political fervor. For zhiqing from low-income families, going to farms or the Corps, where they could earn a wage, reduced their families' financial burden. The zhiqing from politically condemned families also desperately wanted to escape from the depressing and violent atmosphere in the first years of the Cultural Revolution. Many others, curious and adventurous, simply wanted to leave home and see the wider world.

[5] Interview with Mr. Zhu, May 30, 2017.

Thus, when the zhiqing departed, they had a mix of feelings: confusion about the unfamiliar rural life, anxiety about their future, sorrow of leaving parents, some enthusiasm, and much curiosity. Shi Zhi's well-known poem *This Is Beijing at 4:08*, written on December 20, 1968, vividly captures the mixed feeling in the farewell scene at a train station (Shi 2012, 33):

> This is Beijing at 4:08
> An ocean of waving hands
> This is Beijing at 4:08
> A grand train whistle trailing off
> …
> My heart shudders in pain; it must be
> My mother's sewing needle runs me through
> At this moment my heart transforms into a kite
> Tethered to her hands
> So tight it may snap
> I have to stick my head out the train window
> Up till now, till this very moment,
> I begin to understand what has happened
> …
> Once more I wave to Beijing
> And I want to grab her by the collar
> And shout to her
> Remember me, Mother Beijing!

Shi Zhi's poem corroborates with my interviewees' accounts. For example, when Mrs. Hu left Shanghai in 1969, she just had had surgery on her tonsils and could not swallow food. After she packed all her luggage, Hu said goodbye to her mother. Her mother was sick and had been lying in bed for two weeks but suddenly sat up, saying nothing but letting her tears trickle down her face. Afraid of losing her courage to leave, she ran down the stairs, feeling like her heart was being pressed by a huge rock and trying to fight back the tears. Yet the tears finally streamed from her eyes when her neighbor saw her leaving and said, "Good girl! I saw you grow up since you were a baby!" Later, her sorrow of departure was diluted by excitement and a sense of honor, when she got to her school, joined a crowd of her fellow zhiqing, wore a big, red "flower of honor" on her chest, and boarded a bus to the railway station.[6]

This brief exuberance, however, quickly dissipated. When her train whistle blew as it slowly moved away, a deafening cry burst out: "Goodbye, papa and mama! Goodbye, sis and bro!" Everyone on the train and on the platform wept and waved. The thunderous cry

---

[6] Interview with Mrs. Hu, November 12, 2013, and her unpublished, personal memoirs.

immediately overwhelmed the loud, heroic marching songs playing over the public announcement system. Many other zhiqing also said that the farewell at railway stations was the most memorable moment in their lives. Mr. Yao, a Shanghai zhiqing who went to Xinjiang in 1964, described that the "ground was shaken by our cries."[7] Mr. Ying, who went to Jiangxi in 1969, put an apple into his mouth to stop himself from crying loudly.[8] The imprints of this sorrow on their memory were so profound that when they described the farewell scene to me, forty-some years after the departure, many choked back and even shed tears.

What was common to most zhiqing's experience in the countryside was their hardship, including strenuous work in the field, inadequate food, and isolation from cities. Note that the zhiqing were teenagers with no labor or life skills. In some places, the zhiqing fell victim to sexual assaults, torture, and political persecution. In 1973, the situation was so dire that the state, taking an unusual step, investigated cases of abuse and rape and punished some perpetrators (Liu 2009, 186–94). The state also adjusted policies to improve the zhiqing's living conditions, to provide nonagricultural jobs such as those of factory workers and village school teachers, and to allow some of them to go to college through recommendations (Liu 2009). Source cities like Shanghai sent delegations (*weiwentuan*) to their youths' sent-down places to solve practical problems and even build economic connections between the sent-down places and Shanghai (Honig and Zhao 2019). But those adjustments failed to bring about substantive changes. Even the rare opportunities generated by the policy adjustments, such as college and urban jobs, were unequally distributed, depending on many factors other than work performance – for example, political chushen and *guanxi* (personal connections) with the local cadres.

The zhiqing's personal experiences varied greatly in different periods and locations. For example, most interviewees said that in the first year or so, labor in the fields was unbearable to them. After that, many got used to the workload and even became skilled. Others started slacking off, since they did not see the clear correlation between hard work and desirable opportunities. In terms of political restrictions, the Corps had tight control over everyday life, while in villages there was some room for individual zhiqing's own activities, such as reading books, although the room was certainly as limited as everywhere else during the Cultural Revolution. New studies and anecdotal evidence show that the zhiqing contributed to the improvement of the rural economy, agricultural

---

[7] Interview with Mr. Yao, November 4, 2014.
[8] Interview with Mr. Ying, June 10, 2007.

technology and production, healthcare, and education with their knowledge, skills, and connections with urban resources (Honig and Zhao 2015; Schmalzer 2016).

Individual zhiqing's relations with the locals and among themselves also varied. Some had warm and meaningful relations with the locals, especially when they as urbanites witnessed the poverty in grassroots China. In this sense, the official story about Xi's connections with the local peasants contains reasonable elements and resonates with many zhiqing. The unbearably long stay in the countryside was alleviated by moments of friendship, affection, and romance, which formed and grew in young hearts and bodies, despite or probably "because of" all the difficulties, since the hardships of daily life made interpersonal sentiments sweeter (Pan 2002). This common bittersweet experience contributed much to the zhiqing generation's nostalgia today.

Nevertheless, the program floundered and eventually failed. Historical studies, including a book by a former zhiqing-affairs official in the central government (Gu 2009a), have reached a consensus on this point. Bonnin aptly describes the program's implementation as "high on fervor, low on organization" (Bonnin 2013, 78). The program did not achieve its socioeconomic goals. A folk saying, which was circulated at the central government's zhiqing work conference in 1978, summarized the problems with the program as "four dissatisfactions" (Gu 2009a, 123–26). The peasants were dissatisfied because the influx of zhiqing resulted in overpopulation in some areas and created significant food shortage and productivity issues. The zhiqing and their parents were dissatisfied because of the tremendous human costs, such as the delay of marriage and other life events, the lack of opportunities for education, and the constant remittances parents sent to the chadui youths whose incomes were inadequate. The danwei in the source cities were dissatisfied because they had to use personnel to mobilize youths to go down and, after going down, sent reluctant cadres to join the delegations to stay in the countryside to handle various problems. Finally, the government was dissatisfied because the spending on the send-down program (7,542,970,000 yuan from 1962 to 1979, after 1973, 1 percent of state revenue each year) did not produce tangible outcomes.

Most zhiqing and their parents painfully felt the failure of the program, worried deeply about their future, and tried to change their own fate before the state changed its policy. Urban jobs and recommendations for college often generated cutthroat competition among zhiqing. Some attempted to work the system. Common strategies included bribing local cadres and faking sicknesses to get a "sick return" (*bingtui*).

Many who were reluctant or lacked resources to perform those tricks had to wait in the dark.

No words can better describe the deep melancholy and chaotic individual-based pursuits in the last several years of the send-down program than those in a brief recount of Wang Anyi, a renowned writer and former zhiqing (Wang 2014):

> "Do we have to do pointless things over and over again on this black soil?" This poignant question marked a farewell to our youth. The legendary feature of the grand history eventually faded, leaving individuals to take responsibility for their own fate. The glittering spectacle gradually dimmed. Life exposed its mundane aspect, which turned out to be gloomy.

Soon after the Cultural Revolution, the send-down program imploded. Protests, poster campaigns, and demonstrations broke out in major source cities like Shanghai and send-down provinces like Yunnan and later Xinjiang (Yang, Bin 2009). The demonstrators demanded to go home to get their urban hukou back; those who had already arrived in their hometowns demanded jobs (McLaren 1979; Gold 1980; Liu 2009, 476–81). Dreading the possibility of the zhiqing protest converging with other collective actions, such as the Democracy Wall movement, the state began to loosen its control. At the zhiqing work conference in November and December 1978, before most protests, policymakers had already decided to limit the scale of mobilization significantly. The conference was the beginning of the end of the send-down program (Gu 2009a, 137–48). By 1980–1981, most zhiqing – except for many in Xinjiang and those who were married or had urban hukou in their sent-down provinces – were allowed to return to their home cities.[9]

The program ended, but its impacts had just begun. The returning zhiqing found their places in their home cities awkwardly undefined and embarrassing. Most of them were unemployed for a while or under-employed, performing low-skill jobs with meager wages in small factories

---

[9] The unique returning path of the Shanghai zhiqing to Xinjiang is worth mentioning here (Xu 2021). About 97,000 Shanghai zhiqing were mobilized by the Chinese state from 1963 to 1966 to migrate to the Xinjiang Production and Construction Corps. After a series of petitions and protests in 1979 and 1980, which culminated in a hunger strike in Aksu in December 1980, some of them were allowed to return to Shanghai and Haifeng, a farm in Jiangsu but administered by Shanghai, whereas many remained in Xinjiang. Thousands of others, however, rushed back to Shanghai and stayed there without hukou for three decades. They suffered from long-lasting, accumulative impacts of the program, such as an unstable life, low-paying jobs, low pensions, limited healthcare benefits, and various problems with their families and children. Some of them kept petitioning the Shanghai government in the past three decades to solve those "historically remaining issues" (lishi yiliu wenti) until a major leader, Zhang Weimin, was arrested and sentenced to three years of probation (Xu 2021).

in the street administration. "Delay" was the keyword to describe this generation's life course. Their education, marriage, and careers were delayed by the send-down program, and this delay effect was more serious for people who stayed longer in the countryside (Zhou and Hou 1999). These impacts, however, were unequally distributed. Those with higher-class family backgrounds may have been less severely affected; they later "recovered" sooner and better, thanks to the protection provided by their families' privileges (Zhou and Hou 1999; Bonnin 2013). Sociological studies show this generation's disadvantages as cumulative effects of the send-down program and other policy changes, such as the SOE (state-owned-enterprises) reform in the 1990s, in which countless zhiqing-turned workers were laid off. In an article based on interviews in 1999 with laid-off zhiqing workers, Hung and Chiu suggest that "at almost every critical transition in their life history – education, work, marriage, parenthood, and retirement – the state introduced policies that permanently affected their later chances in life by depriving them of certain opportunities" (Hung and Chiu 2003, 231–32). Qian and Hodson also show that the send-down program is less a passing structural turbulence than a "system shock," which shifts the working of a social system and permanently shapes individuals' lives. More specifically, the zhiqing suffered disproportionately at the end of their careers, with men experiencing atypical levels of unhappiness and with both men and women being forced into early retirement, a common phenomenon in the SOE reform (Qian and Hodson 2011; also see Lin 2013).

The Chinese state has been fully aware of the legacies of the send-down program. In 1981, a report by the State Council Zhiqing Work Office explicitly acknowledged that the program was intended to solve the unemployment issue but was implemented as a political campaign. The consequence, said the report, was that "the serious mistakes in the work resulted in the exhaustion of the people and a waste of money, as well as the people's dissatisfaction" (Gu 2009a, 243–44). Such a candid assessment disappeared from later official documents. Nevertheless, the local governments in the source cities, such as Beijing, Shanghai, and Tianjin, have been busy responding to the zhiqing's grievances during the past forty years. The governments made incremental, ad hoc policy changes to mitigate the negative impacts of the program. For example, from 1988 to 1989, major source cities issued new policies to allow those zhiqing remaining in sent-down provinces to send their children back to their home cities to receive a better education (Gu 2009a, 185) – this was how Gu Huifang's son returned to Shanghai.

Even those policy changes, however, have created further problems and provoked more grievances. The 1988–1989 returning child policies, for example, changed many zhiqing's life trajectories again. Many of them decided to accompany their children to return to home cities mostly because they worried about their underaged children. Some also found that even if they did odd jobs in Shanghai or Beijing, they still could earn higher wages than in their send-down provinces. The obvious downside was that they lived in their home cities as strangers in both institutional and social senses. They had no hukou or other formal identities. They also had conflicts with their families who were unwilling to accept their children's hukou, a requirement according to the policy. Many believed their life after returning in the 1990s was tougher than their years in the countryside. In the countryside, they were young and single, and at least had a formal identity. In the 1990s, they were over forty and had to raise their children with their meager, unstable wages earned through sometimes legally dubious jobs like selling breakfast as unlicensed street vendors or through working in hazardous jobs in places like printing factories without much personal protective equipment.

Since the 1990s, some of these returning zhiqing and other groups have been protesting to press local governments to grant their source city hukou and corresponding social welfare benefits. In responding to the mounting grievances, some local governments, such as Shanghai, changed relevant policies but also suppressed the zhiqing's collective actions by arresting leading activists and harassing participants. The Shanghai zhiqing sent to Xinjiang before the Cultural Revolution have been protesting for almost two decades and successfully forced the Shanghai government to adjust the healthcare policies, even if their leader was arrested and indicted (Xu, 2021). Nevertheless, many other groups do not get as much response from governments as the Xinjiang zhiqing. While I am finalizing this book in 2020, some of them are still holding regular gatherings and protests in Shanghai.

Difficult Memories

The memory of zhiqing started immediately after the Cultural Revolution and shows no sign of fading. Such abiding memory reflects the zhiqing's strong emotional identification with their generation. With the shared experience of a massive migration, especially in their formative years, the former zhiqing understandably like using phrases such as "we zhiqing generation": we "ate bitterness" together in the past, so we now gather together to commemorate our bittersweet youth.

Nevertheless, this ubiquitous use of "we" belies the complexity, nuance, and variation in zhiqing's memory. Their evaluations of the send-down program include outright condemnation of it as a "complete disaster," enthusiastic praise that the program helped develop the frontiers and the rural areas, political ambiguity ("it was valuable but way too long"), apolitical indifference ("rarely thought about those issues"), and helpless fatalism ("it was bad, but I could do nothing about it"). Adding to this convolution, their evaluations of personal experience do not always correspond to their historical evaluations of the program. Some have a positive, "redeemable" view of their personal past ("suffering to success") but still hold an unambiguously negative view of the program. Others remain silent on the program, despite their obvious pride about their personal achievements. This complexity goes beyond any linear generalization.

Public memory also varies in form and content. In the 1980s, some literary works – for example, Liang Xiaosheng's short story "A Land of Wonder and Mystery" – depicted a heroic image of the zhiqing and praised the moral–political values the generation cherished, such as endurance, self-sacrifice, and collectivism. Nonetheless, many other zhiqing, who were having a hard time getting back to normal urban life after they returned to cities, did not buy this upbeat story. They flocked to TV sets to watch *The Wasted Years*, a drama series adapted from Ye Xin's best-selling novel of the same title. The title of the novel said it all – since our years were wasted in the countryside, what's the point of talking about "wonder and mystery"?

Exhibits and museums in the 1990s and 2000s showed another pattern of complexity. The organizers of the exhibits and museums purposefully highlighted the zhiqing's tough character, important contributions, and memorable youth without directly commenting on the send-down program. Nevertheless, while the exhibits and museums wanted to detach "youth" from the program, the audience tended to "reattach" the zhiqing's youthful memory to the program and criticized the zhiqing's political ambivalence about their own responsibilities for the atrocities committed during the Cultural Revolution. Unsurprisingly, the literary works, the exhibits, and the museums provoked serious public controversies.

Complexity also appears in the frequent and ubiquitous zhiqing-related activities in recent years. At first glance, most of the activities look like normal reunions filled with nostalgia and exuberance; or they may appear like Maoist diehard activities with nostalgia for their good old days. Nevertheless, my observation shows that the commemorative gatherings could be as politically contested as the public discourses. The pattern of memory in the activities varies across different groups, ranging from outright Maoist nostalgia, oppositional memory expressed in protests, "the people but not the event," to the completely apolitical pattern of "being happy together." All these views and group interactions are complicated by the state's political interventions and companies' commercial interests in the elderly zhiqing as their target consumers.

All these memories occurred against an ambiguous political background. The state mostly remains silent on the program but highlights the political–moral values represented in the new leadership's zhiqing experience: youth should integrate with workers and peasants; youth should fulfill their responsibilities to the nation by going to villages and frontiers; hardship can build youths' character. Even the critical 1981 report from the State Council Zhiqing Office confirmed the benefits of the "tempering" experience in the zhiqing's sent-down years and their contributions to the rural areas. The state's ambivalence toward the program both constrained and enabled the memory boom.

These complexities challenge the homogeneity assumption underneath popular images of the zhiqing generation and scholarly uses of the term "generation." How to "thickly" describe – in other words, not just describe what they say and do but what they *mean* – all these forms, patterns, and trajectories of the zhiqing generation's memories (Geertz 1973)? What factors and mechanisms can account for these variations? In answering these questions, I dialog with two bodies of literature: the substantive literature on memories of the Mao years and the theoretical literature on generation and memory.

The Red Legacies: Memories of the Mao Years

Zhiqing are no strangers to China scholars. Before China opened up in the late 1970s, overseas scholars relied on the zhiqing-turned-émigré to Hong Kong as a major source of information due to the blocked access to mainland China (Walder 2004). Later, the zhiqing generation became the main characters of many academic narratives in history, sociology, anthropology, and public administration (Bernstein 1977; Rosen 1981; Chan 1985; Zhou and Hou 1999; Pan 2002; Chan, Madsen, and Unger 2009; Liu 2009; Bonnin 2013; Rene 2013; Honig and Zhao 2019). In other scholarly works, they have been hiding behind their primary identities as youths in the 1980s (Siu and Stern 1983), laid-off SOE workers (Lee 2002), and so on.

While we know much about the zhiqing generation's past, we know less about how they perceive their past. Only a handful of articles and book chapters have dealt with the memory of the zhiqing generation. Michel Bonnin's article provides a succinct history of the zhiqing memory from the 1980s to now (Bonnin 2016). His recent book chapter shows that scholars and zhiqing alike use unofficial sources and alternative narratives to counter the official memory about the zhiqing's return in the period of 1978–1980 (Bonnin 2019). Guobin Yang's article on zhiqing memoirs shows that the zhiqing generation's nostalgia was their cultural resistance to the rapidly changing Chinese society in the 1980s and 1990s (Yang 2003). A chapter of his book on the Red Guard generation develops this idea and touches on some new forms of memories, such as gatherings and revisit trips to their sent-down places (Yang 2016). A few other articles have studied the old zhiqing restaurants and old images of zhiqing in publications as commemorations of the Cultural Revolution (Davies 2005; Hubbert 2005). These valuable studies, however, are all that we have now. Much of the memory boom remains unaddressed or needs in-depth research – for example, personal narratives in private settings, the mushrooming zhiqing-themed exhibits and museums, and ubiquitous groups that hold commemorative activities. This book is intended to fill this gap.

In studying the memory of the zhiqing generation, this book also attempts to enrich our scholarly and public knowledge about memories of the Mao years or "red legacies" (Lee and Yang 2007; Li and Zhang 2016; Veg 2019). To study the red legacies is to explore "meanings of the past in the present, or what the past does *for* and *to* the present" instead of examining what "really happened" (Li and Zhang 2016, 5, italics original).

An important line of this literature is to examine how such legacies linger in various groups' mentality because of their different socialization processes under Mao and post-Mao lived experience (Chan 1985; Lee 2000, 2002; Jennings and Zhang 2005; Hershatter 2011; Yang 2016; Huang 2018; Xu 2019). At the heart of this line of research is the intersection between personal biography and history, or, more specifically, how different social groups remember their personal experience as part of the history of the Mao years and how such remembrance varies across their social positions and characteristics.[10]

Unsurprisingly, the generation of "Chairman Mao's children," who grew up "under the red flag" and received a full political socialization under Mao, has been the focal point of this line of research. Immediately after the Cultural Revolution, scholars and the public reflected on some

---

[10] Some works have focused on symbolic practices and cultural objects as remainders of the collapsed Maoist cultural system, such as Mao badges and artistic practices, which have been reenacted, altered, commodified, and juxtaposed in various new forms in the post-Mao era (Hubbert 2005, 2006; Jiang 2007; Chen 2016). Others examine memory and memorialization of the Mao era, including officially sanctioned or tolerated sites of memory (Leese 2012; Zhang 2013; Ho and Li 2016) and alternative cultural objects, such as memoirs, documentaries, and literary works (Veg 2014, 2019).

important and painful questions pertaining to this generation – for example, as Anita Chan stated at the very beginning of her book: "How and why did some of China's urban young people become fervent political activists?" (Chan 1985, 1). This question lingers on in later studies of the Red Guards' memorialization (Zhang 2013), contested memories about their guilts and responsibilities (Weigelin-Schwiedrzik and Jinke 2016), the lineage from the activism of the Mao years to political action now (Yang 2016), etc.

These valuable studies, however, have yet to look beyond the most politically active members of this generation, often with the identity of Red Guards.[11] "Zhiqing" is a better lens than "Red Guards" through which to examine the memory of this generation. From a realist perspective, this lens of "zhiqing" has a wider angle. It includes those in this generation who were not Red Guards activists for various reasons. Their more diverse experiences lead to more diverse memories. From a constructivist perspective, in choosing "zhiqing," a less stigmatizing label, as their generation identity, members of this generation try to link their personal biography to a controversial but less notorious event, emphasizing their identities as patriots, victims, winners, and so on, rather than aggressors. Their identity choice itself reveals their painful struggle to find the right way to talk about the meanings of their personal history in light of their shared history. This less unsavory label of "zhiqing" also enables them to express more multivocal feelings and meanings about their past. In sum, I use "zhiqing" instead of "Red Guards" as a heuristic tool to examine the various ways in which contemporary Chinese who lived through the Mao years define meanings of their personal past and come to terms with the red legacies.

Generation and Memory

We cannot choose our generation. We are thrown into this world at different historical moments. Our personal fate is inevitably entangled with some events, reaping the benefits they generate and carrying the burdens they leave. Thus, every generation's unique position in historical temporality and their life cycle leads to different memories.

Sociologist Howard Schuman and his associates find that members of a generation tend to remember the significant historical events that happen in their adolescent years and early adulthood (Schuman and Rodgers 2004; Corning and Schuman 2015). This *critical-years hypothesis*

---

[11] Some memoirs, rather than scholarly works, do present the varying degrees of political activeness, among them Zhong, Wang, and Bai (2001) and Ye and Ma (2005).

can explain why it was the "youth" at the heart of the zhiqing generation's memory. Because people in different age cohorts experience different significant historical events in their critical years, they tend to remember different historical events. This leads to their second hypothesis: there is a repeated pattern of *intergenerational difference* in memory. The two hypotheses are supported by analyses of data from different contexts and are among the most solid findings in the sociology of memory (Schuman and Rieger 1992; Schuman and Corning 2000; Schuman and Rodgers 2004; Corning 2010). The tenet of this approach is that a generation's lived experience plays a consequential role in remembering their collective past.

Nevertheless, our knowledge of generation and memory remains incomplete. There are three significant gaps in this literature. First, the Schuman–Corning approach relies on a cognitive–psychological concept of "memory," operationalized as "recalling" or "naming" some events as the most important. It does not tell us much about how members of a generation interpret the *meanings* of the event they have experienced: Why are the events important to them? How do they evaluate the event? How do they talk about the intersections between their generational experiences and their personal lives?[12] In other words, what matters most is not only *what* people remember but also *how* and *why* they remember (Young 1993; Simko 2015). All these meaning-making processes are essential to the sociology of memory and even to sociology as a whole. Human beings are social animals hung on the web of meanings (Geertz 1973). Meanings work like a "switchman" that determines the track along which action has been pulled by the locomotive of interests (Weber 1946, 280). Palmberger's research on generations' remembrance of Mostar, a Bosnian-Herzegovinian city with an ethnically divided and painful history (Palmberger 2016), is an important starting point for this agenda. It shows how the people there make sense of and give meaning to a past event according to their recent life situations. But more studies are needed along this line.

The second significant gap is that the existing scholarship almost exclusively focuses on *intergenerational* differences in memory. This focus certainly corroborates our conventional understanding of generation, such as the "generation gap." But shared experience of a historical event does not mean identical response. Only when we examine how a

---

[12] In one of their writings, they attempt to remedy this issue by defining collective memory as "how ordinary people make sense of cultural representations of the past" (Corning and Schuman 2015, 14). This conceptualization is limited to "reception," a small part of meaning-making processes in memory.

generation reacts to their collective fate *differently* can we fully understand how they make sense of the intersection of biography and history, in other words, to acquire the "sociological imagination." The zhiqing generation is a strong case to illustrate this point. The dramatic variations in their memory suggest the importance of *intragenerational* differences, even though they are often assumed to have more commonality than variation because they grew up in a homogeneous, draconian political culture.

The third gap in the literature has to do with the level of analysis. The dominant Schuman approach mostly focuses on memory at the individual level. A complex phenomenon like generation and memory, however, also appears at the levels above individuals – for example, what is conventionally termed as "collective memory," practices and collective representations in the public settings (Olick 1999) and what Jan Assmann terms "communicative memory," interactions and communications at the local level, beyond individuals and relatively independent of the public sphere (Assmann 1995; Fine 2012). Cultural properties at different levels are interlinked but cannot be reduced to each other (Jepperson and Swidler 1994). For example, one cannot infer the state's official memory from individuals' life stories or the other way around without a careful examination of both the state and the individuals. Some individual memories are suppressed and silenced by the state (Trouillot 1995). Some memories are also tacit knowledge in a local community but have never made it into the public sphere. Thus, we need to have a more differential frame of levels of analysis of generation and memory.

Addressing these gaps requires a discussion about how to define "generation" and "memory," two common but thorny terms. Here I draw insights from Karl Mannheim and Pierre Bourdieu to lay the conceptual foundation for the analysis in this book.

Mannheim offers a few key concepts: generation as age cohort, actual generation (or "generation as actuality"), and generation units.[13] *Age cohort* is not generation but "generation location." Just as people who have a similar socioeconomic status are in the same class location of a society, people of the same or similar age occupy a location in the temporal order of society (Mannheim 1952 [1923], 290–91). An age cohort becomes an *actual generation* only when the members collectively experience the same historical events or processes, usually in their formative years. "We shall therefore speak of generation as an actuality only where a concrete bond is created between members of a generation by

---

[13] For other concepts of generation, see David Kertzer's overview (1983).

their being exposed to the social and intellectual symptoms of a process of dynamic de-stabilization" (Mannheim 1952 [1923], 303). For example, a young Prussian peasant living at the time of the wars against Napoleon certainly did not belong to the same generation as a young Chinese peasant in the same age cohort. In this sense, we can use the term "zhiqing generation" as an actual generation, because they have experienced the same historical event.

"Actual generation," however, still contains only the potentiality for a generation to shape cultural and social processes. Realizing the potentiality requires more concrete bonds carried out by sectors and groups within an actual generation. Mannheim terms those sectors and groups *"generation units."* The basis of a generation unit is having the same response to a common generational experience. The same generation who grew up in the same era may have different and even oppositional views about some key issues, and they engaged in various sociopolitical processes in quite different ways. One gains awareness as being a member of a generation through one's generation unit instead of the whole generation because the generation units are where people develop "the ability to see things from its particular 'aspect,' to endow concepts with its particular shade of meaning and to experience psychological and intellectual impulses in the configuration characteristic of the group" (Mannheim 1952 [1923], 306).[14]

Mannheim clearly states the importance of generation units (Mannheim 1952 [1923], 304) (italics original):

The generation unit represents a much more concrete bond than the actual generation as such. *Youth experiencing the same concrete historical problems may be said to be part of the same actual generation; while those groups within the same actual generation which work up the material of their common experiences in different specific ways, constitute separate generation units.*

Without examining "actual generation" and "generation units," Mannheim warns (1952 [1923], 311):

---

[14] Schuman and his associates recognize the potential issue of artificial homogeneity in their emphasis on intergenerational differences and have gradually examined other mediating factors, such as education (Schuman and Corning 2000). He and his colleagues do discuss "generation units" in some of their articles, but the discussion strays from their main hypotheses and is not well articulated. A few recent studies based on surveys address this gap by using different generation units to examine memory in different contexts, such as the role of race and region generational memory of the Civil War (Griffin 2004; Griffin and Bollen 2009) and political ranks in Chinese rural memories of past events (Jennings and Zhang 2005). This book follows in the footsteps of these studies but advances from them by paying more attention to how different generation units make sense of the meanings of their distinctive life paths under their shared historical fate.

We risk jumbling together purely biological phenomena and others which are the product of social and cultural forces: thus we arrive at a sort of sociology of chronological tables, which uses its bird's-eye perspective to "discover" fictitious generation programs to correspond to the crucial turning-points in historical chronology.

Let me use an analogy to illustrate Mannheim's point. Imagine the send-down program – or any significant historical event – as a huge tidal wave. Some people who happened to be caught in the wave were submerged, while others were tossed onto beaches. Some lucky ones may have been riding the wave. When the wave has passed, they end up in different locations and have different stories to tell about the wave and themselves. A cursory observer, who stands far away, may only focus on the wave taking away the "whole generation" and tend to use homogeneous terms to describe their common features, vis-à-vis other generations. A better observer usually goes beyond the false impression of homogeneity and listens to how the people in different locations talk about their fate in the huge historical wave.

This book defines "memory" as "mnemonic practice" and its outcomes, including various cultural objects, such as memorials, memoirs, and so on (Olick and Robbins 1998). Mnemonic practices include individuals' narration of their past; communications and symbolic practices about the past in small-group, community settings, such as conversations, commemorative rituals, and so on; and large-scale symbolic practices and cultural production about the past in public, organizational, or institutional settings (Olick 2007). In this book, however, I use the conventional terms "memory" and "remember" instead of the jargon "mnemonic practice," but readers should keep in mind that "memory" is not a "thing" but a practice.

Moreover, "practice" in this definition is not a generic term but a concept from Bourdieu's theory. According to Bourdieu, practice is the "social alchemy," a process incorporating and realizing both objective forces and subjective agency. The social alchemy involves conversions of capitals, in which an individual, or a group, or a community, or a nation-state uses all kinds of substantive *capital* – cultural, economic, and social – to restore, maintain, and enhance their "symbolic capital," a type of capital that takes the form of recognition, prestige, distinction, legitimacy, and so on (Bourdieu and Wacquant 2013). In other words, people want to be respected, recognized, and legitimized by an already established system of distinction, and they achieve that goal by using the capitals they have (Bourdieu 1984). But what capitals matter and what is a recognized symbolic capital depends on the *field* of the actions, that is, a social space with a network of positions and interrelations (Bourdieu and Wacquant 1992, 97): publishing an academic book with a top university press is a mark of distinction in academics but means little in the business world, especially given that such books only sell several hundred copies. The social alchemy, however, needs a critical component inside everyone – "habitus" –to coordinate all other components. Bourdieu defines habitus as "a disposition that generates meaningful practices and meaning-giving perceptions" (Bourdieu 1984, 170). Habitus forms in one's interaction with social structure, especially class position, usually in one's formative years (Bourdieu and Wacquant 2013). Bourdieu summarizes these ideas in a famous formula: *[(Capital + Habitus)] + Field = Practice* (Bourdieu and Wacquant 1992).

If these points sound all too familiar to scholars, then this book offers something new. "Mnemonic practice," I argue, is also social alchemy. Individuals, groups, and organizations engage in mnemonic practices to restore, maintain, and enhance their symbolic capital. Individuals tell life stories to present respectable self-images. Ethnic groups build museums of their ethnic history to highlight their contributions to the country and maintain their dignity. Perpetrators and victims debate over war atrocities to struggle for the legitimate authority to claim historical truths. All these practices need material and cultural resources, including money, power, symbols, and ideas. People with different capitals have different abilities to mobilize the resources. Capitals also have to be reproduced and converted to symbolic capital by the people with the right habitus in the right field. Abundant material resources may be sufficient for building a large museum, but the inadequacy in the museum organizers' habitus – lacking the cultural tastes that are regarded as legitimate and "high-brow" in a certain field – would only lead to negative reviews from elite critics.

Finally, both "generation" and "memory" have different meanings at different analytical levels. Here, I adopt a three-level frame: individual, group/community, and public. At the *individual* level, generational memory mostly means "autobiographical memory," individuals' memory of their personal experience in the historical event that shaped their generational experience; "generation" is a cognitive category in individuals' social frameworks, which links the personal experience to the historical event. At the *group/community* level, "memory" means mnemonic practices in the form of face-to-face interactions and communications, including symbols, words, and rituals at the local level (Assmann 1995; Fine 2012); "generation" is both a cognitive category and a cultural identity used by the participants to label themselves in their interactions. At the *public* level, "memory" means mnemonic practices in organizational and institutional settings and their products available in the public sphere, such as memoirs, exhibits, memorials, and museums. At this level, "generation" is more a cultural identity than a cognitive category. It is socially constructed to enhance cultural influence of the generation (Eyerman and Turner 1998; Edmunds and Turner 2002, 116). The generation label is often selected from the past events the generation has experienced to present a respectable image or avoid a stigma, for example, the "zhiqing" generation versus the "Red Guards" generation.

A Theoretical Framework on Generational Memory

Drawing on the conceptualization of "generation" and "memory," I work out a theoretical framework to capture a colorful, "high-definition" image of generational memory. This framework incorporates different strands of sociological theories of interrelated topics, including memory (Halbwachs 1992; Fine 1996; Olick 1999, 2010), class and habitus (Bourdieu 1984; Bourdieu and Wacquant 2013), generation (Mannheim 1952 [1923]; Eyerman and Turner 1998; Edmunds and Turner 2002, 116), cultural production (Griswold 1987b; Bourdieu 1993), and groups and interactions (Eliasoph and Lichterman 2003; Fine 2012). This framework, however, is not a result of abstract thinking but an outcome of a "theorizing" process (Swedberg 2014; Tavory and Timmermans 2014), a long and constant traveling between data and theory. The theorizing process started when I was amazed by some puzzles – for instance, the unexpected significance of class. The theorizing continued through a longtime immersion, intended to discover new facts and generate new theories, creatively use heuristics, infer the best explanations, and test the theories in various types of data. In every step of this process, I asked myself: "What does this idea mean *historically?*" so that the theoretical thinking makes sense in the historical contexts of the case (see Appendix for details).

In the rest of this section, I provide a synopsis of the theoretical framework, leaving detailed discussions to subsequent chapters.

Individual Memory and Generation: Class, Habitus, and Autobiographical Memory

At the individual level, "autobiographical memory" is the major form of memory. Members of a generation tell their life stories to present respectable self-images (symbolic capital) and link their personal past to a shared event. Thus, such a life story usually consists of two intertwined components: the story about his or her *personal experience* and *historical*

evaluation of the event. The interconnection between the two components is where one's perception of a personal issue connects to one's view
of the event, for example, whether one's current troubles in job, healthcare, and pensions are caused by the long stay in the countryside.

Personal experience and historical evaluation, as well as their intercon-
nections, vary. Many factors can explain variations in autobiographical
memory. For this case, *class* is central for two reasons. First, the send-
down program has caused negative impacts related to class, including
education, income, and jobs, but some members of the generation are
better off than others (Zhou and Hou 1999). Thus, class positions of the
zhiqing *in the present* are part of the social framework for their autobiographical memory (Halbwachs 1992). When they tell their life stories, the
zhiqing use their personal experience in the past to explain their class
positions in the present. For example, President Xi tells a different story
from that of the Shanghai retiree Gu: the higher the zhiqing's present
class positions, the more likely they hold a positive view of their personal
experience in their sent-down years and its impacts on later life. In this
sense, autobiographical memory functions like Bourdieu's famous aesthetic taste, expressing and justifying one's objective class position in the
present and its trajectory from the past to the present (Bourdieu 1984).

Second, "class" has its historical specificities in this case. When the
zhiqing generation grew up, "class" (*jieji*) meant "political class" or
"chushen" (political family background), a highly politicized, caste-like
categorization system, in which, in Bourdieu's terms, political capital – a
subtype of social capital – carried much more weight than economic and
cultural capital. The youths in the 1960s were pigeonholed in "red" or
"black" or "middle" chushen (Chan, Rosen, and Unger 1980; Kraus
1981; Chan 1985). In their response to the opportunities and limitations
of the political class system, they correspondingly developed habitus with
a strong political component. For example, those with bad chushen
would either perform super actively to prove that they were as revolutionary as their red peers or simply stayed away from politics to avoid trouble.
In my analysis, I identify four types of habitus along two dimensions
(chushen and political performance): the faithful red, the indifferent red,
aspirants, and withdrawers.

Once formed, the political habitus can endure through all the dramatic
changes in the society and personal life and remain robust enough to
shape the zhiqing's present views of the political events in the Mao years,
especially the send-down program and the Cultural Revolution. In other
words, the zhiqing's different types of habitus shape their *historical
evaluations* of the send-down program. This theoretical idea "upgrades"
Schuman's critical-years hypothesis by incorporating more social

and historical processes into the early socialization and individuals' remembrance.

Nonetheless, habitus is not a deterministic, static concept; rather, it changes over time. Bourdieu is famous for his insistence on the importance of early experience and durability of habitus, but he also believes that habitus is "an *open system of dispositions* that is constantly subjected to experiences" (Bourdieu and Wacquant 1992, 133). How much the initial habitus has changed or retained is an empirical and historical question. In this case, two historical specificities are important. First, the zhiqing generation's political habitus might be unusually robust because it was formed in a one-dimensional, over-politicized, and closed political system in the Mao years. Second, at some moments of political transformation in China, their political habitus dramatically changed through, as Bourdieu suggests, self-analysis or an awakening experience (Bourdieu and Wacquant 1992, 133): after the Lin Biao incident in 1971 when many became disillusioned with the state propaganda and the personality cult; right after the Cultural Revolution, the zhiqing joined the rest of the country to reflect on the political system and ideology they once embraced. Both were the moments when this generation's personal biography intersected history.

Group Memory and Generation: Memory Entrepreneurs and Group Styles

Memory at the group/community level takes place in face-to-face social situations, most of which are "autobiographic occasions," such as reunions, commemorations, revisits, and so on. On autobiographic occasions, people are expected, encouraged, and required to bring their personal past forth to the interactions to commemorate their shared past (Vinitzky-Seroussi 1998; Zussman 2000). They often interact in groups and thus form group memory. Group memory is not a replication of public discourses or private thoughts. Instead, it contains norms, styles, and ideas that emerge from interactions, group processes, and dynamics (Fine 1979; Eliasoph and Lichterman 2003; Lichterman 2006). The intragenerational differences in memory at this level are the differences of group memories. The groups, rather than individuals, are the "generation units" of memory. "Memory entrepreneurs," who devote themselves to memory work (Fine 1996), certainly play a pivotal role in shaping group memory. But they have to negotiate with other members of their groups to present a "group version" of the past to maintain the "interaction order" among them (Goffman 1983).

Groups also constitute a "memory field," a field in which groups and individuals discover, preserve, produce, and promote memory. Memory fields mediate the interactions between groups and the macro-level social and political structures (Fine 1991; Bourdieu 1994; Goldfarb 2006). The major struggles within the memory field revolve around symbolic capital, in this case, of generation, including recognition of their worthiness and their authority to claim historical truth. Interactions within and between groups are shaped by the dynamics in the memory field and its relations with other fields, such as the field of political power and the field of economy.

Public Memory and Generation: Fields and Institutions

In public memory, "generation" is a cultural identity, and the struggle for the generation's "symbolic capital" is focused on their cultural influence (Eyerman and Turner 1998; Edmunds and Turner 2002, 116; Bourdieu and Wacquant 2013). Not everyone of a generation is engaged in this struggle. Rather, some individuals, groups, and organizations attempt to turn their versions of the past into the universal, authoritative, and true public memory of the whole generation's past. Such a process usually happens in a memory field but could also happen in other cultural production fields – for example, literature – particularly when the memory field has not taken form (Griswold 1987b; Bourdieu 1993; Peterson and Anand 2004). The institutional and organizational relations between the memory field and other fields, such as the field of power, are essential to public memory, because the field of power provides accesses to acquire many material and institutional resources.

The role of memory entrepreneurs in public memory is central. They are regularly involved in mnemonic practices that often lead to the production of cultural objects, such as publications, memorials, museums, archives, monuments, and so on. They are what Mannheim terms "nucleus groups," the people at the center of a generation unit who develop essential conceptions for the generation unit (Mannheim 1952 [1923], 307). Memory entrepreneurs' class positions and habitus shape what autobiographical memories they choose to advocate – usually their own – and how the memories are represented at the public level.

★★★

In sum, this theoretical framework specifies and describes "memory" at different analytical levels in different ways. To explain the commonalities and variations in generational memories at those levels, this framework

Table I.1. *The theoretical framework*

Level of memory	Mnemonic practices	Explanatory factors
Individual	Autobiographical memories	Individuals' class positions and habitus
Group/Community	Group memories	Memory entrepreneurs (with class positions and habitus) Group dynamics Memory field and other fields (especially power)
Public	Public discourses Cultural production	Memory entrepreneurs (with class positions and habitus) Memory field or field of cultural production and other fields (especially power)

identifies several essential explanatory factors, including class, habitus, field, and group dynamics, and explores the mechanisms of interactions among them (Table I.1).

Preview of Arguments and Chapters

In this book, I tell a story of how the zhiqing generation has come to terms with their difficult past in the forty years since the end of the send-down program in the late 1970s. They struggle to deal with the tension between two entangled aspects of their generational memory: their desire to remember their youth and confirm their worthiness, on the one hand, and their difficulty in evaluating the controversial send-down program and other political upheavals in the Mao years, on the other. Such tension is manifested in various patterns of memory in their individual life stories, public debates over literary works, exhibits and museums, and groups' commemorative activities. I explain the variations in their memory by several factors and their interactions at different levels, including class, habitus, field, and group dynamics.

The pattern "remembering the people but not the event!" gradually dominates the public and group memory, although other patterns still exist. This pattern attempts to decouple their youth from the controversial program and its detrimental aftermaths. It is used by the powerful and the successful in this generation to construct their uplifting, ascending life stories to confirm their personal achievements. It has also been used by the state to construct the mythic past of President Xi Jinping, which weaves his "adversity-to-success" zhiqing experience into an upbeat story of the "China dream" but avoids addressing the controversial event.

This self-important pattern of memory, however, marginalizes those zhiqing who are still suffering from the harmful impacts of the program and veils the voices of self-reflection on their moral responsibility in the political upheavals in their formative years. Outside their comfort zone, their effort of decoupling is often interpreted as coupling: nostalgic remembrance of their youth is viewed as a positive evaluation of the send-down program and the Cultural Revolution. As their memory is booming inside their own circle, its cultural influence is declining in the general public.

In short, this generation of "Chairman Mao's children" are still caught between the political and the personal, past and present, nostalgia and regret, pride and trauma.

This story is presented in six substantive chapters.

In Chapters 1 and 2, I use qualitative and quantitative analyses of the life history interviews with the zhiqing to describe and explain various patterns of their autobiographical memory. Their autobiographical memory varies greatly, and the variation can be explained by "class," including their present class positions and their chushen and habitus formed in the Mao years.

Chapters 3 and 4 focus on "public memory." I do not follow the analytical order from micro to meso to macro – that is, presenting "group memory" right after individual memory – because the public memory of the zhiqing generation happened first in time order: literary memory in the 1980s and exhibits in the 1990s before group memory emerged in the late 2000s. Chapter 3 focuses on various patterns of literary memory in the 1980s and later and shows that the pattern of "the good people but the bad event" became dominant. The variations and trend in the literary memory can be explained by the interplay of several factors: the dominant realism and unusual dynamics in the literary field in the 1980s, major authors' habitus, the lower-class position of the returning zhiqing, and the state's political use of the Maoist past. In Chapter 4, I examine "sites of memory": the exhibits in the 1990s and museums since the 2000s. I show that memory entrepreneurs and dynamics of cultural production fields result in a pattern of representation centered on "the people but not the event." Such a pattern, however, provokes even more public debates than expected.

Chapters 5 and 6 focus on generation and memory in group interactions. In Chapter 5, I describe different patterns of group memory – including "socialist nostalgia," "rightful resistance," and "the people but not the event" – which are manifested in narratives, symbols, rituals, speech norms, and other practices. I explain those patterns by examining the interaction between memory entrepreneurs' class positions and habitus and their group processes. In Chapter 6, I focus on intergroup activities. As the activities are booming, conflicts and tensions also emerge along the fault lines of class and ideology, and the cultural influence of this generation outside their memory field is limited.

In the Conclusion, I return to where I began. I first discuss how the research presented in this book can help us understand the Chinese state's official memory of President Xi Jinping's zhiqing experience. Then I recapitulate the major arguments and discuss in detail the broader empirical and theoretical implications of this study. I end the book with a discussion of the political ethics of the zhiqing generation's memory, the normative goal of my book, to reflect on the ethical issues in similar cases of memory.

Researching Memory across the Generation Gap

This book is based on a long-term, multi-stage, and mixed-method research project. Technical details of data and methods can be found in the Appendix. Here I want to share some methodological self-reflection, which I believe is also crucial for understanding some of the key substantive issues such as memory and generation.

The first methodological reflection has to do with how to study memory. I am primarily interested in how people actively create meaning through remembering and what the meaning-making process can tell us about the people involved in the memory and the larger society in which they are embedded. This approach is in line with the major paradigm in the sociology and anthropology of memory (Cole 2001; Olick 2010) and the new cultural history of memorial culture, mnemonic practices, and museums (Mosse 1990; Young 1993; Winter 1995, 2006).

This approach is self-evident in some parts of this book, especially the chapters about museums, memorials, literary memory, and ethnographic analysis of commemorative activities, all of which are "classic" topics in memory studies. But in the chapters on autobiographic memory, the "life history" or "life story" interviews, could be misidentified as "oral history." Life history interviews differ from the conventional oral history interviews in that they intend to identify, analyze, and explain the patterns of meanings in their storytelling practices rather than to know what really happened. In life history interviews, "personal narrative can illuminate the operation of historical forces and of public or historical narratives as they influence people's motivations and their self-understandings as historical agents" (Maynes, Pierce, and Laslett 2008, 44). Admittedly, this difference between life story and oral history is subtle. Some oral history projects take a more constructivist view and examine how memory provides a window onto the subjective world of the narrators, a goal similar to that of memory studies. For example, Roseman examines the complex layers of memory of a Holocaust survivor, even the discrepancies in her memory, to show the strategies she adopted to cope with an unbearable past and her guilt (Roseman 1999). Alessandro Portelli suggests that "memory is not a passive depository of facts, but an active creation of meanings" (Portelli 1991, 52). In the field of China studies, Gail Hershatter's *The Gender of Memory* (2011) discusses how rural women's recollection of the past, including of the socialist state and themselves, may have been shaped by present experience and gender identity. These uses of memory in oral history projects share with my approach some common-ground ideas, and I regard these similarities as a result of healthy cross-fertilization between disciplines and perspectives (Tumblety 2013). I do not see the need for the action of patrolling the disciplinary borders.

The second methodological reflection is the understanding of my identity in my ethnographic fieldwork. Ethnography "rests on the peculiar practice of representing the social reality of others through the analysis of one's own experience in the world of these others" (van Maanen 2011, xiii). Ethnographers need to have a reflexive understanding of their own identity and meaning systems when they are interacting with the observed. Such a reflexive understanding reveals some of the fundamental things in the world of the observed that may not be visible without the ethnographers' intervention. This methodology is in sharp contrast to the positivistic assumption that observers should act like human cameras to record actions in an "objective" manner – a practically impossible and epistemologically unproductive stance. For ethnography, what matters most is not to present a mechanistically defined "objective" reality but to present an "intersubjective reality," which emerges in the interactions between the ethnographer and the observed (Schutz and Luckmann 1973; Mead 2015). This intersubjective reality provides interesting data that otherwise would not demonstrate themselves. Put in a metaphorical way, the presence of the observer in the ethnographic encounters is not a "noise" but "music."

Let me illustrate this point in an account of how my multiple identities in the field, including their ambiguities, fluidity, tensions, and advantages, constituted part of the intersubjective reality. My self-presentations are not simply a "research strategy" but became part of my ethnographic "data" for analysis.

I presented my primary identity as a researcher (a professor) with serious, scholarly interests in this generation's past and present. When asked, "Why are you interested in researching us [zhiqing]?," I usually answered: "The history and present of this generation of 17 million people are important and shouldn't be forgotten, but people haven't paid much attention to this part of history." This standard answer was much appreciated because most of them have felt that their extraordinary past – traumatic or heroic or whatever – had been neglected by the public, the younger generations, and even their own children. Indeed, most of my interviewees said their children were not interested in their zhiqing experience at all. Now, a young professor with a serious interest in this generation had come to conduct well-prepared interviews and followed them around in many activities; this fact itself confirmed their public worthiness – in Bourdieu's terms, a form of symbolic capital.

The other side of my ethnographic encounters has to do with class, a central factor of this study. The identity of "professor" implies a high volume of cultural capital, which most zhiqing lacked, and higher overall class status, at least in China. Thanks to this identity, I was invited to various activities because the organizers wanted to use my presence to show that, in an organizer's words, their activities were "classy" or "upscale" (shangdangci). Consequently, my name was announced at the activities as one of the "distinguished guests"; my image appeared in various social-media reports of those activities, which described me as a "famous expert on zhiqing," sometimes with incorrect affiliations and titles. My mild protests and reluctance to accept those privileges were regarded as modesty, a quality that earned me an even better reputation. In many activities, some zhiqing dragged me by the arm to take pictures with them, as if I were a celebrity. While my "social self" enjoyed this unexpected stardom, my "sociological self" kept reminding myself that "your identity is not you" or, as ethnographers usually say, "use yourself as an instrument." In other words, it was the professor identity – more precisely, the cultural capital attached to the identity, instead of me as a person – that they needed to enhance *their* symbolic capital.

My national identity was also a factor that affected my interactions with the subjects. I was born and grew up in China and am working and living in the United States. This marginal state can put me in both boxes of national identity: Chinese and American. The "Thomas Theorem" worked perfectly here: if I was defined as American, then I became American in consequence. Some zhiqing held a deeply rooted distrust of Americans or Westerners for fear that they might use the information about the zhiqing's painful past – or any negative information – for political purposes. This distrust partially came from their upbringing in the Mao period, when the United States was labeled as "American imperialism." I was told by my key informants that a couple of zhiqing were reluctant to talk with me because of my "American" identity. Once, I received a call from an unknown zhiqing who was interested in telling me her stories but curious about my purpose: "Are you going to relay the information to the American media so Americans can make fun of us?" One of the zhiqing who organized the Yunnan protest in 1978–1979 refused to be interviewed because "we are still patriotic and do not want to talk with anyone from overseas." At a supposed welcome dinner party for me in a museum in the Northeast, the museum's director, emboldened by alcohol, rebuked me for being an "American professor," two identities combined, both of which he resented deeply.

In contrast, a few people were eager to talk with me *because of* my American identity. For example, in an activity, the organizer reminded the participants to give their best performance because "Dr. Xu will take our pictures to America!" On other occasions, informants had political purposes. A zhiqing who regularly went to the Labor Bureau to petition wanted me to "publish" her petition files in a newspaper she described as "the Monitor" (*zhengyanbao*), by which I guess she meant *The Christian Science Monitor*. I refused and explained that I didn't know how to publish her petitions and that I was only a researcher with a non-political purpose. She gave me a suspicious look. Soon after the interview, she phoned one of my informants to say that I must be a "spy" sent by the Chinese National Security Bureau because I claimed to come from the United States but refused to publish her petition in foreign media. My informant laughed over the phone and immediately called to tell me of this mini-drama.

In addition, *generation*, the central concept of this study, also has both methodological and substantive implications. I am one full generation younger than my subjects. In many informants' views, I was not an ideal scholar to research them mostly because I am too young to have had firsthand experience. This is where "experiential authority" was in play. Many zhiqing feel they "own" their past or, in their words, they have the "authority to speak" (*fayanquan*) about *their* past. At first contact, some of them challenged my experiential authority, in either open or roundabout ways, expressing their suspicion of my ability to understand them due to my age and "foreignness." For example, when I first met Mr. Shu, who later became one of my key informants, he lectured me on "sociology." After our interview, he sent me a text message: "Little Teacher Xu: I advise you to read *Introduction to Sociology* edited by XXX, which can help you understand Chinese society." The word "little" (*xiao*) was the key: here, it meant "young," and using it is to convey a sense of superiority based on seniority. If this message was comically condescending, others were blunter, bordering on being offensive. The Yunnan activist mentioned above rejected my interview request also because, in addition to my American identity, as he said in our brief conversation, "you are too young to know our past."

Nevertheless, all these identities – professional, national, and generational – are fluid and ambiguous, very much depending on how the researchers "perform" them to fit the situation (Goffman 1983). Every identity discussed above has another side, which I utilized to minimize the potential constraints from the other side. For example, my "American" identity is balanced by my "Chineseness." I decided to pursue a PhD in the United States at a relatively advanced age after I got my master's degree and worked for a few years in China. My complete socialization experience in China may be a big "delay" factor in my career but also produces positive side effects for my ethnography. I look, talk, and walk like an ordinary Chinese man with no discernible traces of experience of living abroad. My southern-accented Chinese does not mingle with English words. As a kid who grew up in the 1980s, I was familiar with the old songs and novels that the zhiqing generation loved but that younger generations do not even know. I did not have to make much effort to manage my impression to be accepted as an ordinary Chinese because I am one. Furthermore, when asked, I emphasized that I was a Chinese professor working at an American university, an identity different from a Caucasian-looking, "real" American. For most interviewees, my marginal national identity was not an obstacle.

My younger age also has its positive side. On many occasions, I told my interviewees that my mother was a zhiqing and I grew up in her sent-down place. This life history background provided a convincing narrative that could explain my scholarly interest and was emphasized by key informants who helped me recruit other zhiqing interviewees. It also considerably eased the tension caused by my American identity by subtly emphasizing my Chinese lineage. When I told my life story, some otherwise suspicious and even stone-faced people became friendly. Some voluntarily offered their explanation of my motivation for this project: "So you do this research because of your emotional attachment to the zhiqing; that makes sense!"

In sum, I view every ethnographic encounter in the field as a symbolic interaction among people with different positions in the temporal and social order of society. The interaction itself provides intersubjective data. The aforementioned condescension based on generation ("you're too young to know our past!") was more than just an awkward social moment. It was part of my "data" about how the zhiqing patrolled the generational boundary to claim their ownership of their past (see Chapter 6 for details). Their delight and surprise at seeing my serious interest in their memory revealed their sense of insecurity about the diminishing cultural influence of their past. All those encounters relied much on my unique combination of generation and national identities; a zhiqing-turned-professor or a Western researcher might not have the privilege of getting these "data."

The final reflection is about what Arlie Hochschild terms the "empathy wall," which "is an obstacle to a deep understanding of another person, one that can make us feel indifferent or even hostile to those who hold different beliefs or whose childhood is rooted in different circumstances" (Hochschild 2016, 5). My differences from my informants are more than evident. I was intellectually baptized in the "culture fever" in the 1980s and studied and worked in American universities. Politically, I can be categorized as "liberal," broadly defined in both countries. I am a fan of both classical music and contemporary singers like Cui Jian and Beyond. I share almost no ideological, intellectual, or cultural common ground with many from the zhiqing generation, especially those who remain staunch supporters of Maoism. But I also do not necessarily agree with the "liberal" wing of this generation on many things, especially their habitual idealizing of America as a way to criticize Chinese politics and society.

To cross the empathy wall, I did what Hochschild suggests: "without changing our beliefs, to know others from the inside, to see reality through their eyes, to understand the links between life, feeling, and politics" (Hochschild 2016, 5). In interviews and activities, I listened and observed without expressing my opinions. I made it clear that I would listen to all kinds of ideas from different perspectives to have a more comprehensive understanding of this generation. This statement was well received and even praised by the zhiqing across the political spectrum. The zhiqing on the left – people with political views farthest from my own – particularly appreciated my respect for their "traditional" views, which were usually mocked and condemned.

This presentation of myself was not simply a research strategy but was also based on some of my basic convictions. I agree with the Maoists on many pathologies of the current society, such as the huge disparity between the wealthy and the poor, a pressing issue around the world. I am also sympathetic to their difficulties and believe that many of them were victims of the pathologies. Even if I did not agree with their solutions, I rarely expressed my disagreement, which was unnecessary for my fieldwork. As a result, the people on the left maintained warm relationships with me, inviting me to their activities, treating me to meals, helping me recruit interviewees, and so forth. After observing my research activities for a long time, Mr. Zeng, the leader of Black Soil (Chapters 1 and 5), and a well-known Maoist, praised me: "your best quality is to be fair to all kinds of views." People on the right often took it for granted that an American-educated intellectual would certainly be more liberal, and thus, they did not hesitate to express their ideas in a blunt way. In retrospect, I do not see a significant correlation between the interviewees' political views and their willingness to be interviewed and observed.

Needless to say, after the project was completed, my political views and cultural habitus remained unchanged and unconverted. But the research was an enlightening experience for me. It provided me with an opportunity to cross the empathy wall to understand how the zhiqing think, remember, and feel. At some moments, my empathy became deeper and stronger, for example, on those days when Shanghai's temperature reached 38° Celsius (100° Fahrenheit) but the elderly zhiqing protesters still stood in front of the Labor Bureau, sweating and chanting. Sometimes I even asked myself what I would do if my mother was one of those protestors. Join the crowd to fight for my mom? Or still sit in an air-conditioned room to write a book on her twisted life? My mother's now comfortable life temporarily released me from this potential ethical–political dilemma, but this does not mean all these uneasy questions have just vanished. The "sociological imagination" might be the best I can do: even if I myself do not have these kinds of personal troubles, it is still my responsibility as a scholar to reveal the "public issues" that have caused millions of people's personal troubles (Mills 1959).

When the project ended, some of my informants became my "friends who forget their ages" (wangnianjiao), as described in a Chinese phrase. I sociologically translate this phrase as "friends across the generation gap."

1   Winners' Stories

> I have no regrets about spending my youth in the countryside. My youth shone more than others'. I ate more bitterness [endured more hardships] than others. Those who stayed in cities couldn't even imagine that bitterness.   Ms. Lu[1]

Mrs. Lu, then a small but energetic girl, spent her elementary and middle school years attempting to outperform her good-chushen classmates in everything, from political activities to academics. Despite or, more precisely, *because of* her bad chushen ("landlord"), she strove to prove that she was a genuine revolutionary successor, not by birth but by action. In the Cultural Revolution, she organized a few students to go to Beijing to see Chairman Mao without telling their parents, who were desperately paging them for days via a public address system. Their pilgrimage ended earlier; when they got to Nanjing, one of them was sick, and they had to return home.

After Lu went to the Heilongjiang Production and Construction Corps in 1969, she continued her superb work and political performance. Her effort was handsomely rewarded. She was promoted to commander of her platoon and later her company, and she joined the Party in 1974 as a model "child who can be educated" (*kejiaoyu haode zinv* or *kejiaozinv* in short) – a rare honor and opportunity given to bad-chushen zhiqing. Since she returned to Shanghai in 1979, she had worked in the government and retired as a *chu*-level (a middle-ranking) official.

Lu does not try to hide her pride in her achievements: a moderately successful career and comfortable living conditions. She believes that the harsh but "tempering" experience in Heilongjiang prepared her to overcome troubles and setbacks in her later life and work. Thus, in her view, the send-down program was not wrong; instead, it was beneficial.

How about those zhiqing who have not "made it"? Lu believes that it is pointless for those losers to blame the program for their own failure:

---

[1] Interview with Ms. Lu, July 13, 2007.

Some zhiqing … they believe … [if we zhiqing were fruits] they want to put all of us in the same basket. But how come some fruits in this basket are so big while you are so small? So, this is not really about the zhiqing [program]. Really not.

Lu carries the deep imprints from her upbringing in the Mao years. Even today, when she encounters a problem, she usually flashes back to her sent-down years and compares the current problem to a daunting task in that period, like carrying a heavy load. She also takes courage from the methods she used to accomplish those insurmountable tasks, such as chanting Mao's words, reciting a mantra, and singing a revolutionary song. For example: "Be resolute, fear no sacrifice, surmount all the difficulties, and win a victory!" When feuding with an obnoxious colleague, an old battle hymn may help her muster up the courage to fight, like "The People of the World Will Surely Be Victorious," which she stood up and sang in the interview:

> The east wind is blowing, the war drums are beating,
> Who fears who in today's world?!
> It's not the people who fear American imperialism,
> But American imperialism who fears the people!
> A just cause enjoys great support, an unjust cause enjoys none!
> The laws of history can't be broken, can't be broken!
> American imperialism will certainly perish,
> And the people of the world will surely be victorious,
> The people of the world will surely be victorious!

Mr. Yang, another zhiqing from Shanghai, went down to Anhui also in 1969, out of the enthusiasm to "make a difference in the vast universe of the countryside." Like Lu, he wanted to "use my sweat to prove I am also progressive," despite his bad chushen.[2] Every day, he rose early and started to work immediately until breakfast. In all the years in the countryside, he never missed a single day of work.

Yet Yang kept getting doses of harsh reality. He was recommended for factory jobs four times but failed to pass the political vetting of chushen. His repeated rejections wasted the recommendation opportunities that other zhiqing could have taken. Consequently, his relations with his peer zhiqing became strained. Yang once thought about killing himself. "Back then, I realized that I did not belong to the society," he said, "No matter how hard you worked, it was always futile." Later, after all other zhiqing left the village, he finally got a less desirable job as a miner in Anhui.

Yang is what Lu would call a "small fruit." He is now living in Shanghai with a meager pension (less than 3,000 yuan a month in 2017, from his Anhui mine job) and limited healthcare benefits. He is

[2] Interview with Mr. Yang, June 15, 2017.

still fighting with the mine administrators on various issues, such as compensations for his silicosis and housing. During the interview, he spoke with audible hisses in his voice, which he believed were symptoms of his silicosis due to his longtime work as a miner. He underwent multiple tests in two designated hospitals, but none of them verified his illness. The mine did not accept test results from hospitals other than the two designated ones. He suspected complicity between the hospitals and the mine. According to the labor protection laws and the mine's regulations, workers with silicosis can receive subsidies, and their children can get jobs in the mine. Yang said the silicosis quota was filled by the officials who were healthy but acquired fake verifications from the mine hospital, while sick but powerless miners like him got nothing.

Yang lamented: "I've been devoted to Communism and all the positive-energy (*zhengnenliang*) pursuits but ended up having no dignity at all." He unambiguously expressed his resentment toward the send-down program – in other words, he blamed the "basket." His troubles cannot be easily "overcome" by chanting upbeat mantras. He said:

> They say "we have no regret for our youth" [*qingchun wuhui*]. I say, "I have lots of regrets for my youth!" ... If you're better off today, you can say your experience [in the countryside] tempered yourself and your youth is regretless. But when your life is getting worse and worse, [you have] too much to regret!

Both Lu and Yang were "Chairman Mao's children": born in the early 1950s, socialized into the Maoist ideology, and politically enthusiastic. Nevertheless, their life courses diverged. So do their memories. Lu praises the send-down program for building her character and contributing to her later career success. Yang blames the years wasted in Anhui, a result of the send-down program and the chushen-based policies, for his present troubles.

Over the years, I have sat down and talked with many former zhiqing like Lu and Yang to learn their life stories. I wanted to understand their "autobiographical memory," individuals' memory of their personal experience in historical events that have affected their lives, in this case, the send-down program and related events like the Cultural Revolution. In autobiographical memory, a historical event permeates individuals' personal experience, and generation becomes part of individuals' social framework for memory (Halbwachs 1980, 58; Steinmetz 1992; DeGloma 2014).[3] Various forms of public and group memory, such as literature, memorials,

---

[3] This book does not speak to the psychological studies of "autobiographical memory," which focuses on how one constructs his or her self through personal life events, cognitive memory of events that happen in one's life courses, instead of how one's memory is intertwined with history, although the studies do talk about cultural context and social

and commemorations, can be viewed as selective uses of autobiographical memories in public settings. To understand generation and memory, we should start with autobiographical memories.

In this chapter and Chapter 2, I present a qualitative and quantitative analysis of life stories of eighty-seven former zhiqing (see the Appendix for methodological details). I examine both the content and form of their life stories and identify patterns in their ways of connecting personal experience to historical events (Labov 1972; Riessman 2008; Maynes, Pierce, and Laslett 2008; DeGloma 2014). I also link the patterns to their social characteristics to explain *why* they remember in distinctive ways. The two chapters should be read together as a whole analytical narrative.[4]

Personal Experience and Historical Evaluations

Every life story serves as a way for a member of a generation to remember his or her personal past and understand the intersection between personal biography and macro history (Mills 1959). To "operationalize" this idea, I unpack every life story into two intertwined but distinctive components: *"personal experience"* and *"historical evaluation."*

The *"personal experience"* component, which represents personal biography, refers to "a report of a sequence of events that have entered into the biography of the speaker by a sequence of clauses that correspond to the order of the original events" (Labov 1997). Every narrative of personal experience is not just a matter-of-fact description of what happened but a mini-drama with characters, plots, and morals. In the present case, it implicitly and explicitly conveys messages about their understanding and evaluation of their sent-down experience and its consequences on their later life and career.

The *"historical evaluation"* component is an evaluative account of the send-down program as a historical and political event. Some zhiqing have unambiguously positive or negative views of the program. Either they praise the program for nurturing a generation of tough people and contributing to the development of the frontiers and rural areas. Or they blame it for this generation's unsatisfying present life and, in an interviewee's words, "barbarian manners." Between the two extremes are three types of views. Some confirm the ideological and moral values of

---

situation (Brewer 1986; Rubin 1986; Berntsen and Rubin 2012). See (Schuman and Corning 2014) for a discussion on this disciplinary difference.

[4] Parts of Chapters 1 and 2 appear as my 2019 article "Intra-Generational Variations in Autobiographic Memory: China's 'Sent-Down Youth' Generation," *Social Psychology Quarterly* 82 (2): 134–57.

the program, such as its "tempering" functions, but criticize its policy details, particularly its length. When I asked those people about the idea of an alternative plan with a limited duration, say, three or four years, they said, "That's exactly what I thought." This is the pattern of "positive with ambiguity." The flip side is the pattern of "negative with ambiguity": they dislike the program but choose to be at peace with it or fatalistic about it. The real neutral or indifferent attitude also exists: some say, "I don't care" or "I haven't thought about it" or "It was just a period of history you had to live through."

The two components are intertwined in various ways. In Lu's and Yang's narratives, their "personal-experience" components are consistent with their "historical-evaluation" components, either both negative or both positive. More life stories, however, have conflicting links – for example, a negative "historical-evaluation" combined with a positive "personal experience" component, or a completely apolitical "historical evaluation" with a positive or negative "personal experience" component.

I identified and coded the two components in each story, and pinned down several major narrative patterns in the zhiqing's life stories (Table 1.1):[5]

1. *"Double Ascending"* (12.8 percent, n=12): One extends his/her positive evaluation of personal experience to a positive evaluation of the program, strongly identifying personal life course with fate of the nation, as expressed in a popular slogan: "We share the same fate with the Republic!"

2. *"Contentment with Ambiguity"* (14.9 percent, n=13): This narrative remains positive about both the personal experience and historical evaluation, but with a lower degree of positivity in their historical evaluations (positive with ambiguity).

3. *"Single Ascending"*/*"Contentment with Unconcern"* (10.3 percent, n=9): Stories about personal achievements or at least a satisfying career and life are detached from their historical background and are not accompanied by explicit historical evaluations.

4. *"Success/Contentment Despite Suffering"* (33.3 percent, n=9): Personal achievements are highlighted against an outright negative evaluation of the program as a "disaster" or a "wrong policy." As a popular saying expresses: "What did not destroy me made me stronger!"

[5] The reason for the dichotomous "positive-negative" code of personal experience component instead of a three-code set with a neutral view is more empirical than theoretical because there is no interviewee who does not care about his/her personal experience or does not stress one side of the dichotomy.

Table 1.1. *Narrative patterns*

Personal experience		Historical evaluation			
	Positive	*Positive with ambiguity*	*Neutral or indifferent*	*Negative with ambiguity*	*Negative*
Positive	Double ascending	Contentment with ambiguity	Single ascending/contentment with unconcern	Success/contentment despite suffering	Success/contentment despite suffering
Negative	Nostalgia	Nostalgia	Single descending	Tragedy	Tragedy

45

5. "*Nostalgia*" (5.7 percent, n=5): This pattern presents the negative impacts caused by their sent-down experience but frames them as their "contributions" to or "sacrifice" for the country, which, however, are not appreciated or recognized. The years in the countryside were their "good old days" when they worked with passionate idealism and a strong work ethic.

6. "*Single Descending*" (5.7 percent, n=5): This pattern recognizes the negative impacts of their sent-down experience on their present life and career but does not attribute them to the send-down program as a political event. Instead, the story often ends in a fatalistic sigh.

7. "*Tragedy*" (16.1 percent, n=4): This type of story constructs an explicit causal link between the send-down program and their personal difficulties during and after their sent-down years.

Class in the Present: Explaining Personal Experience

What can explain these intragenerational variations? Through a long theorizing process, I discovered that social class – including class positions and habitus – provides the best possible explanation. The concept of "class" used in this book consists of two aspects: "class in the present" and "class in the past." Both are derived from a Bourdieusian theoretical framework.

Let me start with "class in the present."

In my first several interviews, "class" emerged as the pivot of the zhiqing's autobiographical memories. None of them used the Chinese word "class" (*jieji*), which is too reminiscent of Maoist politics to be used in today's everyday conversations. Nor did they have the same explicit expression of their class identities as Americans, such as "I'm a middle-class person." Nevertheless, they expressed a no less clear sense of where they are and how they have moved in the stratification system. Their stories revolve around their class positions and mobility, including opportunities for jobs, education, incomes, Party membership, career success or failure, ups and downs in life, and so on. This emphasis on class surprised me, because I expected them to wax sentimental on their youth instead of stressing the mundane aspect so directly. But I then realized that this central role of class in life stories makes historical sense because the impacts of their long stay in the countryside mainly involved class-related factors, such as education, incomes, jobs, and so on (Zhou and Hou 1999; Qian and Hodson 2011).

I also found another important pattern: they linked their present class positions to the "personal experience" part of their life story. Those with higher class positions in the present seemed to tell an affirmative and "redemptive" story – that past suffering has been redeemed into today's satisfaction. For example, Xi Jinping and Mrs. Lu, two "big fruits" in the basket, think of the past as assets that contribute to their later success. Those who have a lower class position are less likely to tell such a story. This pattern repeated itself in almost all the early interviews.

In explaining this pattern, I found Bourdieu's class theory useful. When life stories revolve around one's class positions, telling a life story about personal experience is like making a statement about one's aesthetic taste, Bourdieu's famous subject, expressing and justifying one's objective class position in the present and its trajectory from the past to the present (Bourdieu 1984). In other words, the *personal experience* part of autobiographical memory expresses one's position in the social hierarchy through words about one's sense of success or failure, satisfaction, or frustration, and one's social image as a respectable person, a "symbolic capital." Such expressions justify one's class position in the present by causally linking it to one's past experience.

To develop and test this preliminary finding, I conducted more interviews through "literal" and "theoretical replications" to see if the personal experience narrative varies across different class positions and if other factors have stronger effects (Small 2009). To make the replications more systematic, I operationalize "class" by drawing on Bourdieu's and other stratification scholars' theories and studies as well as historical specificities (see the Appendix for details of the operationalization). "Class" here includes three forms of capital (economic capital, cultural capital, and social capital) with a scale of 1 to 5 for each (Erikson, Goldthorpe, and Portocarero 1979; Lin and Wu 2009; Bourdieu and Wacquant 2013). With this operationalization, "literal replication" was to look for and compare interviewees with the same class position, and "theoretical replication" compared interviewees across class positions.

Class in the Past, Habitus, and Historical Evaluations

Nevertheless, when I did more interviews, I found that *historical evaluation*, the other part of the zhiqing's generational memory, cannot be adequately explained by class in the present. The variation in historical evaluation is not correlated to the variation of the personal experience. A convenient explanatory factor can be their "political views," but this explanation would be tautological because historical evaluation of the event is part of one's political views.

Moreover, much evidence from prior studies has shown that this generation's political views, at least of the events in the Mao years, are closely correlated to their socialization experience in the 1950s–1960s, when "class" (*jieji*) was an essential political category in both ideology and practices (Unger 1982; Chan 1985; Gold 1991). This brings the inquiry back to the richer and deeper historical meanings of class in contemporary China. In other words, it can be hypothesized that the zhiqing are still "Chairman Mao's children" (Chan 1985), in the sense that the political classification of "class" (*jieji*) left strong imprints on their mentality, has weathered the dramatic social changes since then, remains a pivotal part of their social framework of memory, and shapes their *historical evaluations* of the send-down program. This hypothesis also corroborates Schuman's critical years argument that people's experience in their adolescence and early adulthood greatly shapes their later memory.

Nevertheless, several questions need more precise answers. What exactly are the "imprints on their mentality"? What are the mechanisms that link their life experience to the class system they grew up in? Furthermore, how can we effectively describe the imprints but also avoid painting an Orwellian picture of a generation of "brainwashed" kids?

I am convinced that Bourdieu's theory of class can provide the best possible answers to these questions. First, Bourdieu's multi-capital approach facilitates a historically specific concept of class: the class positions in the Mao years were not an exception but a special configuration of capitals in which "political capital," a type of social capital (Bourdieu 1991, 194–97; Swartz 2013, 64–68), especially "chushen," carried the most weight.

Second, Bourdieu's concept of habitus effectively theorizes and "upgrades" Schuman and Corning's cognitive theory of critical years as well as the "imprints" idea. "Habitus" in Bourdieu's theory includes one's dispositions of action and schema of perceptions, which are formed in a particular social environment and generate new practices in one's constant interactions with other social environments. It is a "structured structure," largely shaped by the class structure in which one is socialized in his or her critical years. In this case, political habitus, including schema of perceptions of political issues and dispositions for political actions, was central to this generation's coming-of-age experience because the class structure in the Mao years was centered on the political class categories.

Third, habitus is also "structuring structure." Once formed in the critical years, habitus is fairly durable and continues to interact with the social structure in the present to generate practices. This argument also provides some insights for today's sociology of memory. Bourdieu (1990) asserts that habitus is a "present past" and a "product of history" (italics mine):

The habitus, a *product of history*, produces individual and collective practices – more history – in accordance with the schemes generated by history. It ensures the *active presence of past experiences*, which, deposited in each organism in the form of schemes of perception, thought and action, tend to guarantee the "correctness" of practices and their constancy over time, more reliably than all formal rules and explicit norms. (54)

A theoretical deduction from this point is the two ways in which the structuring structure function works: one realist and the other constructivist. The realist way is that the zhiqing with different habitus experienced the send-down program in different ways, as a revolutionary pilgrimage or as a reluctant journey. This experience laid a foundation for and set limits to their memories today. The constructivist way is that their habitus, or core parts of their habitus, remains as part of their political-cognitive schema and shapes their evaluations of the program. In this way, the current habitus may revise or selectively use some experience to organize into a coherent narrative.

Fourth, their political habitus also changes at crucial historical moments and in their daily interactions with the political system. How and how much their habitus has changed is an empirical and historical question. Incorporating the possibility of habitus change into the analysis and specifying its ways of change can avoid the deterministic tendency in the habitus concept.

In sum, Bourdieu's theory of class theoretically pins down what "Chairman Mao's children" exactly means. What is usually called "imprint" can be theorized as the zhiqing's political habitus, which formed in the political class system in the Mao years, remains robust, and still shapes their historical evaluations of the send-down program. In this case, "class" is where history meets theory, past meets present. This brings us from theory back to history, to the zhiqing's formative years.

Coming of Age in the Mao Years

The class structure in the Mao years was a rigid political categorization system. One's political class position was determined by at least three factors. First, chushen (family class background), in its narrow sense, meant one's occupation and properties before 1949; or, for zhiqing and other children who grew up after 1949, their parents' class positions (Whyte 1975; Kraus 1981; Gao 2004). Chushen-related policies and practices were derived from the Marxist class theory and the Soviet practice of purging cadres based on their class background. After 1949, the new Communist regime used chushen to gauge people's loyalty, eliminate potential traitors and dissenters, and consolidate its social foundation (Gao 2004). Second, *historical record*: one's or one's parents' engagement in all kinds of political activities before 1949. In practice, one's historical record often merged into chushen. Third, *political engagement in campaigns after 1949*. Frequent political campaigns after 1949 kept reshuffling the class categorization. An individual's class label could be changed from "good" to "bad" if the individual, for example, was defined as a "rightist" in the "Anti-Rightist Campaign" in the 1950s because of his or her blunt criticisms of the Party.

In this book, for terminological parsimony, I use "chushen" in its broadest sense, as a shorthand for the zhiqing's "political class position" or "family class background," which includes the above-discussed three factors. Such a terminological choice was also consistent with usage by many scholars such as Gao Hua and people's everyday use in the 1960s.[6]

When the zhiqing generation grew up in the 1960s, the chushen system was getting more stabilized and rigid. Their parents' political engagement in various campaigns had already been on record and predetermined their class positions. The youths were pigeonholed into three categories: the good ("red"), bad ("black"), and the ordinary (*yiban*). The "red" included those from families with chushen of workers, cadres, poor peasants, soldiers and military officers, and so on. The "black" categories included not only those under the popular term "five black categories" (landlords, rich peasants, counter-revolutionaries, "bad elements," and rightists), but also others defined as "class enemies," for example, as specified in an official document in 1968, the capitalist roaders, present counter-revolutionary elements, and reactionary capitalists. Everyone else in between was in the "ordinary" category, including petty bourgeoisie, staff, intellectuals, and so on. People with ordinary chushen were neither stigmatized nor privileged but were "trapped in the awkward position of being at once trusted and distrusted. Their children at school had to learn at times to walk the same tightrope" (Chan 1985, 5).[7]

---

[6] In everyday discourses, chushen and chengfen are used interchangeably, but they were slightly different. For the zhiqing generation, chengfen refers to one's own class position, which, for the zhiqing, was "student," while chushen referred to their parents' class positions.

[7] A more complex reshuffling process took place in the Cultural Revolution when the officials were in power at the beginning, soon purged, but rehabilitated later before the Cultural Revolution ended. Children from those families experienced both ups and downs of their chushen. I still categorize those youths' chushen as "red" because (1) they grew up in an environment with their parents still in power; (2) many of their parents were rehabilitated soon after the peak years of the Cultural Revolution (1966–1968), and they again benefited from their family privileges. Note that they were different from those "black" youths, including Xi Jinping, whose parents were purged long before the Cultural Revolution and did not get rehabilitated until after the Cultural Revolution.

Important opportunities, especially those related to social mobility and privileges, such as education, promotion, Party membership, and so on, were given mostly to the red chushen youths. On the other hand, the state also deliberately left the door slightly open for those with non-red chushen to achieve upward mobility through super-active "political performance" (*zhengzhi biaoxian*). The state and its propaganda organs assured people that, as stated in a widely spread slogan, "you cannot choose your chushen but you can choose your road" (*chushen bu youji, daolu ke xuanze*). But this slogan belied the fact that to acquire important opportunities the zhiqing with non-red chushen had to make much more effort than their red peers: doing extra work, actively participating in political activities, taking a leadership role, demonstrating adherence to the official ideology, and so on.

Even so, performance was often overridden by chushen, especially when the zhiqing were competing for desirable opportunities, such as recommendations for college, Party membership, and administrative positions. Sometimes, the local authorities used bad chushen as an excuse to make some zhiqing, who usually did not possess good guanxi with officials, ineligible for important opportunities. Only very few opportunities were given to those model "children who could be educated" (*kejiaozinv*), youths with black chushen but with superb political performance, such as Lu at the beginning of this chapter.

In sum, the youths in the late 1960s faced a political class structure with an asymmetrical duality of chushen and political performance. As a "structured structure" (Bourdieu 1984, 170), the habitus of the zhiqing internalized this duality. Note that the political habitus was not simply a copy of the class structure; rather, it formed in the zhiqing's *response* to the class structure. They could choose to have active or inactive political performance. Defiance was not an option. Each habitus included two aspects: (1) *Disposition of action*: The degree of activeness and aspiration in political participation (including holding institutionally sanctioned political positions), taking part in all kinds of political campaigns (especially the Cultural Revolution), everyday political performance, attempting to obtain Party or Youth League membership, and so on (Shirk 1982; Chan 1985). (2) *Schema of perception*: Subjective adherence to the official ideologies.

Consequently, there were four types of habitus (Table 1.2). Numerous memoirs, scholarly studies, and my own interviews provided ample cases for each political habitus.

Faithful Red. The good-chushen youths often felt that they had a natural affinity with the political regime. They often expressed their pride in this affinity in phrases like "naturally red" (*zilaihong*) or its extreme

Table 1.2. *Political habitus of youths in the Mao years*

		Political capital/chushen	
		Good chushen	Middle-to-bad chushen
Political performance	Active political performance	Faithful red	Aspirant
	Inactive political performance	Indifferent red	Withdrawer

version, the "bloodline theory" (*xuetonglun*). Thus, many of them developed habitus with a disposition for active political performance and adherence to the official ideology. I term this type of habitus the "faithful red." For example, Mr. Qian, from a workers' family, wrote an application essay in his own blood to go to Heilongjiang, when he had already been assigned a factory job in Shanghai. He articulated the indoctrination he received in his formative years: "We received the education of Mao Zedong's thoughts, heroism, and patriotism so deeply that these things have infiltrated into our blood and bones."[8]

Indifferent Red. Nevertheless, just as owners of higher economic capital have the privilege of being indifferent to material necessity, as Bourdieu famously suggests (Bourdieu 1984), some red-class youths demonstrated little interest in or held a taken-for-granted attitude toward their high political capital. They unreflexively and naturally accepted the official ideology and followed the convention of political practices without using active political performance to prove their revolutionary character. Meanwhile, they were indifferent to politics because they did not have to worry about political persecutions. They took for granted the benefits brought by their chushen but did not try to use their privileges for political purposes. I term this type of habitus the "indifferent red."

For some working-class youths, such indifference to politics might also result from their primary concerns with their family's living conditions, which overrode their political interests. Mr. Song, for example, went to the Heilongjiang Corps largely because the stable wages he would earn in the Corps (35.2 yuan, including 10 percent "frontier subsidies") could help his family. His mother, as a single parent, had to raise him and his younger brother with her meager wages (39 yuan per month). When he went to Heilongjiang, his only luggage was a cardboard box with very few items inside. After he got his wages at the Corps, he remitted 20 yuan

---

[8] Interview with Mr. Qian, May 18, 2017.

every month to his mom until his younger brother graduated from school and started to work.[9]

Aspirants. For the middle- and bad-class youths, the only way to enhance their political capital was political performance. Many demonstrated their strong political aspiration in their enthusiastic political performance, mostly to prove that they were as revolutionary as their red peers. I term this type of habitus "aspirant." Both Lu and Yang, whose life stories were presented at the beginning of this chapter, were aspirants. Mr. Ming, another zhiqing with a capitalist chushen, developed an aspiration to demonstrate his revolutionary character by outperforming his peers, often in a desperate way. He was the first one in his school to sign up to go to Inner Mongolia when his classmates were still hesitating, because "I had that kind of youthful enthusiasm, fearing nothing, more than ready to sacrifice my life for the country if the country needed me."[10]

Withdrawers. Many middle- to bad-chushen zhiqing, however, were repeatedly denied access to all kinds of political opportunities and publicly humiliated. They were afraid of getting into trouble due to their chushen, particularly in the first few years of the Cultural Revolution. They felt frustrated and stayed home to avoid trouble, killing time by doing a variety of things, such as reading, fixing radios, or playing instruments. They were the "wanderers" (*xiaoyaopai*) in the Cultural Revolution. I term this type of habitus "withdrawer" – middle- to black-chushen with inactive political performance.

Has their political habitus, which was formed decades earlier in the peculiar political context, weathered the sea changes and remained a pivotal part of their social framework for memory today?

Answering this question requires an in-depth inquiry into life stories. The zhiqing's life stories tell us about how they have traveled their life paths, celebrated their achievements, lamented their fate, and expressed and justified their class positions. Life stories can also show how their habitus interacts with all these personal experience components and shapes their evaluations of the send-down program. I group their life stories by their class in the present and then by their habitus. In each group, the zhiqing share common traits but subtly differ from each other. I examine how the commonalities and similarities in their class positions and habitus lead to the variations in their autobiographical memories. To test the findings from the in-depth qualitative analysis, I draw hypotheses from the analysis and test them in a data file that includes thematic codes

---

[9] Interview with Mr. Song, May 15, 2017.
[10] Interview with Mr. Ming, November 9, 2013.

of narratives, class positions, and habitus (see the Appendix for the hypotheses, coding, and statistical analysis).

This chapter focuses on those with upper-middle-class to upper-class positions today (11–15 on the class scale) – the so-called winners. Chapter 2 will focus on those with lower-, working-, and middle-class positions.

The Faithful Red

Mr. Zeng was born in 1947 and grew up in a cadre's family in Shanghai. A typical "faithful red" youth, Zeng attended an elite high school and held various student leadership positions. He was an avid reader of Soviet literary works, which, in his words, were "positive, sunny, and upbeat" and had a significant influence on his worldview.[11] During the first years of the Cultural Revolution, he devoted himself to various political activities: posting "big-character-posters" on buildings on Nanjing Road, going to Beijing to see Chairman Mao, and writing essays for the *Red Guard Battle Paper* (*Hongwei Zhanbao*), an influential self-published newspaper. Zeng and other cadre-chushen kids organized a conservative Red Guard group "32111 Steel-Stick Old-Conservative Battle Team" (32111 *ganggan laobao zhandoudui*), a name that drew on the "32111" oil-drilling group in Sichuan, then a revolutionary model work group. Zeng's "battle team" engaged in verbal and physical fights with their rivals, which quickly escalated to bloodshed. In a fight, Zeng was badly beaten and even stabbed in his buttock, whereupon he was sent to the emergency room.

In 1968, as the Red Guard movement subsided, Zeng was assigned a job in Shanghai. But he turned it down. He did not want to become one of those students who had sworn to sacrifice themselves for revolution a few months earlier but now desperately tried to stay in Shanghai. To prove his genuine spirit of revolution, he broke a glass bottle, used the shattered glass to cut his finger, and wrote his application essay in his blood, entitled "[My] Determination to Go to the Front of the Anti-Revisionist Struggle." The "anti-Revisionist front" meant the Heilongjiang Corps, which was adjacent to the area where China engaged in an armed conflict with the Soviet Union.

Soon after his arrival in Heilongjiang, because of his excellent writing skills and his red chushen, he was promoted to a position of propaganda worker in the Corps. In 1977, Zeng and his wife passed the newly

---

[11] Interview with Mr. Zeng, June 3, 2014.

resumed college entrance exam (*gaokao*) and were accepted into a local petroleum college. After graduation, he worked in a government bureau in Daqing and later relocated to Shanghai, where he worked as a propaganda official until he retired with a chu-level position.

Zeng tells a "double-ascending" life story. The first ascending is a typical "redemptive" account of his personal experience: the difficulties in his life in the sent-down years have been "redeemed" into his later success. The backbreaking field labor in his sent-down years caused some health issues, such as chronic arthritis and back pains. Nevertheless, the physical difficulties of the field labor, he said, "tempered" his character and nurtured his ability to "eat bitterness." With this ability, he could easily handle the challenges in his later life and career. This ascending story uses his zhiqing experience to explain and justify his present class position: four-year college education, which was rare among the zhiqing, a middle-rank position in the government, and good pensions constitute an overall class score of 12 out of 15, a typical upper-middle-class position among zhiqing.

Zeng's second ascending story is a positive historical evaluation of the send-down program. Zeng spends much time in the interview lecturing me on the political significance and consequences of the send-down program, such as "ten great historical contributions" of the send-down program, including stabilizing the employment situation in urban areas, preparing for a potential war with the Soviet Union, constructing large-scale hydraulic systems, providing impoverished areas with teachers, establishing the rural healthcare system by turning zhiqing into "barefoot doctors," and so on.

This historical evaluation can be explained by his habitus in two different ways. First, a realist explanation is that Zeng's experience did not contain much pain. He thought of his going to Heilongjiang – a war front – as a revolutionary pilgrimage. His privileged chushen protected him from political persecutions. The "bitterness" for him was merely physical difficulties instead of a political, psychological ordeal. Even the physical difficulties were exaggerated. Zeng worked in the field for less than two years before being promoted to an administrative position. Zeng was among those zhiqing who "ate" the least bitterness in the sent-down years. His sent-down years did not have much negative impact on his career. He joined the Party and started his career in Heilongjiang. With no painful political experience in the past, he naturally tends to be positive about the send-down program.

From a constructivist perspective, Zeng's faithful red habitus remains a robust part of his social framework of memory. Zeng is an open Maoist. He says he has read Mao's writings many times and learned a great deal about "how to view Chinese society and history correctly." He still cherishes some of the ideologies he grew up in: that the youths need to go to the countryside and the frontier to receive reeducation, endure the test of hardship, and make a difference. This stubborn political habitus has been strengthened by his career as a propaganda official. His job was to propagate the official ideology through various activities, including writing reports, editing Party-sponsored magazines, newspapers, and newsletters, and organizing all kinds of political and propaganda events.

The two parts of his life story – the personal experience and the evaluation of the program – reinforce each other and converge in his strong identification with the nation. Such identification is common among the zhiqing generation who grew up in a collectivistic world and tended to tie their personal fate with the nation's history. As the saying goes: "We share with the Republic the same fate!"

Not all "faithful red" are as entirely positive as Mr. Zeng. Some have reservations about the methods, length, and other policy details of the program. For example, Mrs. Yu, from a worker's family, feels that her long stay in Heilongjiang and the resulting inadequate education limit her knowledge and scope. Mr. Kang even expresses some criticisms. In the late 1970s, Kang, already a farm official, was tasked with inspecting the zhiqing dorms. He was shocked to see that the zhiqing were drinking and smoking heavily and that some were lying on the ground and apparently intoxicated. They did not even bother to greet him, their superior. Kang understood the zhiqing's despair because they did not see their future in the farm and were desperate to leave.

Nevertheless, those complaints about the program are mainly about the details of the implementation of the policy and constitute a minor part of their overall positive historical evaluations. They remain convinced of the merit of the program's ideological goal: young students should be connected to workers and peasants. The program would have been more effective in achieving its goal if it were shorter, they believe. Moreover, their exposure to the program's damages was mostly secondhand – seeing other people's suffering instead of theirs – or, even if they have difficulties, their later career and lives are not seriously impacted.

The Indifferent Red

Of all the life history interviews I conducted, the one with Mr. Zang was the only technical failure. It lasted only forty-two minutes and mostly followed a Q&A model because he could not articulate his ideas. Zang could have told an ascending story. From a working-class family in Shanghai, he was sent down in 1969 to Wannan (pseudonym), a county in Anhui Province, and stayed in the countryside until 1977 when he was recruited into a factory in Anhui. In 1993, he retired early to take care of his daughter, who returned to Shanghai for school. After doing a few odd jobs, he soon demonstrated his management skills and was promoted from a security guard in a marketplace to the security manager and then the executive manager. Later, he started his own business. He now owns a few small hotels and other facilities in Shanghai. By any standard, he made an enviably successful career through fighting uphill battles and making persistent efforts. Nevertheless, he talked about all these in a matter-of-fact way, and, when asked his opinion of the send-down program, said: "You should ask those who have ink in their bellies" (a Chinese expression meaning cultivated people).

The brevity of the interview with Zang does not mean he is unwilling to tell his life stories. He tells his story not in the formal, recorded interview but through casual conversations and actions, especially on a trip to revisit Wannan. He invited me to go along with him. The trip had two purposes: to revisit his sent-down place and to organize and host a "zhiqing festival of culture and tourism" with hundreds of participants.

According to Chinese cultural expectations, homecoming trips are often imbued with not only nostalgia but also ritualistic actions that express class positions. As a proverb goes, a wealthy and successful man (usually a man) is supposed to wear a silk gown on that trip to garner admirations from his old neighbors and friends. This display of success can bring "face" (*mianzi*) – a Chinese form of symbolic capital, meaning reputation or prestige (Hwang 1987) – to his extended family.

Zang did not wear a silk gown but was no less eager to demonstrate his "face." He called on local officials, company managers, and ordinary peasants to come to his activities. The local government sent a minivan with a driver to take him to his sent-down places. The vice-magistrate of the township where he was sent down accompanied us. Every meal was hosted and paid for by local companies and governments. Zang apparently enjoyed this stardom. He drank very fast over the meals. At the first lunch, he finished about a half bottle of liquor (42 percent alcohol). Several hours later, at dinner, he finished another whole bottle. But when he tried to stand up for the bathroom, he instead skidded down under the dinner table. It took two of the guests, who were sober enough, to lift him to another room and then send him to the emergency room. The next morning, he was sent back from the hospital but said:

Whenever I come back to Wannan, I always drink like this: finish all the liquor in the cup when other people make a toast for me. The liquor is good, so I never got drunk here. Never got drunk. Don't worry about me. I won't get drunk in Wannan.

Zang attributes his tremendous "face" and career success to his sent-down experience, including the great work ethic he developed, his wide connections, and the good reputation he accumulated in Wannan over the years. An ascending story indeed.

Nevertheless, Zang's story is a "single-ascending" one: with no evaluations of the send-down program. Not just in the interview but also in the activities we both attended, I have never heard him talking about political issues related to the send-down program. Whenever such a debate began, he yawned, went to the bathroom, or smoked outside.

Zang's silence on the political aspect of the send-down program can be explained by his habitus as "indifferent red." In the first years of the Cultural Revolution, he stopped attending school and simply idled his time away. In some sense, such indifference was a privilege: his red chushen protected him from political persecutions and punishment. For example, soon after going to Anhui, he established his reputation as a troublemaker and was detained by the local authorities for his fistfights with the locals. Not long after he was released, he had another skirmish with a peasant and got so infuriated that he killed a small pig the peasant was raising. Then he cooked the pig's meat and invited the peasant for a "reconciliation" dinner. Over the dinner, the peasant enjoyed the meat and attempted to repair their strained relations, until Zang told him the meat he ate was from his own pig. The reconciliation dinner ended in a fight. Despite all the trouble he made, Zang was never politically punished: there were no public struggle meetings and no loss of any important opportunities – mostly thanks to his red chushen.

After the Cultural Revolution, when chushen-based political capital no longer determined one's class position, his "indifferent red" habitus further deemphasized the political aspect of class position and highlighted other forms of capital, especially economic and social capitals. To a lesser degree, his indifference to political discussions of the send-down program is also a defensive strategy to conceal the deficit in his cultural capital, because he believes such discussions are only for "those cultured people." Zang normally shunned people with higher cultural capital. I was introduced to Zang by another zhiqing, but, as Zang later told me, he was reluctant to see me at first because he believed I was an "intellectual," the kind of person with whom he did not really have anything to talk about. Nevertheless, after a few chats and drinks, he was convinced that I was not "that kind of intellectual" and was happy to take me to the revisiting trip, his distinctive way of telling his life story.

Other "indifferent red" zhiqing tell life stories with the same pattern but less drama. For example, Mr. Cui is now the head of a Cultural Department in a small city, a reputable position with a decent income that sustains a comfortable living. When the Cultural Revolution started, he was briefly enthusiastic but soon lost interest and spent much time making and playing musical instruments. Because of his musical talent, only three months after he arrived in the farm, he was selected to enter the farm's propaganda team and left field labor for good. He has experienced very few physical difficulties due to his shorter stay in the countryside. His red chushen also protected him from political persecutions. Thus, he has the luxury of being apolitical and taking his chushen for granted: "Since I don't have chengfen [chushen] problem, I didn't even feel it." With this "indifferent red" habitus and smooth career, he tells a "single-ascending" story with a focus on his personal experience and successful career with only passing, neutral comments on the program, and only when he was directly asked about it.

Other "indifferent red" zhiqing have a "neutral" rather than "indifferent" evaluation of the program: they admit both benefits and problems of the program but do not have strong opinions. For example, Mr. Gong acknowledges that the program was too long and delayed his education. Nevertheless, his complaints are limited to the policy details rather than the program's main direction. He says he is neutral in all the debates about the program: "I don't say it's good or bad. I'm quite neutral on these [political issues]. At least we [zhiqing] shared the same experience and have quite warm feelings with each other [now]."

Aspirants

Mr. Feng grew up in a family cursed with their bad chushen. In the 1950s, his father, a businessman, was convicted of being a "counter-revolutionary" and sentenced to nine years in prison. After release, his father was transferred to Baimaoling Rectification Farm and then died of a stroke. Feng was an academically stellar and politically progressive student. He published essays in newspapers and magazines, held the position of class president, and ran the school newspaper. He truly believed in the propaganda of Lei Feng and other Communist heroes. Nevertheless, his family's chushen shattered his dream for college. In 1964, when his street administration mobilized him to go to Xinjiang, despite his mother's objection, he signed up out of his belief that youths should go to the impoverished areas to contribute to the country's development and his desire to prove that he was also revolutionary.

Only one year after Feng arrived in Xinjiang, he was promoted to "cultural teacher" (*wenhua jiaoyuan*) and was in charge of daily office work and propaganda. Later, he made his way up in the propaganda system and became the vice editor-in-chief of a provincial-level state media outlet in Xinjiang, a vice-*ting* rank, rare among the Shanghai zhiqing to Xinjiang. During the interview, he proudly presented the newspapers that carried his reports on national leaders and the prestigious national awards he won. Feng now enjoys a decent pension, lives in a spacious condo, which is usually a local source of pride in Shanghai, and actively participates in government-organized activities for retired officials.

With obvious contentment with his career and life, Feng attributes his success to the zhiqing years in Xinjiang. If he had stayed in Shanghai, he says, he might not have all these achievements. Moreover, this personal affirming story is linked to a grand narrative of national development, which closely follows the official ideology:

[The zhiqing] are the pioneers of the state's program of frontier development and large-scale send-down, witnesses of this period of history, practitioners of the state's frontier reclamation and defense, the distributors of the combination of the eastern ocean civilization and yellow-earth civilization, and a generation of good youths educated by the Communist Party of China. ... As a centralized state, to maintain long-term stability, there must be a group of Han Chinese, especially in today's Xinjiang, to face the threat of the Xinjiang independence movement.

But how can a bad-chushen youth tell such a "double-ascending" story, given that his father suffered from and died because of political persecutions?

The answer to this question is his typical "aspirant" habitus, which drove him to perform superbly in work and politics to erase the scarlet letter of his black chushen. His effort was decently rewarded by positions and honors within the political system. Consequently, the pain brought by his family tragedy had fewer impacts on his career and subjective experience. Moreover, his career as a Party propaganda news official has reinforced the political belief in his "aspirant" habitus. As for his father's ordeal and death, Feng blamed "ultra-leftism," but those mistakes, he said, had been corrected by the Party. This was a typical post-Mao official narrative about the past. His father's mishap was mentioned only in passing.

Other aspirants also tell "double-ascending" stories with some variations, for example, a positive story with a somewhat ambiguous positive view of the event, given that explicit praise of a controversial event in the Mao era is rare in the today's China. For example, Mr. Xu, now the president of a Shanghai university, claims that "ordeal is an asset, without which one can't mature." When asked about his view of the program, Xu emphasizes: "Some elite emerge from this generation, become the backbone of society, and know ordinary people's life." The elites he refers to are the current Chinese leaders, especially Xi Jinping and Li Keqiang. Xu believes that, like the zhiqing-turned-leaders, he developed his emotional attachment to ordinary people in his sent-down years. The emotional attachment served as the basis for his later "down-to-earth" (*jiediqi*) leadership style. He worked in the field for long hours and sometimes slept in pig sheds. Other generations do not have that kind of experience and thus do not understand ordinary people's lives. Even the most negative impact of the zhiqing years, the delay of education, he believes, has been redeemed into his stronger motivation to study when he got an opportunity to do so. Like Premier Li Keqiang, in college, he always carried flashcards of English vocabulary with him and studied whenever possible.

This self-identification with the leader, however, does not come naturally from his chushen but his aspirant habitus. Xu's father worked overseas before 1949 and had a "complicated historical record." Their house was raided by the Red Guards in the Cultural Revolution. He was mocked and bullied by his red chushen classmates. Even when he was in the countryside, some zhiqing with better chushen filled his shoes with human waste. Xu did not dare to fight back but was determined to use work and political performance to prove his revolutionary spirit. This typical aspirant habitus included an actively pursued identification with the state and its ideology, and it was reinforced by his later career in the administrative sector of universities, which, in China, follow the same institutional logic as the state system.

Withdrawers

Mr. Yu grew up in a family with a seemingly red chushen, his father being a manual worker and his mother a cadre in a factory. He wholeheartedly admired Mao and felt extremely lucky to live in the new, red China. He still remembered his excitement and pride after a school field trip to "Pumpkin Alley" (*fangualong*), a place that used to be a slum but was rebuilt into a "workers' village" equipped with tap water, gas, electricity, and other modern comforts (Ho 2018).

This otherwise typically "red" coming-of-age experience, however, was shattered when he applied for a Little Red Guard (*hongxiaobing*) membership at the beginning of the Cultural Revolution. His application was denied because "your father was a rightist." "What? Rightist? My father?" Yu could not remember how he got home on that day but remembered that he lay on the bed and stared at the ceiling for the whole afternoon. In the evening, his father tearfully told him that he did not reveal his rightist background to Yu and his brother because he did not want this stigma to impede their political performance. Meanwhile, violent struggles spread in his school. Yu and his brother stayed away from the upheavals to avoid potential troubles. They spent most of their time reading books at home. This solitude forged his introverted personality, sensitivity to misery, and calm and critical view of the world. Unlike in the reckless "red indifference," there was much pain underneath the timid calmness in his "withdrawer" habitus.

Yu uses "despair" to describe his years in the Yunnan farm to which he was sent down. With no chance to be recommended for college due to his chushen, he felt as though he were walking in a long, dark tunnel without light at the end. While his fellow zhiqing began to indulge themselves in alcohol, absenteeism, and dating, Yu tried to soothe his anxiety by reading books. One day, he copied the poem "Mad Dog" (by Shi Zhi) from his Beijing friend, who warned him "absolutely not to circulate" this unpublished, politically dangerous poem. Forty years later, he can still recite several stanzas, which fit his feeling of being abandoned so well back then:[12]

> After suffering heartless ridicule
> It's hard to see myself as human
> It's as though I have become a rabid dog
> Wandering unstrained through the world
> Yet I am not as good as a rabid dog!
> It would jump these walls if forced
> But I can only endure those silently
> My life holds more miseries

This melancholic narrative, however, has an ending of personal success. Yu finally returned to Shanghai in 1979 to replace his father in an SOE. Later he studied part-time, got an associate college (dazhuan) degree, and became a chu-level administrator. At the time of the interview (2017), he was still working after his official retirement because his old danwei invited him back with an extra salary. He is now earning an income of 20,000 yuan per month, one of the highest among my interviewees.

Yu's high-class position shapes his autobiographical memory. His career success, Yu believes, benefits from some lessons he learned in the zhiqing years, for example, that "things will work out in the end, no matter how difficult the situation is." Once he went to the county seat about 70 kilometers from his farm but missed the last returning bus. The only way for him to get back was to walk, probably for a whole night.

---

[12] Jonathan Stalling's translation with my revision of the last two verses (Shi Zhi 2012).

Vehicles were rare in that area. He had nothing but a packet of cigarettes with him. In despair, he decided to walk in the pitch darkness. Miraculously, after he had walked for 5 kilometers, a military truck showed up, stopped, and picked him up and drove him to his farm. Yu said that later when he was facing difficulties, he always flashed back to the night on the country road and encouraged himself that "there is always a way out, and you just need to wait."

In contrast, Yu has an entirely negative evaluation of the send-down program and the Cultural Revolution: both, in his view, were complete disasters and historical tragedies. He kept a blog and later a WeChat public account to criticize the send-down program and the Cultural Revolution, and the blog made him a famous "right-winger" in the field of Shanghai zhiqing.

Yu's whole life story follows a typical pattern of "success despite suffering": the resilient and successful "I" at the center of the stage of the mini-drama, against the grim background of a catastrophe caused by the state's wrong policy. The main message is: "That which did not destroy me makes me stronger!"

Other withdrawers tell similar stories. For example, Mr. Yuan, who went to a farm in Chongming Island in Shanghai's suburb, is now a full professor at a prestigious university. Yuan's narrative about his life resembles Yu's. He confirms the benefits of the difficult years in the countryside for building his character but stresses an exorbitant price of the benefits:

The send-down program was definitely a waste. If someone still says the program was good, okay, an easy way [to test it] is that you send your children to the countryside! ... Our willpower was built and strengthened in that environment. But we didn't choose that life! It was something we had to accept in a situation we had no other options. That life was imposed on us. Let me put in this way: if someone were simple-minded enough, [back then] he would have thought of killing himself. We didn't know where our future was.

This narrative pattern can be explained by Yuan's "withdrawer" habitus. His father was an editor for a newspaper sponsored by the Nationalist Party before 1949, and this occupation naturally made his chushen black. In the Cultural Revolution, their home was raided several times by the Red Guards. Yuan was regularly humiliated at school but did not dare to respond to the insults – for example, once his classmate with good chushen pointed a finger at his nose and told him, "Behave yourself or else!" Yuan withdrew from political activities, stayed home, and occupied himself with reading books. Upon his arrival in Chongming, he soon found that many of his fellow zhiqing – more than half – had similarly bad chushen and similar withdrawer habitus. An atmosphere of pessimism and misery dominated the farm: "[The authorities] kept saying that you should put your root down (*zhagen*) in the countryside ... we were told [the meaning of life] was for revolution. But what did the revolution try to eliminate? What was the revolution for?"

The only comfort for the zhiqing withdrawers in his farm was reading books. They smuggled banned books into the farm, where, unlike in the military corps, political surveillance was fortunately loose. When the authorities occasionally raided their dorms, the zhiqing played some tricks on the illiterate supervising peasants: for example, claiming that *The Red and the Black* by Stendhal was a book about "two lines of class struggles." *Les Misérables?* That was a book about the "miserable life of proletariats in a capitalist society." The zhiqing-turned-cadres themselves too read the books secretly, and therefore only paid lip service to the authorities. Several years later, when Yuan took a course on "Western Literature" in college, he was surprised that he had already read half of the books on the reading list. His withdrawer habitus remains strong even today, largely thanks to his career as a professor, which is conducive to the elements of sober observation and critical thinking inherent in his habitus.

Other withdrawers went even further and denied a link between the past suffering and present success. "That which does not destroy me" does not "make me strong"; the only reason is "me!" – my own character and quality, which remain the same everywhere, sent-down or not.

Mr. Zong was such a case. Zong's family had "two black generations." His grandfather, a small private entrepreneur, was sentenced to five years in prison in the 1950s as a "counter-revolutionary element." His father, a well-trained historian, was labeled as a "reactionary academic authority" in 1966 because his scholarly view was similar to Wu Han's, one of the first targets of the political attacks that triggered the Cultural Revolution. The children in their neighborhood threw stones and spat at Zong. On every holiday, Zong's family had to put up two "confession posters" on their front door. Zong described that situation as a "mental hell." In the early years of the Cultural Revolution, he stayed home, dreading becoming a target of attacks. When the send-down program started, he felt there was no choice but to sign up for Jiangxi. He even secretly hoped that a red poster that praised his voluntary decision to go down would be posted on their front door and that their stigma would be alleviated. That poster, however, never appeared. Feeling cheated, Zong went to Jiangxi in 1968 in the forlorn hope of returning to Shanghai to continue his education.

Soon after his arrival, Zong realized that even that forlorn hope of returning had disappeared. He also found the contradictions between the ideology of "reeducation" and the reality he witnessed in the countryside: the most diligent peasants were former landlords or "rich peasants," while those "poor and lower-middle peasants," who enjoyed the revolutionary distinction in the class ideology, were indolent. Even the slight idealism in his mind quickly evaporated. In 1973, Zong broke his clavicle, and the local hospital's improper treatment only exacerbated the injury. That serious injury, however, turned out to be a blessing in disguise because it gave him a legitimate reason to return to Shanghai for good. A few years later, Zong took the newly resumed gaokao and got into a reputable tech college. The college degree was the starting point of Zong's successful career as a senior engineer in a state-owned enterprise.

Nevertheless, unlike Yu and Yuan, Zong believes that the years in the countryside were neither "assets" nor "character-building experience." "Those were words of winners!" Zong said. I reminded him that he was also a winner. He admitted his moderate success but attributed it to his own dogged determination to improve his life condition and to demonstrate he is not a loser. "This is something in my personality and has nothing to do with my chadui experience," he said.

Mr. Sheng, another "withdrawer," similarly detaches his success from the zhiqing experience. He was one of the very few zhiqing who admit that they neither worked hard in the field nor actively participated in political activities. He believed he did not belong to his sent-down village. He joined a group of zhiqing who regularly stole vegetables and poultry from local peasants' houses. Once he was caught and beaten by the peasants. Commune cadres often criticized him for his "backwardness," but he did not really care. He spent most of his time reading books, from literary classics to secondary school textbooks, and teaching himself English by secretly listening to *Voice of America*. These activities were generated by his withdrawer habitus, somewhat unconsciously ("because I always loved reading") and also strategically ("I realized that even if I performed superbly, I had no chance to be recommended for college due to my chushen and other people's 'backdoor tricks'"). His persistence in the study was rewarded handsomely after the Cultural Revolution. He succeeded in the gaokao and got into a college in Shanghai. His professional rank before retirement was "professor-level senior engineer" – the highest possible in his profession. His highest income before retirement was about 600,000 yuan, ten to fifteen times that of his fellow zhiqing's average. He believes this hardworking attitude is just a personal trait that has nothing to do with the zhiqing experience. Even in other situations and professions, he says, a person like him could also excel.

The withdrawer habitus has real-world consequences. The withdrawers used the time that other people spent on extra work and political performance to read and study. Consequently, with better preparedness, they fared well in the resumed gaokao. In the 1980s, a college degree not only served as a source of tremendous pride – students wore their school badges, especially those of elite universities like Fudan and Tsinghua, to garner admiration from strangers – but also almost guaranteed an administrative or professional job. The withdrawers in the upper- and upper-middle-class position have the highest volume of cultural capital (mean=4.3), second-highest monthly income (mean=10,050 yuan), and tie with the aspirants as the highest overall class positions (mean=13).

Habitus Changes

At some moments of the zhiqing's life courses, the zhiqing's political habitus dramatically changed through self-analysis and political awakening. Those moments were also the critical junctures of political transformations in China, including the Lin Biao incident in 1971 when many became disillusioned with the state propaganda and personality cult; the "thought liberation" movement right after the Cultural Revolution, when the zhiqing joined the rest of the country to reflect on the political system and ideology they once embraced; the "culture fever" in colleges in the 1980s; and so on. Habitus change also happened at "normal times" and at a gradual pace: one's superb political performance was rewarded with chushen-based discriminations, one witnessed corruption of government officials, and, as the ideological obsession gradually faded, one's pragmatic concerns with life and career took priority. Consistent with the societal changes, all the changes led toward a declining faith in the official ideology and a neutral to negative evaluation of the send-down program.

The habitus change happened to all kinds of habitus (28 out of 87, 32.2 percent), but it was most dramatic among aspirants: 18 out of 27 (66.7 percent) changed; among the high-class aspirants, 7 out of 13 (53.8 percent). The aspirant habitus was particularly precarious and subsequently malleable. The superb and revolutionary performance in the habitus was a response to the humiliation and inferiority imposed by the political class system. The aspirants' pain caused by their chushen did not disappear but was suppressed. If one's performance was rewarded duly by the system, as in the cases of Feng and Xu, their success would overshadow the pain. If not, they tended to experience an "awakening moment" when the suppressed humiliation and resentment were "reactivated." In fact, frustration was the norm and unshakable belief an exception.

For example, Mr. Ming, a private entrepreneur whose assets are worth several hundred million yuan, is such a case. I interviewed him in his company's display room filled with expensive redwood furniture. Ming was born into a family cursed by a full collection of black chushen: his father was a capitalist; his uncles included a big landlord, a capitalist executed in the 1950s, a Nationalist Air Forces pilot, and a collaborator working for the Japanese Imperial Army during WWII.

Because of this condemned background, Ming aspired to demonstrate his revolutionary character by outperforming his classmates. He promptly signed up to go to Inner Mongolia when his classmates were still hesitating. His effort, however, was rewarded by denial of access to all the important opportunities. Not until 1975 was he recruited into a geological team, a less desirable job that required longtime, outdoor fieldwork. A few years later, after the Cultural Revolution, he was recruited into a local task force to investigate the victims of the 1957 Anti-Rightist Campaign, another less desirable job requiring extensive travel and much archival work.

This otherwise tedious work, however, was his moment of political awakening. He found out that the politically condemned "rightists" he visited committed no serious crimes and that some were even completely innocent. Some of them knelt down and tearfully begged him to plead their cases. Their misery shocked him and reminded him of his family's trauma. Nonetheless, his superior seemed unmoved and said, "Those people would be defined as 'rightists' even today." Infuriated and disillusioned by the officials' aloofness, Ming quit the job immediately. He then moved to Hong Kong to join his mother, who had already migrated there after his father died. Ming said that he decided to leave the Mainland mainly out of his disappointment with the political system:

I aspired to change my situation and hoped the Communist Party would embrace children with bad chushen like me. Our hearts were red. We were ready to sacrifice anything, including our lives. But, when I was investigating [the rightists], I realized for the first time that the Party did so many horrible things.

This habitus change shaped the "historical evaluations" part of his memory. Ming criticizes the program for interrupting the life courses of a whole generation. Those people with bad chushen like him have too many painful experiences to sing the praise of the send-down program. Ming tells the story of "success despite suffering." Unlike Feng, the editor of a Xinjiang newspaper, his success was achieved outside of the state system. Ming was the unrewarded Feng, and Feng was the unawakened Ming.

In some cases, habitus changed when the zhiqing's diligent effort to achieve practical goals was thwarted due to their chushen and local politics. They then contemplated the discrepancies between the loud ideological slogans and the sordid reality. Mr. Gui was such a case. Gui's father was a cadre in a factory but had complicated "overseas relations" and historical problems, for which his father was detained in the first years of the Cultural Revolution. Gui remembered that his mother and he secretly burned books and documents at home and flushed the ashes down the sewer. "It was so horrible, so horrible," Gui murmured when he recalled the appalling experience. In his sent-down years, Gui gained acclamation from the local peasants and the authorities. But when it came to distributions of urban jobs and recommendations for college, local officials appropriated them to their own children, who could count as "returning zhiqing" (*huixiang zhiqing*, those rural youths who went to school in towns and returned to villages), using his problematic chushen as a pretext. Gui gradually lost his belief in the official ideology he once cherished. So did most of his fellow zhiqing.

After the Lin Biao incident in 1971, the local authorities organized a meeting to criticize the "571 Project Outline" drafted by Lin Biao's son Lin Liguo. When the zhiqing in his team read Lin's attack on the send-down program as "a form of rectification through labor camps," they all kept silent. The atmosphere at the meeting became so awkward that the local official had to end the meeting hastily. In private conversations, however, everybody said: "that [the labor camp remark] was so true!" The biggest pain, Gui said, came from the schizophrenia between their public expressions of their determination to "put down our roots in the countryside" and their private concerns about their future. Years later, Gui became a successful engineer; he even received the award of "national model worker," a prestigious honor only a few people in his province received in a year. Nevertheless, he still believes that the program was a "catastrophe of culture and education." He attributed his personal success to his resilient effort to struggle out of the dire situation.

Such political awakening also happened to some of the "faithful red" when they were exposed to new political ideas even if they did not encounter frustrations in their career. They often seemed unlikely to change their habitus because they were among the very few lucky ones who benefited instead of suffered from their chushen and zhiqing experience. Nevertheless, it was the greater transformations in society and politics that prompted their personal awakening. Mr. Hui was such a case. Hui joined the Party in the Heilongjiang Corps and then was selected as one of the very few zhiqing for college in 1974. When he was in college (1974–1977), however, as the whole society cooled down from political fanaticism, he read books and began to reflect on some political issues. But he did not dare to question the dominant ideology until the April 5 Tiananmen incident in 1976, when the poems and posters circulated in and beyond the square resonated with his private thoughts. His final moment of disillusionment and enlightenment came as the whole country was rocked by a series of dramatic changes in politics and culture, including the fall of the "Gang of Four," the debate over "truth criteria," and the "scar literature" that revealed the atrocities and pains caused by the Cultural Revolution. Hui now confirms the positive function of his personal sent-down experience on his later career but regards the send-down program as a disaster that inflicted damages on a whole generation and deprived them of the right to education. He said, "We so-called educated youth indeed lacked education." This view was extraordinary because he was recommended for college and enjoys a higher class position today (13 on the class scale). Thus, his strong criticism of the impacts of the program on education does not apply to himself. This puzzle can be explained by his college education. Howard Schuman made the point that education allows people to go beyond their personal experience to gain a broader historical view of political issues (Schuman and Corning 2000, 922); Karl Mannheim has a similar but even more famous point that intellectuals are a "free-floating" group whose views are not exactly bounded by their own political and economic conditions (Mannheim 1956). In this case, it was Hui's college education that enabled him to be re-socialized into the transformative trends and intellectual awakening in the late 1970s.

Another type of habitus change involved a personal transformation from a revolutionary idealism to individualism with political apathy. Their ideological fervor faded into indifference and ambiguity instead of challenge and resistance. Therefore, their memory is a "single-ascending story": a redemptive story of personal success with an apathetic and ambiguous evaluative account of the program's effects on personal life.

For example, Mr. Yi grew up in a typical working-class family of five children, relying on his stepfather's meager wages. With red, working-class chushen and superb political performance, Yi signed up to go to the Heilongjiang Corps even before the official call in December. His motivation included the idealism of "constructing and defending the frontier," a practical concern with the family's livelihood, and a desire to stay away from his abusive stepfather. Almost fifty years later, however, the practical aspect remains strong and is even amplified in his autobiographical memory, while the revolutionary idealism has faded. During the interview, he emphasizes his comfortable living. He voluntarily gives me the figure of his family income in 2017: 20,000 per month, including pensions, the salary from his second job, and rental income, in addition to their two mortgage-free properties. "Among my fellow zhiqing, not many are better than me," he says, and then adds, "probably except one of them, who is a high-ranking official and always foots the bills of reunion meals."

He attributes his success to his ability to "eat bitterness," which developed in the strenuous work and punishing weather in Heilongjiang. When asked about his view of the program, he equated the political event to his personal fate, without realizing the mix:

Without experience in Heilongjiang, I wouldn't have my today's [success]. If you want to have a better life, you need to work hard. Only when you eat bitterness and work hard can you have a career. I always say: if you're outstanding in Heilongjiang, you're outstanding in Shanghai. If you're no good in Heilongjiang, you're *nao* [no good] everywhere.

I changed my wording and asked him again about the program. He thought for a few seconds and said there was nothing wrong about the program.

This change from fanaticism to individualism with political apathy also happened to aspirants, but mostly those with an "ordinary" political chushen, because bad-chushen zhiqing may not easily erase the trauma left by their political class background. For example, Mr. Hong, from a family with "office worker" (*zhiyuan*) chushen, an ordinary class background, entered college through the gaokao. Later he went to the United States for study. After graduation, he worked in the financial industry until recently, when he returned to Shanghai. With wealth accumulated in the United States, he continued his business in Shanghai. In his words, he "has developed better than others."

Unsurprisingly, he tells a personal ascending story with a typical "American dream" trope: he arrived in New York with only $45, knocked door by door to hunt for jobs, and lived in a basement for years. All these difficulties he encountered in the United States, he says, were "nothing" compared to the ones he had experienced in the small village in China. Poverty did not matter, because "I didn't even have $45 when I was in the village." A basement apartment? "It was certainly much better than the adobe hut I stayed in the village!" In his story, the "village" was his symbolic crucible, in which he tempered his hardship-proof disposition.

In contrast to his enthusiasm for his personal success, Hong does not comment on the send-down program until asked. He admits in passing the problems with the send-down program and the Cultural Revolution. But he says, "The environment was the same for everyone." The most important thing, he emphasizes, is that "you don't waste time, and you improve yourself." As long as "you absorbed positive stuff from the environment," he says, difficulties and suffering could turn into your blessing.

Winners' Stories

Resilience, perseverance, and, finally, success. Who would not want to hear an inspiring story with these elements? Nevertheless, those stories are winners' stories. They have their limitations and can even go awry.

Remember Ms. Lu, whose story was presented at the beginning of this chapter? She made an interesting comment on "fruits" and the "basket": the "smaller fruits" should blame themselves rather than the "basket" (the send-down program). Some other "bigger fruits" made similar comments. For example, Yi mentioned one of his fellow zhiqing who has a low-paying job and does not even have money to treat his serious illnesses. None of his three sons has a decent job, and two of them over forty have yet to get married – a personal failure in the view of many Chinese. Yi attributes all this to his fellow zhiqing's not making enough effort or lacking the ability to "eat bitterness."

Even those zhiqing with black chushen who criticize the program choose to be at peace with the difficult past – not only their own past but also others' past. Mr. Ming, the private entrepreneur disillusioned with the ideologies, said:

So [people in] every historical period have their own suffering. Don't exaggerate your suffering. Of course, don't ignore your suffering. [The send-down program] certainly brought about suffering to us in our formative years, but you need to draw good things from the suffering. Now on the internet, many people only see the negative side; they use derogation to air their grievances. Those people have no future because they can't bring balance to their hearts. Unsuccess has reasons. Everyone has an equal opportunity. [If you are unsuccessful], you certainly have some problems.

It was surprising to hear his comment that "everyone has an equal opportunity," because minutes earlier he had said many of his opportunities and rights were taken away due to his chushen. But it was not a surprise if we look into his habitus and life trajectory. For Ming, his upward-moving aspiration was finally fulfilled by his later success, and thus he tends to seek reconciliation with his painful past. He tells a story of a personal odyssey, in which politics is downplayed into something certainly not pretty but that one has to adjust to. He elaborates on this point in a metaphor that could be easily found in books like *Chicken Soup for the Soul*:

Life is a journey. One carries a bag throughout the journey and puts everything in the bag. As one grows old, the bag becomes heavier. As one approaches the sunset, the bag is too heavy to carry. But I am a wiser person. ... I throw away suffering and pain. I can forget suffering very quickly but put happiness and other people's kindness in my bag. So now I walk briskly, even if I am approaching the sunset and my weight is 208 *jin* [229 pounds]. I have neither shadow nor resentment in my heart. I forgive everyone who has insulted and hurt me. I have thrown away all the pains in my life. My bag contains only happiness.

For those zhiqing who did not want to bother themselves with the past pains, such a narrative with apolitical, inspiring messages is a perfect justification of their focus on present happiness. As the reader will see in Chapter 5, this "present pleasure" narrative is why Ming's group in Shanghai attracted a huge crowd of the zhiqing retirees who treat the commemorative activities as leisure occasions to enjoy life and, ironically, to forget the past.

This pattern of thinking, however, reduces what Mills (1959) calls a "public issue" – a program that has caused problems to millions of people – to personal trouble which results from individuals' lack of some qualities, such as hard-working and resilience. It does so through cheerleading for the winners and a not-so-subtle boo for the so-called losers, who may not be able to see the light at the end of a dark tunnel.

2 Unequal Memories

The Working and Lower Classes

Not all difficult memories can be "thrown away" so easily. Not every zhiqing can say, "My bag contains only happiness." Not all the "things will work out in the end." These expressions are a kind of luxury, which only people whose painful past has stopped affecting their comfortable present can afford.

For many zhiqing, adversities in the past have not been "redeemed" into satisfying living conditions, let alone "success." The legacies of the send-down program are their day-to-day worries, including limited pensions, inadequate healthcare, and even their children's education and jobs. They tell me their life stories, but not in places like Mr. Ming's display room with luxurious redwood furniture, or coffee shops, where they often feel out of place and worry about the cost, even if I assure them that I will pay. Rather, they invite me to their homes in traditionally working- and lower-class neighborhoods in Shanghai, such as Zhabei and Yangpu, or simply sitting on benches in public parks, which can be accessed for free.

No happy endings for their unhappy stories. Difficult past begets difficult present.

It is tempting to assume that they blame the send-down program for their personal trouble. Some do, but many others do not. While they clearly know the detrimental impacts of their sent-down years on their later life, they have difficulties preserving their dignity when facing such impacts. They take more pains than "winners" to reconcile their personal experience with their historical evaluations.

The Faithful Red

In the early morning of a summer day in 2014, I was walking down a long, rain-drenched alley in a slum-like neighborhood in downtown Shanghai, ironically surrounded by glamorous skyscrapers and luxury stores. At the end of the alley, I found Mr. Zhou's apartment, more precisely, a 10-square-meter (108-square-foot) room with a refrigerator, a dining table, a full-sized bed, two drawers, and a few chairs. There was no toilet in the room, and Zhou had to use the public bathroom in the alley. The walls were made of hardboards; they were so thin that when we were talking, I heard someone next door coughing. Zhou rents this subsidized public apartment from the city government.

Zhou grew up in another neighborhood similar to this one. After he graduated from middle school in 1965, his pure and red chushen secured him a job in a factory in Shanghai. Nevertheless, enticed by the Xinjiang Production and Construction Corps' successful recruitment propaganda, he applied to "join the army" and was accepted. Like many Shanghai youths, Zhou believed that he would become a "soldier" in the "People's Liberation Army Xinjiang Military District Production and Construction Corps," a long, official, military name that effectively aroused a sense of awe and passion among the boys and girls. His parents quietly resisted the propaganda, mostly out of their intuitive perception of Xinjiang as a remote place only for the banished people. They hid from him their hukou certificate, a required document to finalize his transfer. Zhou decided to go to the recruitment office without hukou. The officer refused to issue a transfer for him; Zhou sat on the officer's desk, pleading and throwing a tantrum until they agreed.

Zhou worked in the Xinjiang Corps as a farmworker until the 1990s, when, like many other Shanghai zhiqing in Xinjiang, he retired early and returned to Shanghai for his son's education. Since then, Zhou had been taking odd jobs such as plumbing and repairing appliances. His pension from the Corps was 2,244 yuan per month in 2014, much below Shanghai's average. His biggest worry was his limited healthcare insurance. His insurance policy was from the "Shanghai City Residents' Community Medical Co-op and Assistance Program" (hereafter, "the Co-Op Program"), which covered those people mobilized in the Mao years to go outside of Shanghai but who now resided in Shanghai without hukou. The Co-Op Program was a successful outcome of the Shanghai-to-Xinjiang zhiqing's persistent protests (Xu 2021), but Zhou complained that the Co-Op Program was inadequate for most retirees with chronic conditions.

Zhou recounted the difficulties he had gone through in Xinjiang: backbreaking field labor, hunger, appalling living conditions, and isolation from the outside. Zhou was deeply involved in the Aksu hunger strike in 1980, for which he was arrested and detained for a month. After he returned to Shanghai, he joined the petitions and protests to demand better pensions and benefits.

One might expect Zhou, as an experienced protester, to have a negative evaluation of the send-down program. But he says that he never regrets going to Xinjiang and that the send-down program was absolutely correct. His suffering in the past and difficulties in the present are his sacrifice for the country and his contributions to the development of the frontier. He says:

First, I expanded my scope. Second, most importantly, I lived up to my parents' expectations, right? I made contributions to the country ... the two slogans "Defend the Frontier" and "Develop the Frontier" are not wrong. I went to Xinjiang to defend and develop the frontier. I believed I made contributions. How the government thinks about [my contributions] is their business. I feel I didn't let my country down, didn't let the Communist Party down, and didn't let my parents down, you know? [*Choked and crying*] I kept my parents in my heart. My father ... my father died when I was 18. He taught me (not to let the Party down) ... my father [*choked again*] ... so throughout my life, I am not against the Party at all.

This sense of honor is also manifested in his self-identity as a "Corps soldier" who has fulfilled his duty to "settle in and defend the frontier." Even his involvement in the Aksu incident and later petitions in Shanghai did not change his habitus. Rather, like many protesters, he resorts to the official ideology to demand justice, a typical framing that scholars term as the "rightful resistance" (O'Brien 1996).

Zhou's narrative follows a pattern of "nostalgia," a negative view of personal experience combined with a positive historical evaluation of the send-down program. This paradoxical combination can be explained by his class position today and his robust habitus. His perception of his lower-class position today is expressed in his negative memory of his personal experience in Xinjiang, which he believes is the cause of his trouble. His faithful red habitus, however, leads to a positive view of the program, of which he was proud of being part.

The problem, however, is how to reconcile the lasting difficulties caused by the past with his youthful enthusiasm, sense of honor, and pride in helping to develop the frontiers. A painful question Zhou asks himself is: Why does a person like him, who voluntarily went to the frontiers and sacrificed his youth to the development there, end up being in such misery? This question is even more painful when he compares himself to the "369ers," those zhiqing who returned from Xinjiang and stayed in Shanghai illegally and later got their hukou and monthly stipends of 369 yuan in the 1990s (Xu 2021). He thinks it is unfair that legal retirees like himself who have been faithfully following the Party and obeying the rules are treated worse than those who whine and are unruly.

Was his faith wrong? His answer is no. He finds fault with the present government, which, in his view, is corrupt, dominated by the rich and powerful, and deviates from the "mass line" of the Communist Party, that is, the principle that policies should benefit the ordinary people rather than the powerful. No wonder such a government is aloof to the zhiqing's ongoing suffering and fails to recognize the zhiqing's sacrifice for the country. In his view, Chen Liangyu, the former Municipal Secretary of Shanghai, is the epitome of such aloofness and cruelty: "that bastard said 'Don't bother to talk with them [zhiqing]. Just put off [dealing with them]. They will die soon.'"

In contrast, Zhou says, the Communist Party in the 1960s was more caring. When his father, an ordinary worker, was hospitalized in the 1960s, his father's danwei paid all the medical expenses and often sent officials to visit him. This nostalgic comparison corroborates Lee's study of the laid-off workers in the 1990s who aired their grievances through their fond memory of the Mao years (Lee 2000). A subtle difference here is that Zhou does not remember his own "good old days" but rather his father's. This surrogated memory contradicts his life stories of hunger and strenuous labor in Xinjiang. The contradiction, however, does not seem to bother him. He openly expresses his admiration of Mao on his social media. His ID on WeChat is "Loving Mao and Communist Party" (ai Mao gong).

The working-class "faithful red" are the majority of "grassroots Maoists" among my interviewees, including both Corps zhiqing, who cherish the honor of being "Corps soldiers," and chadui zhiqing. For example, Mr. Liu, from a working-class family, joined a group of youths who walked to Jinggangshan in 1966 but became stranded there, as it was snowing heavily. They barely survived the winter by living off the supplies provided by the People's Liberation Army (PLA). In 1968, he voluntarily signed up to go to Jiangxi. A few years later, Liu was recruited by a factory and had been a worker there until 1996 when he returned to Shanghai for his child's education. He worked at many jobs to survive but finally made an unusual decision: he taught himself to be an astrologer. He started by setting up a roadside stall and then expanded his business to various services, including fortune-telling, checking feng shui for home buyers, giving auspicious names to newborn babies, and so on.

Before our interview, I had Liu tell my fortune. He dissected the word I wrote down into several meaningful parts, linked them to my personality and career, and ended his sleight of hand with a combination of ambiguous predictions and unambiguous compliments. His income from his astrological practice, however, is less impressive, around 3,500 per month. During the interview, he sighed several times and said that his career is far from successful.

Nevertheless, Liu says: "I went down with much enthusiasm. You should not go against yourself, even if you're not successful." He expresses his admiration for Mao and believes that the Chinese society now has lost everything good from the Mao years, including, as he believes, free healthcare, free education, free housing, etc. "Who are happier in the reform period?" he says, "it is political oligarchs and big capitalists." I asked him if he saw the contradictions between his belief in Maoism, which contains a radical iconoclasm of Chinese traditional cultures, and his practice of Chinese astrology. Liu saw no conflict between the two: "Mao is a great nationalist, and I love traditional national Chinese culture."

The Indifferent Red

Mrs. Xue's parents were "Subeiren" – migrants from Northern Jiangsu to Shanghai, who were mostly working-class and lower-class people living in what Shanghaiese called "low-end corners" (*xiazhijiao*, or in Shanghai dialect, *hozego*) and speaking Subei dialect at home (Honig 1992). During my multiple interviews with her, Xue switched freely among three different dialects: Shanghaiese, the Subei dialect, and the Northeastern dialect, which she acquired in her zhiqing years in Heilongjiang. Each interview was long, lasting for a few hours, but was never dull. Rather, the interviews were enjoyable because of her raucous laughter, black humor, and curse words, certainly, in the three dialects as well.

Xue began to do heavy housework for her family of nine when she was young: cooking, running errands, and doing laundry by hand. The heavy housework had formed calluses on her young hands, which itched so terribly that she scratched and peeled them during classes at her school. Once, her teacher discovered her unusually callous hands, learned her stories, and burst into tears.

Xue went to a farm in Heilongjiang in 1971, married a local farm-worker, and led a frugal but relatively stable life there. Her ordeal began in 1992 when she returned to Shanghai for her daughter's education. Her siblings refused to accept her daughter's hukou, fearing that she might use her daughter's name to claim a share of their compensation if the government demolished the houses in the future. Xue promised to give up her share and begged them in tears, but her attempts were futile. Xue was infuriated. She told her elder brother and his wife, for whom she did a lot of housework when she was only a little girl: "Rest assured that I'll never knock on your door. Even if I become a beggar one day, I'll knock on the doors of your neighbors – No. 1, No. 2, I'll skip No. 3 – your address – and go on at No. 4."

Xue later managed to register her daughter's hukou with one of her old neighbors. Since then, she and her husband have been selling breakfast and vegetables without a license to supplement their meager pensions from Heilongjiang. To dodge the patrolling urban administration staff, they had to run and hide; when they got caught, they argued and fought, sometimes adopting a passive-aggressive rhetorical strategy: "If you don't allow me to sell stuff here, can I go to your home to eat?" The last time I saw her in 2018, she was earning small commissions by helping a travel agency by circulating advertisements on WeChat.

In the early 2000s, the government decided to demolish the residential area where Xue lived. She started accosting all relevant government bureaus to get an apartment a little bigger than the policy allowed. She installed herself in the relocation office and threatened the officers in a pitiful but assertive manner:

They [the relocation officers] wanted me to pay for the size over the limit. I said "no"; I wanted the apartment but had no money for you. It isn't easy to make money now, I said. Which danwei was stupid enough to hire a grandma like me? Doing business? No, I don't have start-up money; don't have the guts. Being a vendor? The urban administration chases me around. Oh, yes, I find something lucrative. That guy [relocation officer] asked, "What job?" I said, "Human trafficking, or maybe selling drugs." He was terrified. Then I said, "Since I can't do those, then the most lucrative was to sell my ass [to prostitute myself]. Right, sell my ass to you officials, one or two or even more; if district-level officials aren't enough [to pay for my apartment], I'll go to the municipal government, until you think it's enough!" Then that guy laughed and said, "Xue ayi [Auntie Xue], stop, stop!"

Her perseverance was rewarded with a studio apartment of 17 square meters (183 square feet), with a kitchen but without a living room, slightly over the limit of her family's quota. It was a rare victory amidst many losses in her life.

Like many other working-class zhiqing, Xue gave meticulous accounts about the details of her struggling life: the housework she did when she was young, her wages in 1980, the amount of money she spent on her trip from Heilongjiang to Shanghai, the exact words that the government officials said in response to her requests, and so on. In contrast, Xue's memory of historical events was sketchy and vague. She did not have the memory of the chaos in the early years of the Cultural Revolution mostly because she stopped going to school and occupied herself doing house-work. A typical "indifferent red," she did not play even a minor role in school's politics or any school activity.

When I asked her if she resented the send-down program, she answered with a long complaint about her bad-tempered husband, a Heilongjiang local. I thought she didn't get my question. Later, I brought up the question again. She complained about her ungrateful brother. Again, I tried a third time to ask the same question with different wording: "Do you resent the government for sending you down?" She looked confused and then responded: "It wasn't only me who ate that bitterness." In other words, her resentment and regret were about particular people and personal fate and had not been linked to policies and politics.

Mrs. Xue represents those zhiqing who tell "single-descending stories." They have a clearly negative view of their personal experience but do not attribute their personal trouble to the program as a political event. Sometimes such stories become fatalistic ("It was just my destiny!" or "It wasn't only me!"). Personal troubles are just personal troubles, not public issues. This narrative pattern is caused by several factors, including their class positions in the present and their habitus formed in the past. Her lower-class position in the present makes her clearly understand the detrimental effects of her sent-down years and results in a melancholic, meticulous memory of her struggling. Her good chushen gave her a safety net against political persecutions and discriminations, and, thus, she does not concern herself with the political aspect of the movement. This political indifference is reinforced by the configuration of her capitals. Her habitus developed in her formative years in a poor family led to her focus on meticulous details about survival. Her lack of cultural capital led to her inability to address political and cultural issues related to the send-down program. Her indifferent red habitus has not changed in her relatively similar working environment: from a low-paying job in the Heilongjiang farm to the bottom of the social hierarchy in Shanghai.

Aspirants

The aspirants with lower- and working-class positions tell the darkest stories. Their autobiographic memories follow the *tragedy* pattern with regret, resentment, and even outright challenge to the Party–state's legitimacy. They once were as politically enthusiastic as the faithful red, hoping to be recognized by the state despite their chushen stigma. Nevertheless, their channel of moving upward was blocked. All aspirants with lower- or working-class positions experienced habitus changes. They are keenly aware of the deep divide along the class lines *now* – the socioeconomic disparity they are painfully experiencing – and *then* – the political class system in the Mao years. They are at the bottom of both stratification systems. Thus, their frustration about their personal sent-down experience leads to attribution of their difficulties to the send-down program.

Mr. Xiang, for example, has a life course almost identical to Mr. Zhou's: he went to Xinjiang before the Cultural Revolution, returned to Shanghai in the 1990s for his son's education and better wages, has been doing odd jobs to make ends meet, and participated in the petition to demand adjustment of pensions and benefits. But he differs from Zhou in his "aspirant" habitus and his life story. Xiang's father was a "counter-revolutionary" and sentenced to several years in prison in the 1950s. When the mobilization of youths to Xinjiang began in Shanghai, their family was targeted by the street administration. Xiang's brother's health conditions did not allow him to live in a harsh environment, so Xiang decided to go to Xinjiang to reduce the pressure on the family. Xiang's other motivation to go there was that he could wear a quasi-military uniform, which signified his identity as a "Corps soldier," albeit without the cap or shoulder insignia. Xiang believed that he then could change the fate of his family because "if one person joins the army, then the whole family is honored."

Soon after his arrival in Xinjiang, he realized that his self-identification with the military was his own – and many other Shanghai zhiqing's – wishful thinking. They were simply farmworkers. Like Mrs. Xue, when he returned to Shanghai in the 1990s, he also begged his elder brother to register his son's hukou: "Brother, I exchanged my entire life in Xinjiang for your life in Shanghai!" But his brother replied: "Don't say beautiful words! You went to Xinjiang voluntarily! No way to register your hukou in my household!"

In his life stories, Xiang unambiguously blames the send-down pro-gram and the political class system for his ordeal and trouble. He disdains the slogan "regretless youth" (*qingchun wuhui*) and says he had only "choiceless youth" (*qingchun wunai*). This distinction is also the fault line between classes. The youths from privileged families, he says, went down to accumulate their political credentials, whereas people like him simply had no other options:

XIANG: How can you compare yourself to them [the leaders]? What "gold content" (*hanjinliang*) does their zhiqing experience have? What "gold content" does *your* zhiqing experience have? You have no "gold content"; you have only "water content!" Honestly, people like Xi Jinping went down to be "gilded" or to escape the catastrophe, since his father was in trouble. Their zhiqing years and our zhiqing years were two totally different things. When the send-down program was over, they

Figure 2.1 The residential area where Mr. Xiang's house was located. A large Chinese character, "demolition" (chai), indicated that the area would be demolished. Photo taken by the author in 2017

went back to cities to be officials, and we were still there working in the field. Right? ... They are the "Second Generation Red" [*hongerdai*] or the "Second Generation Officials" [*guanerdai*]. But you are ordinary people. You don't want to think that since they were zhiqing and you were zhiqing they are the same [as you are]. Do they care about you?

XU: Some zhiqing say because Xi and Li were zhiqing, when they become leaders, the [zhiqing's] situation will be better.

XIANG: Give me a break [*bangbangmang*]! He is an official's son, not your son! If he were your son, he would stand with you. But he isn't, and he stands with his interest group.

While Zhou emotionally recalls his father's danwei's paternalistic care, Xiang, also emotionally, remembers that after 1949, the Communist government confiscated his family's house, including a storefront on the ground floor and four rooms on the second floor, leaving only two rooms to his parents. The two rooms are the ones Xiang and his chronically ill wife live in now. The house is supposed to be demolished. On the walls of the house and other houses in that area there is a big Chinese character, "demolition" (*chai*), painted in red. The house looks uninhabitable. Except for the two rooms Xiang and his wife live in, all other rooms are filled with trash and dust (Figure 2.1).

In 2012, Xiang moved into the house hastily on the same day his brother moved out to a new condo the government offered as a compensation for demolishing it. The demolishing office tried to expel Xiang, but he mobilized about 200 Xinjiang zhiqing to occupy their office and forced them to concede. The demolishing office stopped harassing him. Since then, Xiang and his wife have been living in the house without hukou. But this also means that he pays no rent or utilities, because requiring them to pay would mean that his hukou status is recognized and that he would be entitled to have a new condo when this area is demolished. The street administration did not want to get into this Catch-22 mess.

Xiang expects the deadlock situation will end when the government is determined to tear down the houses in the whole residential area, most possibly by force. This scenario is probable because his neighborhood looks like a deserted island surrounded by new, nice buildings, and a public green. He expects a fight instead of a negotiation:

The government now acts like this: When you try to reason with them, they will talk about the laws. When you talk about the laws, they behave like hooligans. When you behave like a hooligan, they put you in jail.

He showed me a picture of him protesting outside of the Municipal Government of Shanghai. He was wearing a homemade paper hat, holding a cardboard signpost and hanging a plate around his neck. The plate reads:

> Zhiqing's difficulties are caused by the government.
> Dogs can register hukou, but I can't.
> People are not as respected as dogs.
> I left home when I was young.
> I've been deceived for a lifetime and [now] resent it.

Unlike the aspirant "winners," who can dilute their resentment by their success – what's the point of asking for governmental compensations when you are well off now? – the aspirant "losers," however, have no comfort zones in which they can be cocooned. It is unsurprising that many aspirants – more than any other type of habitus – defy the authorities and participate in petitions and protests. Mr. Yang, the Anhui zhiqing whose story was described at the beginning of Chapter 1, kept writing petition letters to the central and local governments. Mr. Hong, another zhiqing to Xinjiang, a core activist of the Aksu hunger strike, who is now blacklisted, even more bluntly challenges the legitimacy of the Party-state:

I completely lost my faith in the Communist Party. For a person who was educated by the Party and learned the spirit of Lei Feng, this loss of faith was a total catastrophe. I have no feeling [for the Party]; if anyone is trying to overthrow it, I won't stand up to prevent him. ... Back then, I went to Xinjiang with idealism and had been indoctrinated by the Party, but the positive influence of the indoctrination has been erased by the Party's corruption.

Withdrawers

The withdrawers chose to stay away from politics out of fear rather than indifference. Thus, compared to the indifferent red, the withdrawers have slightly more complaints about the program and tended to link their personal trouble to the program. Nevertheless, their complaints are more ambiguous than the aspirants' explicit resentment and outright challenge. Sometimes they tend to be fatalistic about their lives, of which they feel they have no control.

Mr. Hua, for example, was one of the very few interviewees with a working-class family background who had bad chushen because his father joined the Nationalist Party before 1949.[1] Consequently, his family had double disadvantages: lower socioeconomic status due to the parents' working-class jobs and lower and even negative political capital. This class position shaped his habitus significantly. For example, he repeatedly emphasized the importance of money in sustaining a person's dignity, or, more precisely, in shielding a person from bullying and discrimination:

Those better-off people were talkative and spoke loudly, but our volume was lower. If you are a better-off person or a family, you usually have more capability. And others won't bully you. They will treat you differently. If my family is better ... has better income, people won't look down upon me. If you aren't and have no good income, you can't speak loudly. Other people talk first, and you talk later because you don't have this capability.

Consistent with his words was his timid manner: avoiding eye contact, speaking at a low volume, and walking slowly. In the first years of the Cultural Revolution, he could not participate in the Red Guards activities due to his chushen. Throughout his life, he was politically inactive. In the countryside, he first worked hard, hoping to please the local authorities to obtain urban jobs and return to Shanghai, but soon realized work performance did not really matter. He began to shift his attention to how to improve his living conditions. He meticulously – sometimes proudly – recounted how he managed to survive without his parents'

---

[1] Interview with Mr. Hua, November 2, 2013.

support: raising chickens for eggs, planting vegetables, bartering his produce for peasants' grains, and so on.

With this withdrawer habitus, Hua did not see his suffering as his honorable contribution to the country. Nor did he demand compensations and policy adjustment. Instead, he believed that his life course was controlled by invisible yet formidable forces. Since his return to Shanghai, he had been doing low-paying odd jobs to supplement his meager pensions from his Jiangxi danwei (2,200 yuan in 2013, about 1,000 less than a Shanghai retiree with the same job and number of work years). At the time of our interview, he had an additional worry: his son, due to his lack of education and poor health condition, had neither a job nor a girlfriend. Nevertheless, he was ambiguous about the program. But he did not link his personal troubles to the political aspect of the program.

That [program] has become history. Back then, even the best leaders were not perfect. There is no perfect person in the world. And the state has already done a little to solve the problem, but it can't satisfy everyone. No country, even if it is rich, can satisfy everyone. Now we are OK, basically fine. So, it's fine.

At another time, he said that the only negative impact of the send-down program was the low incomes of the zhiqing like him. Compensation for the zhiqing would be great. But he believed that the state had its own priority. The money could be better used in national defense because a stronger nation is necessary for ordinary people's peaceful life. He believed that the government would consider compensating for zhiqing as soon as it gets stronger, like better-off parents will give their children more money.

In 2017, I heard from another zhiqing that Mr. Hua passed away after a stroke. The government compensations he was hoping for never came.

The Middle

The zhiqing with middle-class positions – 8–10 on the class scale – regard their present class position as "acceptable" – not high enough for them to congratulate themselves but not low enough to air their grievances. With only very few exceptions, their views of their personal experience are either moderate contentment or moderate dissatisfaction. Their historical evaluations of the send-down program largely depend on their political habitus.

The Faithful Red

Mr. Yao, a working-class youth with red chushen, voluntarily went to Xinjiang in 1964 out of his enthusiasm for the great project of defending and developing the frontiers. Also, as the oldest child in the family, he felt obliged to shoulder the responsibility to reduce the family's financial burden and to make room – in a literal sense – for other family members. His family, including his parents and five siblings, lived in a room of only 10-something square meters. Xinjiang, as described by the recruiters, was a place where one could earn regular wages and become an honorable "Corps soldier." Upon departure, he was appointed as the leader of a team of students from Yangpu District, a traditionally working- and lower-class area.

Yao's experience in Xinjiang was different from most zhiqing's. He was assigned to a staff position in the Headquarters of the Tenth Division in Yili. But Yao was frustrated because he wanted to go to tough places to prove his revolutionary spirit instead of doing paperwork in an office. He sneaked into a truck heading to farms but was discovered by his superior, who threw his luggage out of the truck and ordered him to stay. His later life and career were stable and smooth: a teacher first in Xinjiang, then in Haifeng, and he retired from a salesman position in a factory. He now lives in a small condo in Yangpu he bought before the housing market skyrocketed.

With a typical middle-class position now (scoring 9 in the class scale), Yao highlights his "ordinariness" and the character-building values of his sent-down experience:

People like me have no great achievements, but we worked hard in our ordinary positions. We have done something for the nation and for the development of the frontier area. So, we have no regret. This was like in *How the Steel Was Tempered*, [in which] there is a sentence like "when I close my eyes, I have no regret because I did not idle my time away."[2]

Yao also believes that the send-down program in Xinjiang was a necessary solution to various problems, including the development of the frontiers, the urban youths' unemployment, and the ethnic conflicts in Xinjiang. In short, he tells a life story with a mild version of a "double ascending" pattern: discernible contentment with his personal experience and a positive evaluation of the program.

Other zhiqing's faithful red habitus does not always lead to such an entirely positive view of the program but a pattern of "positive with ambiguity," which generally affirms the program's political and ideological principles but complains about its policy details. For example, Mr. Hai, in his own words, "grew up in an environment of collectivism,

---

[2] *How the Steel Was Tempered* by Nikolai Ostrovsky is a Soviet war hero novel, popular in China in the 1950s and 1960s. Yao's words are slightly different from the original quote.

patriotism, and Lei-Feng-type altruism" and preserved a "red heart" for the Party and nation throughout his life. Nevertheless, he started his story by describing how he and his fellow zhiqing desperately struggled for the opportunity to get into college and leave the Corps. He also regarded the send-down program as a terrible mistake. But the mistake was not about its principle – sending youths to the countryside to be re-educated – but its method and length. To make sure I understood him correctly, I asked: "If the send-down program was not that endless but had a specific length, say, two or three years, then would you support it?" Hai immediately said, "I would raise my two hands to support it!"

For other zhiqing, especially those with cadre chushen, being in the middle is disappointing, a downward mobility from their privileged family background. Sometimes, they may have to adopt a defensive mechanism to protect their dignity by telling a "double-ascending" story. Anita Chan argues that the youths from cadre families fully demonstrated the "authoritarian personality," such as uncritical acceptance of the dominant ideology, a self-identification of themselves as "revolutionary successors," and a sense of superiority based on an identification of individual life with the political system (Chan 1985). If the controversial term "authoritarian personality" is replaced by "habitus," then her observation is substantiated by my interviews.

For example, Mr. Shu was from a high-ranking official's family. His mother, an Organization Department official, was detained and interrogated in the first years of the Cultural Revolution but cleared and rehabilitated in the early 1970s. Shu wrote a "blood application" to go to a village in Anhui, where he was established as a model zhiqing and promoted to a local official position. His career since his return to Shanghai in 1979, however, has been mediocre: first as a staff member in his mother's university and then in a company affiliated with the university. His highest position was below the chu level with an average income.

Nevertheless, Shu still tells a "double ascending" life story, as positive and heroic as those zhiqing with upward mobility. Even more surprisingly, he compared his zhiqing experience with President Xi Jinping's: he transformed himself from a privileged kid loafing around in the village to a revolutionary successor, who rose early every day, worked diligently, and actively participated in political activities. This transformation happened when his aunt criticized his behavior and inspired him with the revolutionary tradition. The fundamental reason for the transformation, Shu says, was the "revolutionary education" Xi and he received in their red families, or what he calls "software" but I would term "habitus."

Mr. Shu also is passionate about "sociology." He was eager to discuss with me some of his "sociological theories." Shu believes that his love of knowledge, deep thinking, and theoretical analysis distinguish him from other zhiqing. Such a symbolic boundary helps Shu redefine his class positions today. He identifies his class position as "definitely in the upper class" (*shangceng*), emphasizing his cultural practices, although, as he admits, he has a much lower income and rank than his parents. His ascending story ends in his self-perceived high cultural capital. This perception is also a result of his habitus nurtured in his family, whose high-class position – total volume of capital – led to his higher self-expectation. When this self-expectation is not met on the political dimension, he uses a rhetorical emphasis on his self-accumulating cultural capital to subjectively compensate for the loss in his other capitals.

His view of the send-down program also demonstrates a sense of superiority based on his nonmaterial, cultural pursuit. He does not think the years in the countryside were wasted for zhiqing because "the program and the Cultural Revolution helped us understand the laws of historical development." He believes one should not judge a historical event by its material gains or loss. I reminded him that most people care more about their material living conditions. He agreed but made a distinction between "people like me" with such a lofty pursuit of knowledge and "those people without this kind of 'software'"; and, "we shouldn't impose our thinking on them." In his view, the send-down program was problematic because the policies did not take into consideration "those people's" material needs. In other words, he believes that the program was too idealistic instead of wrong.

The Indifferent Red

The "indifferent red" zhiqing with middle-class positions tell their life stories with mild contentment with their personal sent-down experience and moderately positive or apolitical evaluations of the program. In some cases, they evaluate the program by their personal experience, and, in others, they simply do not have any evaluations.

For example, after his zhiqing years in Anhui, Mr. Guang has worked as a factory worker, a middle-level manager, and now a freelance swimming coach and pool maintenance contractor. Guang is moderately satisfied with his present life, including his income and housing. A politically inactive youth in the Cultural Revolution, Guang spent most of his time on sports, except for briefly following bigger kids to raid homes and a church. During his zhiqing years, he continued to play sports and engaged in a few fistfights, but showed no interest in field labor or political activities.

Guang evaluates the send-down program by drawing on his own experience, and, therefore, his contentment with his present life leads to a mildly positive evaluation of the program. Even the most obvious negative outcome in his case, lack of education (only nominal middle school education), is not his worry. Neither his parents nor he himself had a higher expectation for his education. He says he does not have a "cultural" (*wen*) career but a "manual" (*wu*, literally meaning "martial") one. "As long as I can read instructions and understand books' titles," he says, "[my middle school] education is adequate for me to manage my business."

Those "indifferent red" from families of officials, however, are less at ease when they end up in a middle-class position. They take pains to reconcile their self-important habitus with their awareness of their downward mobility. For example, Mr. Li was from a high-ranking official's family with an exceptionally privileged and comfortable life. His family had maids, telephones, and a car with a chauffeur. All of those were unimaginable luxuries for ordinary Chinese families in the 1950s and 1960s, and they were provided for free by the government.

During his sent-down years, Li benefited much from his family background. His parents – two officials in the healthcare system – helped the local officials in Li's sent-down place find doctors and hospitals in Shanghai. In return, the local officials promoted Li to a position in an urban danwei, after only a year and a half on the farm. Li's career since his return, however, has been far from successful. He started as a staff member at a university. After a few years at that sleepy position, Li became restless. Without much education or professional skills, he hopped from one job to another, engaged in a few failed projects and businesses, and ended up as a tour guide with an average income. This career is acceptable for many in this generation, but for Li is a clear trajectory of downward mobility from his family's privileged background. He clearly knows that. He says that his sent-down years have made his life and career "unstable." Nevertheless, Li's habitus of self-importance alters his life story from a downward trajectory to a somewhat "single-ascending" one. Instead of focusing on career success, he talks about his character. He says that without the "tempering" experience in the countryside, he probably would have become one of those decadent and corrupted "children of high-ranking officials." A cynic might point out that he did not even have much "tempering" experience, because he lived in the "countryside" for only a brief period before he moved to a town and that the move was also one of the benefits of being a "child of high-ranking officials."

The Aspirants

Similarly, for aspirants, the same middle-class position today can be viewed as a less desirable outcome for the ambitious or a satisfactory status for those who have striven to obtain it. In both cases, because of their heavily politicized habitus, they connect personal experience to historical evaluations.

Mr. Ji was a case of unachieved ambition. Ji's family was cursed by his father's "historical problems." Before 1949, Ji's father applied to join the Nationalist Party. Even though his father was not accepted and quickly forgot the application, that piece of application form was discovered in the Cultural Revolution and haunted the whole family. Every day, as Ji remembered, his father lowered his head, bowed to Mao's portrait, and tearfully confessed his sins. Ji's father was also ordered to clean the streets in the neighborhood. Ji still remembers his embarrassment when he and his friends saw his father sweeping the ground. Ji vowed to change his fate by his superb political performance.

After he went to Yunnan in 1969, despite his hard work, he did not get any important opportunities due to his chushen. Later, Ji was assigned a teaching job in a remote town in Yunnan. The only good thing about this less desirable job was its urban hukou, which, however, disqualified him from returning in the late 1970s. Frustrated and infuriated, Ji and other zhiqing abandoned their jobs, returned to Shanghai, and petitioned the Shanghai government to demand their hukou move back to Shanghai. They took to the street, occupied government offices, and even laid themselves down on the railway tracks to block trains. In 1985, his hukou finally moved back to Shanghai. Since then, Ji has been doing different jobs, from manual labor work to running small businesses.

Ji evaluates his career as "mediocre" (luluwuwei), much lower than his expectation. He attributes this mediocrity to the send-down program and, more fundamentally, the "indelible mark of chushen." This attribution of personal troubles to public issues resulted from his habitus changes. His first moment of awakening and disillusionment came when he witnessed the hypocrisy of some politically active zhiqing in his farm, who were particularly good at presenting themselves as altruistic heroes but were not sincerely interested in field labor. The aspirant habitus gradually vanished in his longtime fight with the Shanghai government – including petitions and protests – to get his hukou back.

In contrast, Mr. Tai, with a similar aspirant habitus, holds a positively ambiguous view of the send-down program. "The years when I taught at the local school were the most memorable years in my whole life," he said. "I left my youth in Heilongjiang." While he makes passing comments that the Cultural Revolution must be condemned, Tai, somewhat paradoxically, emphasizes that it is pointless to attack the Party and the government for the problems in the past because much of the suffering was caused by the particular "times." Tai says, "Don't hurl insults at the Republic like you don't hurl insults at your parents, even though they have made mistakes."

This paradox in his life story can be explained by the rewards for the actions generated by his aspirant habitus. Despite his bad chushen (capitalist), Tai's career is extraordinarily free from major setbacks. Because of his active performance, he was selected as a model "child who can be educated" to go to the Heilongjiang Corps, which usually required good chushen because of its national defense function. Later in his sent-down years, despite a brief period of persecution, he did not miss any critical opportunity. He was soon selected as a teacher at a local school and left the field for good. He was recommended for an agricultural college but turned it down because he was afraid of being assigned jobs in less desirable places after graduation. After the zhiqing years, he had a stable administrative position in an SOE and did not suffer from the massive layoff in the 1990s. With his effort being duly rewarded and without an awakening moment, he retains his belief in the Party and the core values with which he grew up. Therefore, he tells his story with warmth, contentment, and political ambiguity.

The Withdrawers

The middle-class withdrawers' personal experience stories are less self-congratulatory than the upper- and upper-middle-class withdrawers but more mildly content than those lower- and working-class withdrawers, whereas their historical evaluations are ambiguous, critical, fatalistic, and indifferent.

Mr. Hao grew up in a family with an ordinary chushen ("staff") with some less severe problems, especially "overseas relations." Hao was a typical "withdrawer" in his formative years. He was neither qualified for nor interested in the political activities in the Cultural Revolution and spent most of his time playing the guitar, taking pictures, and, in his own words, "developing some bad habits," such as smoking cigarettes. Hao voluntarily signed up to go down not because of enthusiasm but because he worried that his parents might get into trouble if he resisted. Soon after going down to a village in Anhui, his already feeble idealism was dampened by the living conditions there: backbreaking labor (he literally broke his back and lay in bed for months), hunger, and isolation from urban culture. He wanted to leave.

Hao's pragmatic disposition then began to function in full force. He managed to develop good guanxi with the local officials. Through them, Hao obtained a non-manual-labor job. He was recommended for college twice. The first time, he did not pass the political vetting. The second time, he was recommended for a local vocational college, on condition that he must return to the commune after graduation. Hao turned it down because he did not want to return. The Party secretary of the commune, however, misinterpreted Hao's rejection as his willingness to stay and was so pleased that the secretary pulled out the document about Hao's father's "overseas relations" from his dossier and tore it into pieces. A year later, a large-scale SOE in Anhui recruited workers in the commune. Many regarded the job as the most desirable opportunity in years because of its job security, better benefits, and urban location. Hao decided to leave. Hao worked in the SOE for about ten years and then moved to Wuxi, a city closer to Shanghai, and retired as a financial and HR manager in a hospital.

With this smooth career, Hao confirms the positive effects of his zhiqing experience on his later life. But he still has regrets about his career. He says that he has no passion for his occupation as a financial professional. He wanted to be a musician. In his elementary and middle school years, he learned music from a famous teacher, who, however, was detained and violently tortured during the Cultural Revolution. His music dream was shattered. This led to his reproach of the main effect of the send-down program: lack of education. He also suggested another issue: "Why did the government avoid talking about the class of '69 [middle school]? Because when we went down to work in the field, we were only sixteen. It was a child labor problem!" Hao did not hide his criticism, despite his Party-member identity: "Sometimes people said, 'Lao Hao, you are a Party member, and how dare you talk like that?' I said, 'Because I am a Party member, I know those things too well!'"

Nevertheless, he has a "so what?" turn in his narrative:

Having said that, a policy was a policy. Policies were methods that moved history forward. The send-down program was a solution when other methods were not effective. It was like a war, in which there were always casualties. ... It was unfair. True. But so what? Liu Shaoqi died. Was that fair? He was Chairman of the country. Isn't the case that many people are still suffering from injustice? Things happened. Let them go. The Tiananmen incident? So what? Many things are like that. Let them go.

To "let them go," as Hao himself acknowledges, is easier for a person like him – at least with a decent pension – to say. This slight fatalism – "nothing I can do to change this" – is also a result of his withdrawer habitus: political detachment combined with a pragmatic disposition.

In sum, Hao's life story is a pattern of "contentment despite suffering" with moderate fatalism and a considerable amount of ambiguity.

Other withdrawers also hold this "let them go" attitude, despite their families' ordeal in the Cultural Revolution. For example, Mr. Xin, whose father, a university professor, committed suicide during the Cultural Revolution, says that the whole generation wasted about ten years in the countryside and that the loss of this generation was too enormous to be measured in any quantity. But he also says that the loss was a burden the whole generation had to bear. It is useless now to think about the trauma and pain. "I'm looking forward instead of backward," he says.

Their fatalistic view of the event, however, dovetails with their emphasis on effort to change their personal fate. Sometimes, the withdrawers with satisfying middle-class positions even express a mild sense of superiority over those with lower present class positions. Mr. Wei, who later became an engineer, claims: "There were many opportunities [to study] after the zhiqing years. Did you ever make an effort to seize any of them? ... Regretting a while is fine. Regretting for your whole life is pointless." Similarly, Mr. Geng, a Hangzhou zhiqing who went to chadui in Heilongjiang, generalizes his own satisfaction with his current life, albeit with an average income, to a need for "good mindset":

When we have reunion gatherings, I often say to them: "You're always complaining about this and that, but what on earth are you complaining about? With that mindset, even if you stayed in Hangzhou, you would not have a good life. We're at the same age and have the same experience. Why am I better off? Your personality is problematic. Do some self-reflection!"

Habitus Change

Habitus change also happened among the zhiqing who have working- and middle-class positions now. The patterns, causes, and directions of the changes were similar to those of the upper- and upper-middle-class zhiqing.

Mr. Shang is a representative case of such change. Shang was born into a poor, working-class family in Qiqihaer with separated parents and many children. After the defeat of Japan in Manchuria in 1945, Shang's father, a former Manchurian army soldier under Japan's reign, accommodated and later married a Japanese settler woman, who stayed in Manchuria after Japan's defeat because she was too feeble to flee. Because of the Japanese woman, whom Shang called "little mom" (xiaoma) or second mom, Shang was called "Japanese devil" at school. More importantly, his little mom's Japanese identity added one more political trouble to his father's troubled historical record of being a Manchurian army soldier. Shang's political and educational aspirations were thwarted. Even today, Shang keeps a letter from the provincial college admission office, which informed him that he was rejected because of his family's "historical issues." His relationships with a few girls also ended up nowhere because they and their family worried about his chushen. "Those failed relationships cast a huge shadow over my heart," he said.

Distressed by the stigmatization, he vowed to "prove that I was also revolutionary." Shang fanatically joined political activities in the first year of the Cultural Revolution. Shang was one of the very few interviewees who confessed they "struggled" – verbally attacked and physically beat– with their teachers. Years later, he apologized to them and was forgiven. Later he voluntarily signed up to go down to a farm in Heilongjiang.

In 1972, Shang's elder brother took great pains to get an opportunity to transfer Shang back to Qiqihaer, through his guanxi with some of his classmates from privileged families. On a snowy day, his brother rushed to his farm to tell him the good news, but Shang refused to leave because he wanted to stay and "construct the frontier." His brother was shocked, wept, and begged him to leave, but Shang was unmoved. Even when Shang later left the farm and went to a local vocational school to study, he truly believed that he would return to the farm to fulfill his obligation.

This uncritical acceptance of the official ideology was not shaken until the 1980s, when his danwei sent him to study as a "visiting and training teacher" (jinxiu jiaoshi) at two prestigious universities in Dalian and Hangzhou. That was a time of "cultural fever," when the intellectual atmosphere in Chinese universities was most vibrant, open, and reflexive (Calhoun 1994). Moving from a local school to those universities, he said, was "like seeing the sea for the first time." He attended lots of lectures. Some lectures attracted such large audiences that he had to sit on the floor. He avidly read books of Western humanities and social sciences and began questioning the Communist ideology he once enthu-siastically accepted. The suppressed humiliation and stigma caused by his chushen were reactivated. While he once blamed himself and his family for his troubles, now he realized they were caused by the Maoist political system, which trampled underfoot the ordinary people's family, personal feelings, and basic rights. He finally shook off the imprints of the ideology he so blindly accepted in his formative years.

For Mr. Ye, a super active Red Guard from a working-class family, such habitus change was even more dramatic. In 1967, Ye organized a Red Guard group named "Jinggangshan" and walked for several months from Shanghai to the real Jinggangshan. Now, a retiree from a lecturer position at a university, Mr. Ye often makes political comments completely the opposite to the ideology he was indoctrinated into, condemning Mao and advocating for democracy.

Ye's habitus change happened in a series of incidents in the 1970s, which, in his words, "smashed all the icons." The first big icon was Lin Biao, whose treason shocked many politically enthusiastic zhiqing. Then, his faith in the Maoist ideology faded in his college years, when he extensively read literary and political books. Later, after Mao's death, during the public debate over the truth criteria, he completed his dramatic habitus change. Ye explained his change as a result of "my deepest hatred (toward Maoism), which came out of the collapse of my deepest love (of Mao)."

Gender, Culture, and Habitus

"Does memory have a gender? If so, what does it look like and sound like?" Gail Hershatter asks in her study of rural Chinese women's memory (2011, 24). She gives an affirmative answer to the first question and specifies how the gendered framework in the state's socialist project shapes the rural women's memory of China's collectivist past. My life history interviews and quantitative analysis also show some significant gender differences, but the findings are not conclusive and can be a point for further exploration.

In the logistic regression models on "personal experience" (Appendix, Table A.4), gender has statistical significance: men are more likely to have more positive views about their personal experience in the countryside than are women. This might have to do with women having lower present class positions (5.750 in class as a continuous variable) than men (6.825) ($t = -2.334$, $p = .022$). But the significance does not exist in the models on historical evaluations. This suggests that the significance of gender relies on present class positions. When present class positions are statistically insignificant – in this case, in the relationship between class and historical evaluations – gender also loses its significance (Appendix, Table A.5).

The zhiqing's life stories show some nuances of gender difference, combined with class. For example, when women talk about ups and downs in their lives, they tend to weave family and marriage into a story revolving around class positions. The unhappy ones start with stories about their abusive husbands or family problems and then move on to complain about the unsatisfying living conditions today. For example, Mrs. Zhi, a Shanghai zhiqing with the indifferent red habitus, focuses her story on her unhappy marriage and family. In her years in Jiangxi,

Mrs. Zhi got pregnant and had to marry her boyfriend, another Shanghai zhiqing, and both she and he were punished by the local authorities for their "immorality." Their parents also opposed the hasty marriage because they saw her husband as a "hooligan" with neither a future for himself nor the ability to shoulder family responsibilities. Their words became an eerily accurate prophecy. Their marriage ended after a series of fights. At one time, she attempted to kill herself by drinking two bottles of DDVP (a lethal pesticide) but was soon discovered and sent to the emergency room. She had been working in a production team in her neighborhood until retirement. She complains about the damaging effects of her sent-down experience on her marriage and career but does not comment on the send-down program as a political event.

Mrs. Jin shares with Mrs. Zhi a similar experience: unhappy marriage in the countryside, suicide attempts, and endless regrets over her career and family. Mrs. Jin said she had "very lofty aspirations" (*xinqi hengao*) in her childhood. Her classmate, my informant, described her as a "princess" in her school: from a wealthy family with well-educated parents, Jin was one of the prettiest girls in her school, pursued by boys and envied by girls. She was also a top student in academics and, in her words, would get very upset if she did not get the highest grade in her class. Soon after going down to Jiangxi, this middle school princess was pursued and even harassed by some fellow male zhiqing and local men. Frustrated and afraid, she later married a local peasant, a veteran with pure, red chushen ("poor peasant") but limited education. The jealous men in the village described their marriage as "a lovely flower stuck in a dunghill," a derogatory phrase, which suggested their mismatch and, unfortunately, predicted the tumult in their marriage over the next four decades. Mrs. Jin did not attend many reunion gatherings because "those people who are now professors and engineers were not as good as me in school." Yet, when she told her story, she attributed her lack of success to the marriage that ruined her life rather than the send-down program.

For some other female zhiqing, however, their unsuccessful career was compensated for by their happy families. Mrs. Liu, for instance, worked in a factory after she returned to Shanghai and then was laid off in the SOE reform. She then found a low-income job in a department store until she retired. But during the interview, she emphasized that her family, especially her loving husband, compensated for all her pains over the years. After retirement, Mrs. Liu has been volunteering in a zhiqing association and doing accounting and other administrative work (Chapters 5 and 6). Almost everyone I encountered in this association knew "she has a happy family."

For other women, who had bigger career ambitions than Mrs. Liu but failed to achieve them, such emphasis on family life served as a rhetorical strategy of "switching" the focal point of their life story from career to other achievements. The main characters of their life stories are still themselves, who have "made it," but just in different areas.

For example, Mrs. Gu grew up in a family with middle-to-bad chushen but extremely high cultural capital: her father had graduated from an American university before 1949 and became one of the founders of public health research in China. She, however, did not go to college. She has been working as a physician in a community clinic for her entire career.

Thus, Mrs. Gu has to reconcile her family's higher status and her sense of self-importance with her intergenerational downward mobility in career. Using the "switching" strategy, Gu is eager to show two things: her son's achievements and herself as a gourmet. She arranged our interview in a famous old-Shanghai-style restaurant. Immediately after we sat down, she pulled out a pile of documents from her bag, including her father's books, a copy of her son's MIT diploma, and pictures of him working in a lab at Harvard. Then, she told me she has a fulfilling life as a "life-type" person: a person with a focus on lifestyle, food, and aesthetic tastes. She frequently interrupted our conversation by commenting on the dishes and talking about other food-related topics. She and her husband even raise chickens and turkeys on a small piece of land they rent in a suburban area, an unusual hobby for Chinese urbanites. She does not conceal her self-confidence and pride: "We eat those things that Shanghaiese can't even imagine, like turkey. Even our casual eating at home is well researched and carefully prepared. This can show that we have high IQs." She says she could have easily become a PhD and then a professor, but she does not think of her lack of higher education as a failure. With all her hobbies and interests, she believes she now lives more happily than her father, who spent his whole life on "very boring" research and teaching.

With this rhetoric switching, Gu's memory of her zhiqing years rarely contains painful episodes and sometimes even becomes idyllic: she grew vegetables by herself; she and other girls took a break from field labor, basking in the winter sun, relaxing and chatting. As for the movement, she emphasizes that it is pointless to complain about it; if some zhiqing are living an unsatisfying life, it is mainly because "they didn't grasp opportunities." She said:

I could have complained a lot [because] other zhiqing have already become professors. But I don't think they are as good as I am. I am very happy. I raise chickens. I raise "pearl chickens" [a special type of chickens] and even turkeys. Do you [professors] have this kind of experience? No, you don't!

Such rhetorical switching can find a parallel in Lamont's study of French and American upper-middle-class men: those who experience downward mobility in their careers tend to stress that they have found satisfaction and fulfillment in activities other than their work, for example, playing jazz and reading (Lamont 1992, 164–65). But in the cases of Liu and Gu, the switching is also gendered – to their family life and their domestic role – as compared to the men in Lamont's study.

As the present class position of a woman increases, the family–career link disappears from their narratives. None of the high-class-position women attributes their success to their family. A realist explanation of this gendered memory pattern might be that the harsher environment for female zhiqing and higher expectations for women's domestic role impeded their career development. Therefore, those women with career success are less troubled by family problems brought on by their domestic role. A constructivist explanation also makes much sense: the closer a woman's achievement is to the expectations of the male-dominated society, which emphasizes career rather than family, the more likely the woman adopts this masculine social framework to perceive their past. Yet, some questions about gender remain unanswered and could be good for future research. For example: Why is there no significant gender difference in historical evaluation? Does this mean the gender–politics link is weaker than the gender–class intersection?

Another problem also needs some discussion: How does "culture" matter in the zhiqing generation's habitus? Bourdieu's concept of habitus is illustrated in his examination of cultural tastes and education and their role in solidifying and reproducing class distinctions (Bourdieu 1984). Nevertheless, Mannheim, another source of inspiration for this book, has a seemingly opposite, famous argument about "free-floating intellectuals" (Mannheim 1956). The intellectuals, Mannheim argues, are able to transcend the constraints of class, at least partially, because their education enables them to be exposed to "opposing tendencies in social reality" (156) and they are interested in "seeing the whole of the social and political structure" rather than simply expressing interests of a particular class (161). Both Bourdieu and Mannheim, however, had difficulties in explaining the class system in the Mao years. The political class system significantly downplayed and even condemned the importance of cultural capital – for example, intellectuals were called "stinky

No. 9" (*choulaojiu*), which meant they were both politically despicable ("stinky") and socially low ("No. 9") in the class system. Thus, they were neither dominant in defining cultural tastes nor "free-floating."

Nevertheless, despite the general devaluation of culture, those zhiqing from intellectual families still managed to maintain their highly "cultured" habitus, for example, the regular habit of reading, having a good work ethic in learning, and having a strong education aspiration. How, then, do they now view their personal experience and evaluate the send-down program?

Among my interviewees, eleven (about 12 percent) had highly cultured habitus. They were top students in their schools, regularly read books, and had higher education aspirations. Unsurprisingly, most of them grew up in families with high- or at least middle-level cultural capital, including university professors, high school teachers, engineers, and so on. Also unsurprising is that the zhiqing with highly cultured habitus later have the highest level of education. More specifically, those who kept the habit of reading books and had higher education aspirations were more prepared for gaokao. Several interviewees' stories in Chapter 1 were examples of this typical scenario: Mr. Yuan (the professor in Shanghai) sneaked books to Chongming to read; Mr. Sheng (the high-income engineer) evaded the field labor and listened to *Voice of America*. Both passed the competitive gaokao and had successful careers. Even for Mr. Yu, who did not have a college degree, his reading habit and educational aspiration paid off later in his factory job: he got his diploma through continuing education, was promoted to non-manual-labor positions, and kept a quite influential blog. Correspondingly, consistent with the theory I propose, ten of the eleven high-cultured-habitus interviewees have positive views about their personal experience, mostly because their higher education levels contribute to their higher overall class positions. In this sense, with some modifications, Bourdieu's education production theory can still be applied to this case (Bourdieu and Passeron 1977).

What is interesting and somewhat unexpected, however, is their polarized historical evaluation of the send-down program: seven of them clearly expressed criticism of the program, while the other four gave their positive opinions. There were no middle-of-the-way, ambiguous views. This polarization cannot be explained by quantitative measures, but an in-depth examination of the cases can reveal its mechanism. The eleven people can be divided into two types of zhiqing: the *most* politically active (the aspirants and the faithful red, who had either black or red chushen), and the *least* active ones who harbored doubts and resentments due to their chushen (the withdrawers). Those who had positive evaluations of the program were three aspirants and one faithful red who did not change their habitus, whereas those negative about the program were aspirants who experienced habitus change and withdrawers. Their present jobs have no correlations with their evaluation: among the four positive ones, there are a university president, a poet, and a newspaper editor, who by profession are typical intellectuals.

In sum, neither Bourdieu nor Mannheim provides ready-made answers to the question about cultural capital. The cultured habitus perfectly explains those zhiqing's later education achievements, but it is very much expected and does not offer new insights. In explaining historical evaluations, it is not as strong a predictor as the politics-based habitus and its later changes. Mannheim's "free-floating" intellectuals argument was simply impossible in the Mao years, particularly in the late 1960s, when the zhiqing grew up. "Intellectuals" were one of the class labels, even a class stigma, rather than a "classless" stratum, as Mannheim claims. Children of intellectuals were forced to choose from two options: either demonstrate their revolutionary spirit by adopting the official ideology, or quietly stay in the shadow. Therefore, their political habitus was divided into two clear-cut types, aspirants and withdrawers. The politically divided habitus overshadowed cultural habitus, and this division shaped their memory.

The Big Picture

I coded each life history interview and combined the codes with the demographic information from a brief, after-interview questionnaire. The information was quantified and input into a data file to test some hypotheses generated from the interviews through regression analyses (see the Appendix for hypotheses and regression analyses). The results of the regression analyses satisfyingly corroborate the qualitative analysis.

Here I recapitulate the major findings from both the qualitative and quantitative analyses of autobiographic memories.

First, contrary to the popular stereotype, the members of this generation of "Chairman Mao's children" have diverse autobiographical memories of their personal and collective past. I identify two key components of their autobiographical memories: *personal experience* and *historical evaluation*, which instantiate how personal biography intertwines with history. The two components and their interrelations greatly vary. Thus, the zhiqing's generational memory at the individual level shows significant *intragenerational differences*. In other words, like children in a family, "Chairman Mao's children" share common traits from their coming-of-age experience but differ from each other in how they remember their personal and shared past.

Second, the intragenerational differences in the zhiqing's autobiographical memories can be explained by "class," more specifically, including "class in the present" and "class in the past."

Their *present class positions* play a decisive role in shaping their retrospective views of *personal experience* during and after the sent-down years. Those with higher class positions today tend to have more positive views of their personal experience in their sent-down years.

Their *class in the past*, including their chushen in the Mao years and their corresponding habitus, shape their historical evaluations of the program. Those with "red" chushen in the Mao years are more likely to have positive evaluations of the send-down program and other Mao government policies and campaigns than those with black or middle chushen. But the habitus may also change as a response to the dramatic social transformation in China from the Mao period to the reform period and leads toward more negative historical evaluations. The aspirants more easily change their habitus, and, thus, their memory tends to be positive about the program. But those aspirants whose habitus remain unchanged tend to have positive evaluations of the send-down program.

If the two parts ("personal experience" and "historical evaluation") are put together, we have a complete picture of the zhiqing generation's autobiographical memories. When they remember their personal past, they follow the rules of winning and losing in today's stratification system. Their life stories mirror, express, and justify their present class positions. When they evaluate the send-down program and related events, they follow their habitus formed in the political class system in the past, unless such habitus has changed.

This class explanation also has implications for us to *historically* understand this generation, especially the popular statement that they are "Chairman Mao's children" carrying the imprints from their coming-of-age experience under Mao. These "imprints," as I have specified, are their "political habitus," which formed in the political class system and extended its significant influence from the Mao years to the present day.

Many of the zhiqing link their problems to the send-down program as a policy failure. They follow what Mills advocates, the "sociological imagination." Nevertheless, many others do not make this link. Some of the "winners" highlight their own success without paying attention to their fellow members of the generation who are still suffering from the aftermath of the event. Many "losers" fail to recognize that their troubles are not really their fault but part of the aftermath of the program and the persisting political system.

In sum, when they seek to anchor the meaning of life through their autobiographical memories, they are torn between two class systems, one in the past and the other in the present, and between personal trouble and public issues. They are indeed a marginal generation.

3   The Wasted Years and a Land of Wonder
The Literary Memory

In 1982, Ye Xin, a zhiqing-turned-writer, published a novel, *The Wasted Years* (*cuotuo suiyue*), in *Harvest*, a prestigious literary magazine. The issue that carried the first half of the novel sold a record-breaking 500,000 copies. But the record was soon broken by the next issue, which carried the novel's second half and sold over a million copies. The novel was adapted by China Central Television (CCTV) into one of its first-ever TV series, which wrung tears from an audience of millions. The otherwise little-known, classical Chinese idiom "wasted years" (*cuotuo suiyue*) has been used as a shorthand for a view that holds the send-down program accountable for the zhiqing's traumatic experience.

The sensation of *The Wasted Years* can hardly be explained by its literary values. It is only marginally mentioned or simply ignored in textbooks of contemporary Chinese literature. It has never won any prestigious literary awards. It became a runaway success mostly because it exposed the zhiqing's suffering in their sent-down years and explicitly attributed them to chushen-based political discriminations and other political wrongs in the Cultural Revolution. The title said it all: the years in the countryside were wasted.

In the same year, Liang Xiaosheng, a Heilongjiang zhiqing writer, published a short story, "A Land of Wonder and Mystery" (*zheshi yipian shenqi de tudi*). The zhiqing in the story conquered a marsh and uplifted their morale and spirit, at the expense of three deaths. Set in the Great Northern Wilderness (*Beidahuang*),[1] this story endowed the zhiqing generation with a tenacious spirit and positive qualities like self-sacrifice. But it refrained from making any political judgments about the send-down program.

---

[1] Beidahuang refers to a large land in the northeastern part of China, mostly in Heilongjiang Province. Much of the land used to be uncultivated and uninhabited, although it had been the place for punitive exiles, reclamations, and frontier settlements before the PRC government began large-scale reclamation programs of demobilized soldiers in the 1950s and zhiqing in the 1960s (Wang 2017).

This upbeat story, however, attracted much attention to the part Liang was trying to downplay. An immediate response to his exaltation of the zhiqing's sacrifice was a poignant question: "What did we sacrifice *for*?" This question was painful against its historical backdrop. The whole generation was experiencing disillusionment with the Maoist ideology and anxiety about their future. Some popular texts represented these sentiments. For example, Bei Dao's poem "Reply," in which he screamed for his generation that "I – don't – believe!" The famous letter by "Pan Xiao" to *China Youth* magazine also expressed the frustration in its title: "Why Is Life's Road Getting Narrower and Narrower?" (Siu and Stern 1983). Thus, it came as no surprise that even fellow zhiqing writers criticized Liang's heroic representations of the past. Kong Jiesheng, for example, said:

Liang Xiaosheng tried to create tragic heroes and praised zhiqing's devotion, but he forgot the historical background. I feel that the more he praised the zhiqing's bravery and devotion, the more tragic they appeared to be. (Leung 1994, 77)

Despite their different views of the send-down program, both novels highlighted and confirmed the worthiness of the zhiqing generation. Liang's heroic representation of the zhiqing was obvious. Even Ye Xin explicitly stated his purpose was to show the zhiqing deserved more respect than they had received (Ye 1999, 47). Many writers followed Ye Xin instead of Liang Xiaosheng. They collectively presented a pattern of memory at the intersection of this generation's collective personal biography and the historical event that defined their fate. This pattern is "good people but the bad event": it strives to present a respectable image of the zhiqing against the backdrop of the botched send-down program.

In the late 1970s and early 1980s, for empty-handed zhiqing who just returned from the countryside and were wandering as strangers in their hometowns, writing, reading, and talking about literary works were not ordinary activities. Rather, literature provided them with a medium to make sense of the meaning of their past and express their feelings and desires. The literary works were largely *of* the zhiqing (about zhiqing's life in the past), *by* the zhiqing (most writers were zhiqing), and *for* the zhiqing (most readers were zhiqing). They wanted to tell stories about themselves, to lament their lost youth, to figure out what went wrong, and to find ways to say who they are and who they were. In this sense, the literary works of the zhiqing "help produce collective memories by recollecting the past in the form of narratives" (Erll and Rigney 2006).

In this chapter, I focus on the "literary memory" of the zhiqing generation. My analysis here does not repeat the prior literary studies of the "zhiqing literature," which have offered in-depth interpretations of representative works (Guo 1988; Yang 2002; Cao 2003; Scruggs 2014). Literary values are not my central concern here. Rather, I treat literary works as one of the forms of "public memory," like memorials and museums, which are constructed and reproduced in mnemonic practices, including writing, production, dissemination, reading, adaptation, and public discussions (Erll and Rigney 2006; Padgett 2018). Public memory selectively uses one or more autobiographical memories of various groups in the generation – in Mannheim's (1956 [1923]) terms, "generation units" – and turns them into publicly expressed and disseminated narratives. Which group's memory got represented publicly? Which group's memory becomes the dominant narrative? How? For what purposes? All these questions lead us to the "cultural production" process in which public memory is produced and embodied in cultural products, such as novels, movies, TV series, and museums. Such cultural production also relies on organizations, institutions, and various other social and political factors, which all operate in a field of cultural production (Tuchman and Fortin 1984; Griswold 1987b; Bourdieu 1993, 1996; Peterson and Anand 2004).

I examine four major processes involved in the literary memory of the zhiqing generation: (1) *Reflection*: how the literary works reflect the challenges and opportunities the zhiqing faced in their critical life stages, for example, when they returned to cities; (2) *Representation*: patterns of representation of the past in the texts, including the zhiqing's personal experience and their political views of the send-down program; (3) *Production*: the "field" of cultural production, including institutions and organizations within the field, its relations with other fields (especially the field of power), its dominant logics, major positions, internal dynamics, and trajectories (Bourdieu 1993), and memory entrepreneurs – the people devoted to memory creation and dissemination (Fine 1996) – mostly writers, publishers, reviewers, cultural officials, and so on, and how the entrepreneurs' memory work is shaped by their social characteristics, including class position, habitus, and positions in related social fields; (4) *Reception*: how people within and outside the generation and the cultural production field receive the works and how their discussions about and debates over the works reproduce the literary memory (Griswold 1987a). I believe that dynamic and complex intersections among these processes can explain the contents and forms of the literary memory of the zhiqing generation.

I selected thirty-seven literary texts, including nineteen novels and eighteen novellas or short stories, by fifteen writers (see Table A.6 in the Appendix for a list of texts). In terms of time periods, this list includes only fiction written since the end of the Cultural Revolution (1976), mostly in the 1980s. Because I intend to study memory instead of literature, I chose works that most significantly represent public memory. These works satisfy two criteria. First, the works must have an explicit intention to tell stories *about* the zhiqing generation's life in and after their sent-down years, and the identity of "zhiqing" must be central to their stories. This criterion excludes those works that only use the zhiqing experience and characters as part of another story with purposes other than representing the zhiqing past. For example, Lin Bai's *One Person's War* (1993), a novella that includes the protagonist's zhiqing experience, is excluded, because it neither emphasizes zhiqing as the protagonist's primary identity nor has the explicit purpose of representing the generation's past. Second, the works must have generated influence on public memory of the zhiqing generation within and outside the literary field. For example, they have been adapted into popular TV dramas or movies, or have been discussed and debated in the media, or won prestigious national prizes. Essays, reportage, and poems are excluded because fiction has been the most influential subgenre in the literary memory of the zhiqing generation.

The Lost Generation: Strangers in Their Hometowns

Literary memory of the zhiqing generation emerged and boomed in the late 1970s and early 1980s, when most zhiqing returned to their home-towns and had serious difficulties reentering the labor force and rejoining urban life. Many of them had to come to terms with the legacies of their long stay in the countryside and struggled to find their positions in their cities. In the eyes of many residents in major source cities like Shanghai, the returning zhiqing were a group of dejected youths wandering at the margins of their cities. They became what Michel Bonnin's terms China's "lost generation."

Their difficulties started almost immediately upon their return. For some, the fatigue after years of drifting and wandering was redeemed in their moms' delighted tears. For others, however, such a warm welcome was more imagination than reality. Upon her return from Anhui to Shanghai, Mrs. Wei, one of my interviewees, was met with an unexpectedly cold and awkward atmosphere at home. Her younger sister, also a zhiqing but on Haifeng Farm in Subei, said to her: "You don't want to register your hukou. Let me register first and take the replacement [*dingti*] of dad's job!" Her mom cried and kept repeating a Yue Opera line: "Mom's palm and back of mom's hand; both are mom's flesh!" (*shouxin shoubei doushi rou*) – meaning it was such a pain for a parent to decide between two children. Wei's father finally made a decision. First,

Wei took her dad's replacement job because she had been in the countryside for more years. Second, to compensate her sister, Wei must pay her 6 yuan every month out of her 30-yuan monthly wages. Even now, Wei still lamented that the family relations were reduced to cold, meticulous calculations.

Nevertheless, Wei was still one of the lucky returning zhiqing. Not many zhiqing could dingti their parents, and even fewer could dingti at a desirable danwei like hers, the Shanghai Piano Factory, a state-owned-enterprise (SOE), in which, at least in the 1980s, workers had job security, above-average wages, and good benefits.

If Wei gave up her dingti opportunity to her sister, her option would be to join a "production team" (*shengchanzu*, urban neighborhood workshops), organized by the street administrations, to earn – in her case – 70 fen a day, approximately 17.5 yuan per month, a little more than half of an SOE job wage. The production team job was often low skilled and repetitive (Lu 2019). For example, Mr. Sheng was first assigned to make some parts for sewing machines, then to punch rivets into the old-style menstruation pads, to ride tricycles to deliver products, and so on. For Mr. Huang, his first job was to sweep floors, then lift 60- or 70-pound chains and put them into boxes, and then make nails on a noisy machine. Some returning zhiqing, like Mrs. Zhi, worked in production teams until the teams were disbanded in the 1990s. Mrs. Cai was luckier. Not long after she returned, she was soon assigned an office job in a "Labor and Service Company" (*laodongfuwu gongsi*), a new form of organization established by district and street administrations to gather under-employed youths to provide community services such as house repairs.

Many other zhiqing idled at home and waited to be assigned jobs, joining a crowd of "youths waiting for work" (*daiye qingnian*), a euphemism for unemployed youths. Their waiting time ranged between several months and a year or two. In a few cases, the zhiqing had to improvise to make a living, often through unlicensed work. Mr. Ji, who protested to demand a transfer of his hukou back to Shanghai (Chapter 2), lived in Shanghai without hukou for more than six years, from March 1979 to October 1985. To survive, he started selling vegetables in a local grocery market. He had to bribe the "red armbands" (market administration staff) – 30 fen or so, off the record – to buy a space. Ji also sold fruits, buns, sunflower seeds, "coffee" (made from coffee dregs), "pseudo suit-shirt collars,"[2] and so on. But all these businesses were short-lived due to

---

[2] "Pseudo suit-shirt collar" was a common accessory in the 1970s and 1980s. It was only upper part of a suit-shirt with collars, worn under a sweater, to be used as a partial, cheaper replacement of a real shirt.

the city administration's crackdown. The most organized business he engaged in was his clothing profiteering (*walun*, in Shanghai dialect), partnering with other returning zhiqing. Two of them were selling clothes on a cardboard box on the roadside, and three female zhiqing (*qiaobian-mozi*, in Shanghai dialect) pretended to be "clients" who formed a small crowd, selected and praised the clothes, and tried to attract passersby. Another person kept watch, giving the other zhiqing a coded signal when the city administration's people were coming. In addition, they had to fight with other street vendors to get the best possible spot. Once, they engaged in a conflict with another group of vendors for territories and had to pay some gangsters, in Ji's words, to "solve the issue."

There were about ten million unemployed zhiqing in the early 1980s (Anderson 1984). The central government and local governments in major zhiqing source cities adjusted policies to provide jobs for the millions of returning zhiqing (Gold 1980). For example, in August 1980, the State Council passed a plan to encourage urban residents, especially returning zhiqing and unemployed youths, to start their own small businesses, such as bicycle repair stalls, which were prohibited during the Cultural Revolution, or to organize themselves to start small collectively owned enterprises, such as dim sum restaurants (Gu 2009b, 163–65).

Even among those with jobs, the years in the countryside still caused serious delays in their life courses. The oldest returning zhiqing – those back from Xinjiang – were already about 35, often with spouses and children. The "old three classes" (66–68) of high school were around 30. Many of the middle school classes of 67–71 were also above 25. The Chinese society in the 1980s expected people within this age range to get permanent jobs (not in production teams), get married, have children, and settle down. For many returning zhiqing, those age-based expectations were unrealistic. Besides job and education problems, many found themselves feuding with their siblings, who, several years ago, wept at the railway stations seeing them off to the countryside. Some of the fights were caused by housing – for example, a married older brother occupied the larger room, and an unmarried returning zhiqing had to squeeze into a room with another sibling, parents, or grandparents. The situation could be exacerbated when two siblings had marriage plans at the same time.

Some zhiqing, however, showed remarkable resilience in endeavoring to improve their situation. While very few zhiqing – only seven of my interviewees – passed the newly resumed gaokao and got into four-year colleges (*benke*), many took all kinds of continuing education programs, including Radio Broadcast and TV College (*guangbo dianshi daxue*, or *dianda*), Letter Education (*hanshou*, a type of distance learning through the mail), Adult Self-Learning Higher Education Exam (*chengren zixue gaokao*), and so on. Some programs were not even at the college level: for example, high school or even middle school "make-up study" (*buxi*).

Many zhiqing studied in those programs when they had full-time jobs and families, and at age thirty or even older. For example, Mrs. Cai, the aforementioned zhiqing who entered a "Labor and Service Company," returned to Shanghai with only a nominal middle school education because when she entered middle school, the Cultural Revolution broke out and schools stopped. It took her nine years, from 1979 to 1988, to finish a young workers' buxi program, then get a mid-level associate degree (*zhongzhuan*) through an evening school, and finally a college associate degree (*dazhuan*) through a self-learning program, when she got married and became a mom. The long-time pursuit of education paid off almost immediately. With her degree in economics and accounting, she was promoted to a manager position in her bank.

A common mentality among the education strivers, including those who got the golden fleece of a four-year college education, was to "compensate for the lost years." The story that Premier Li Keqiang carried English vocabulary flashcards with him and studied whenever and wherever he could resonates with many zhiqing-turned-college-students because they did exactly the same. They now had legitimate reasons to pat themselves on the back, because they had paid higher prices for their achievements. For many others, however, the lost years were simply lost without any tangible returns.

Literary Memory: Seeking Meanings in the Present and the Past

Many literary works realistically reflected the zhiqing generation's difficulties after returning. For example, in Wang Anyi's "The Final Stop of This Train" (1981), Chen Xin, the protagonist, finally arrives in Shanghai by train, only to find himself lost in daily trivialities. He gets his job by replacing his mother but at the cost of his younger brother, who fails to get into college and is idling at home. Chen Xin's older brother and his wife occupy the living-room-turned-bedroom, which is also used for dining. Chen Xin shares a bed with his brother. A conflict over space finally breaks out among siblings. Even Liang Xiaosheng's mostly upbeat works on zhiqing do not shun the difficulties; instead, in his *Snowy City*, he presents tragedies of the returning zhiqing, especially those in working-class families: poverty, unemployment, and even death.

Most of the literary works, however, do more than simply reflect the difficult present. They are the medium for the bewildered, frustrated zhiqing to seek meanings through memories. In telling stories about their past, the zhiqing try to find answers to a series of questions: What happened to us? Who or what caused our present mess? Were our best years lost? Who is to blame? What kind of people are and *were* we – Corps soldiers? Victims? Idiots? Losers? Heroes? Or others? All these questions revolve around the intersection between personal biography and history, the core of literary memory (Mills 1959, 5).

To examine the meaning-making in their literary memory, I start with the works and their authors, a conventional starting point in both literary studies and cultural sociology, and then move on to the production process. I unpack every story presented in the works into two components: one is a narrative about the event, the send-down program, and the other about the people, the zhiqing generation. I examine the commonalities and differences among the works in how the two components are represented and how they are interwoven.

To examine the authors, I look at how their writing is constrained and enabled by their social features, including intentions, worldviews, emotions, immediate circumstances of writing, training and professional experience, local conditions, and so on. This analysis is intended to rebuild the writers' "brief," a sociological profile of the writer, and to causally link the brief to the patterns of representations in their works (Griswold 1987b). I found that the central feature of the "briefs" of the zhiqing writers was their political habitus – the political disposition and schema of interpretation they formed in their coming-of-age experience in the Mao years. As discussed in Chapters 1 and 2, such habitus endured and changed, having a significant influence on the zhiqing's views of the past. Moreover, in the 1970s and 1980s, the authors wrote in the "experiential mode," a type of literary memory that draws on writers' autobiographical memories of their "lived-through" personal experience (Erll 2011, 151). They were zhiqing, they spoke to zhiqing, and their zhiqing readers read them as a representation of their collective experience. This makes the authors' habitus even more directly relevant to their works.

Dignity of the Faithful Red and Anguish of the Mistreated Child

Only a few zhiqing-turned-writers have the "faithful red" habitus (good chushen with active political performance): Liang Xiaosheng, Zhang Chengzhi, and, to a lesser degree, Lao Gui. Blessed with the "natural redness" from their chushen, they were fervent believers of Maoism and passionate participants in the Red Guard movement. They voluntarily went down to the countryside and imagined the years ahead as a revolutionary pilgrimage rather than a reluctant odyssey.

Two of them, Liang Xiaosheng and Zhang Chengzhi, did not experience any political ordeal. Instead, they were recommended to study at two prestigious universities, Fudan University and Peking University. Neither of them changed his political habitus significantly, although each made moderate revisions of his political views. They take pains to catch up with the changing vocabulary while offering positive literary memory with considerable political ambiguity. The values of their political belief formed in their youth are subtly confirmed by generic words like "passion," "heroism," and "idealism," which replace the Maoist vocabulary. Meanwhile, their idealism is slightly diluted by passing, vague criticisms of "ultra-left politics," in Liang's case; in Zhang, such dilution does not even appear.

Liang Xiaosheng's works have helped forge the literary memory of the zhiqing generation for almost forty years. Liang grew up in a typical working-class family in Harbin. At an early age, Liang painfully felt the class disparity in living conditions and developed a sympathy toward the underprivileged. In the Cultural Revolution, Liang witnessed and took part in the violent conflicts between two Red Guard factions, who used battlefield weapons in attempts to eliminate each other. At the climax of the conflicts, Liang was dragged out by his uncle from a marching crowd, and his mother used scissors to cut his hair and shoes to prevent him from joining the bloody clash. "When my ghost-looking hair grew, the weather was warm. Then I took the job of sweeping the streets for the wage of fifteen yuan a month, with a complete disappointment: I had achieved nothing, realized nothing, but lost everything," Liang describes in his autobiography *Confessions of A Red Guard* (Liang 2009b, 433).

This disappointment, however, was somewhat overstated, because later he remained politically enthusiastic and active. He mobilized his classmates to go to a farm in Heilongjiang in 1968, before the official call in December. His career benefited much from his good chushen and active political performance. In 1974, he was recommended to get into Fudan University, where he studied literature from 1974 to 1977, before a wave of intellectual awakening swept the university. (Lu Xinhua's *Scar* was put up on a bulletin board at Fudan in 1978, a year after Liang graduated.) Nowhere in his autobiographic writings and interviews does he mention a moment of disillusionment or awakening.[3] Instead, he

---

[3] In his memoirs, Liang highlights his disgust with the ultra-left politics. After the fall of the Gang of Four, he and other students petitioned the university authorities to allow them to hold a parade to celebrate (Liang 2009a). But both his words and practices conformed to

proudly says that he retains the core of his political habitus, including concerns with social equality, compassion with the underprivileged, heroism, and idealism (Leung 1994, 120).

Consistent with this faithful red habitus, Liang's writings confirm the zhiqing's idealism and enthusiasm but remain equivocal about the send-down program as a historical event. In the aforementioned "A Land of Wonder and Mystery" (1982), for example, all the characters have a strong sense of responsibility and the virtue of self-sacrifice. In some places, Liang stops the narrative flow and enthusiastically makes compliments about his generation. The whole story seems to take place in a political vacuum, in which the central conflict occurs between the insurmountable wilderness and the determined zhiqing explorers.

An expedition group of ten something zhiqing started a journey to reclaim the "ghost swamp" and Mangai wasteland in Beidahuang. In the dangerous and tedious reclamation process, the zhiqing put aside their previous conflicts and biases and began to discover the better side of each other. "I" – the narrator – fell in love with Li Xiaoyan, the leader of the group and also began to understand "my" younger sister's relationship with another zhiqing, which brought her disgrace. "My" sister later was swallowed by a swamp when she went out to look for food. Li Xiaoyan, the director, died of an illness. Wang Zhigang, who also loved Li Xiaoyan, left the only gun to "me" but was killed by wolves. Finally, this group of zhiqing conquered the "ghost swamp" at the cost of several lives. A synopsis of Liang Xiaosheng's "A Land of Wonder and Mystery" (1982)

Liang's next major work, *A Snowstorm Is Coming Tonight* (*jinye you baofengxue*) (1983), moves toward realism by directly depicting the Heilongjiang zhiqing's protest and petition to demand to go home. The main character, Pei Xiaoyun, has black chushen and a family tragedy. Nevertheless, these bold changes belie the unchanged narrative pattern: confirmation of the zhiqing's dignity and heroism accompanied by ambivalence about the program. All the main zhiqing characters have some heroic traits, regardless of their personal choice to leave or stay in Beidahuang. Two of them, Liu Maike and Pei Xiaoyun, even sacrifice their lives on their posts. At the height of the protest, Cao Tieqiang, a zhiqing company (military unit) commander, is facing challenges from his fellow zhiqing, who attempt to start a riot to force the Corps to let them go home. Cao makes a speech to dissuade the zhiqing:

Perhaps, tonight is the last page of the history of the Corps. The history of the Corps is the history of Corps soldiers. Every one of us should respect this history. No matter how society will evaluate the history of the Corps, the title "Corps

---

the Party's line right after the Cultural Revolution, which blamed the "Gang of Four" or "ultra-leftism" for all past wrongs and stopped short of a political awakening.

soldier" was imbued with our contributions! No one can insult this title! (Liang 1993, 359)

The speech conveys the main idea of Liang's literary memory: "no matter how the society will evaluate the history of the Corps," the title "Corps soldiers," an identity with the military ethos and pride, retains its glory and dignity and does not allow insults. The tension between self-confirmation and uncertainty about historical evaluations is more than evident.

Snowy City, Liang's next novel, starts with a depiction of urban residents' denigration of the former "Corps soldiers" and moves on to melodramatic stories of their tragedies. Such a realist representation of the returning zhiqing's difficulties, however, is balanced with a rarely noticed but even bolder move: he associates the identity of "zhiqing" with the Red Guards and remains strikingly equivocal about the Cultural Revolution. For example, in the novel, Yao Shouyi, a former Red Guard, recalls his participation in an exuberant protest against the Municipal authorities in the peak years of the Cultural Revolution: "Even today he still believed that their – 1,700 of them – emotions, exuberance, and spirit of being ready to protect something by their blood and bodies were very sincere and authentic." Here, Liang could not help crossing the fine line between two sides of the generation identity: the zhiqing and the Red Guards. This is out of the "sincerity and passion" in his political habitus, which he emphasizes in a 1998 essay (Liang 1998, 20):

Now I look back at my zhiqing novels and find nothing satisfactory. ... The only thing in which I can take solace is that back then I wrote with sincerity and passion. Even though they are superficial and naïve, the sincerity and passion of writing is something I retain forever.

This pattern continues to exist in his later writings, such as *Zhiqing* (2012), a novel adapted into a TV series in 2014. It was widely regarded as a tribute to Xi who officially became China's leader around the time the novel was published. The novel and particularly the TV series were criticized for their "beautifying" the send-down program and the Cultural Revolution, and Liang defended himself by blaming the censorship in the TV adaptation process that deleted much description of the Cultural Revolution. Nevertheless, even the novel, which Liang believed reflected his intention and ideas, did not go beyond the pattern of highlighting the zhiqing but downplaying the event in his previous novels.

Zhang Chengzhi, whose "faithful red" habitus was well known, went even further. He never hesitates to reveal his nostalgia for his Red Guard years. In a 2005 interview, Zhang said that his purpose in writing is to "use my pen to side with the people who are oppressed, who have no discursive power, and who need help" and that this idea is something he has cherished from his youthful participation in the "great revolution in the sixties," which obviously refers to the Cultural Revolution (Liu 2005).

This political habitus led to Zhang's positive memory of both the zhiqing generation and the send-down program. For example, in *The Golden Pasture* (*jinmuchang*, 1987), the protagonist's zhiqing experience in Inner Mongolia is intertwined with his story of Red Guard chuanlian (traveling to make connections and exchange revolutionary experiences with other Red Guards), constituting the "M" (perhaps standing for Mongolia) part of the novel. The M story contrasts with the "J" (Japan) part of the novel, also including two interrelated stories: the protagonist's visit to Japan and his exploration in the Western part of China.

At first glance, the M story appears grimmer than the ones in Liang's novels, featuring the zhiqing's extremely difficult living conditions, their involvement in the local conflicts, their desire to leave, their marriage with the locals, and so on. Nevertheless, two ways of reading reveal some distinctive features of this story. First, as literary scholar Xu Zidong points out (Xu 2011, 284–304), the *eejee* ("mother" in Mongolian) in the zhiqing protagonist's host family occupies a significant symbolic position in the story. Eejee treats the protagonist as her son and gives him a Mongolian name, Temur. The demobilized, dejected Red Guard is rehabilitated by a mother from the *"renmin"* (the people). As Xu insightfully suggests, no matter how emotionally attached to the people, they are only "sons of the people" – not part of them – and eventually will return to cities.

Second, reading *across* the stories shows a tenet of Zhang's literary memory. The Red Guards in the story go on a revolutionary pilgrimage, which is intended to imitate the Red Army's Long March. The Red Guard chuanlian story implicitly connects to the sent-down story through Zhang's idealistic identification with the role of advocates and pioneers for the "poor" people. The "J" story connects to the "M" story through Maoist Japanese students' rebellion against the administration of the University of Tokyo. The underlying pattern revealed in this cross-story reading is evident: the Red Guards are defeated in their rebellious battles in cities but continue their revolutionary pilgrimage to the countryside, where, as zhiqing, they develop their affinity with the underprivileged, lower-class renmin, especially with mother-like figures like eejee.

Unlike Liang and Zhang, Lao Gui (Ma Bo) focuses more on the mistreatment he received from the Party–state that indoctrinated and nurtured him. He was from a family with political privileges – his mother,

Yang Mo, a famous revolutionary writer. He had an unconditional love of the Party and Chairman Mao, a Manichean view of the world, and a stoic doctrine of personal life, as he describes in his autobiography *Blood and Iron* (Lao 2010, 125):

East Is Red, a revolutionary epic of dance [and music], was filled with the love for Chairman Mao. It was like a stream of pure water, cleansing all the organs of my body. It made my mind particularly lofty and made me as loyal as a dog to Chairman Mao. It also made me realize, in my subconsciousness, that revolution was sacred, noble, and beautiful. You won't be respected unless you are revolutionary. You won't get gorgeous girls' attention unless you are revolutionary. Revolution was our youths' only hope.

Nevertheless, in his sent-down years in the Inner Mongolia Corps, Lao Gui was persecuted, detained, and tortured by the authorities mainly due to his mother Yang Mo's political fall and his conflict with the local officers. In his autobiographical novel, *The Bloody Sunset* (written in 1976, published in 1987), Lao Gui revealed the military officers' misconduct, the authorities' abuse of zhiqing, the zhiqing's own violence, and their cutthroat fight with each other for self-protection and scarce resources.

Despite its raw revelation, *The Bloody Sunset* remained ambiguous about the send-down program and the Cultural Revolution. At the end of the novel, Lao Gui seems to attribute all the tragedies and ugliness to individual moral character ("bad guys," *huairen*) and even a specific individual, Jiang Qing, whom he alludes to as an "evil woman" (*yaofu*). The novel reads more like a mistreated child's desperate effort to win back his parents' love than a reflection on whether the parents' behavior is justified. No evidence from interviews or autobiographical writing suggests that Lao Gui has experienced a significant habitus change. His critical tone toward his youthful fanaticism always stops short of an in-depth self-reflection and outright criticism of the Cultural Revolution (Lao 2011).

The Aspirants: Disillusionment and Idealism

All the "aspirant" writers experienced a political disillusionment and habitus change. Consequently, they faced a dilemma: If the send-down program was a disaster, then was our youthful idealism just a stupid, absurd fanaticism or an experience that contained something worthy and good? Their answers to the questions vary: salvaging idealism from the ruins of Maoism, empathetic understanding of the zhiqing, painful self-reflection, and even calls for the zhiqing's repentance. Which ideas they present in their literary memory depends on how far they went in their habitus change.

Lu Tianming, whose chushen was neither black nor red, developed an extraordinary political enthusiasm at an early age. In 1958, when he was only fourteen years old, Lu faked his age to go to Anhui, long before the send-down program officially started, but he was soon sent back because of his tuberculosis. In 1963, as a local Youth League secretary, he was responsible for mobilizing youths to go to Xinjiang. Lu decided to go along with the youths he mobilized, although he could have stayed in Shanghai, out of his conviction that "it [going down to the countryside] was the best future for Chinese youth and the best method to bring a better life to the peasantry" (Leung 1994, 128).

This strong conviction did not change until he was transferred to the Central Broadcasting Station in Beijing after the Cultural Revolution when Chinese society was experiencing a dramatic change in politics and society. He went through a painful process of self-reflection and corresponding habitus change (Li 2003):

I looked back at my works and suddenly found my idea of literature one-dimensional. The idea I believed before that moment was that literature was about nothing but revolution and the Party. I felt worried and painfully decided to look for a new path. I wanted to look for my [own voice] in literature and to resume the independent value of literature.

Nevertheless, the core of his habitus, the moral–political idealism that one should pursue a goal higher than his own career and life, remained unshaken and only changed its direction. The evidence for this robust idealism can be found in his various statements of his purpose of writing: to shoulder social responsibilities and to write about the most important social problems (Jing Yang 2009).[4]

Shaped by the habitus change, Lu Tianming's major work on the zhiqing generation, *The Sun over the Sangna Highland* (1987) presents an unambiguously negative view of the send-down program but also an ambiguously positive view of individual zhiqing's idealism. Xie Ping, the protagonist, has tremendous difficulties reconciling his revolutionary ideals with the bureaucratic, complex reality on the Xinjiang farm. After making a few tactical errors in the micro-politics in his danwei, Xie is sent into exile on a remote farm and gradually absorbed into the violent, hierarchical local culture there. Nevertheless, the core of Xie's

---

[4] His later works with anti-corruption themes demonstrate this purpose: *For Heaven's Sake* (1995), *No Footprints on Snow* (2000), and *The Provincial Secretary* (2002). These novels explicitly address social problems and aim to reach wider audiences.

youthful idealism remains robust enough to compel him to make some uncalculated moves to protect his dignity and moral principles against local tyrants. In the end, Xie leaves Xinjiang. Xie's painful defeat could have been avoided if he had bowed to the local strongmen and their political networks. Through this tragic hero figure, Lu conveys a clear message that while idealism might not work, the idealism itself should not take the blame.[5]

Han Shaogong is another writer with "aspirant" habitus. Han's father committed suicide during the Cultural Revolution to protest the political persecutions he received, but his problem was posthumously cleared. Despite the family tragedy and his dubious political background, Han still enthusiastically participated in Red Guard activities to prove his revolutionary spirit. He joined a "moderately rebellious" Red Guard group, wrote essays, avidly read revolutionary classics, engaged in both verbal and physical fights, and even trained for using weapons (Wenxue Bao 2012).

In 1968, Han voluntarily went down to Miluo in Hunan but soon realized that his disillusioned fellow zhiqing desperately wanted to leave the village. Han was disappointed and joined a small group of intellectuals, including some later well-known writers and scholars, such as writer Mo Yinfeng and economist Yang Xiaokai, to reflect on the problems of autocracy and mayhem in the Cultural Revolution. In 1977, Han got into Hunan Normal College, where his long-time doubts culminated in a systematic rejection of the official ideology (Kong 2008).

Nevertheless, like Lu Tianming, Han Shaogong keeps his idealistic core, in an even more high-profile way. Critics regard him as a "New Left," a label he rejects, because of his strong concerns with social and political issues and his vocal opposition to the tyranny of the market. He also emphasizes the function of literature to express people's grievances about injustice, a conviction similar to Lu's (Yang 2011). This habitus leads to a pattern of literary memory similar to Lu Tianming's. In his "Looking Westward at Cogon Grass Land" (*xiwang maocaodi*), he presents the zhiqing's disillusionment with the propaganda, their resentment toward the local officials' authoritarian style, and their pragmatic consideration about their career. Nevertheless, Han shows his ambivalence toward the idealism by adding complexity to the head of the farm,

---

[5] Lu Tianming's younger sister, Lu Xing'er, who had the same habitus of aspirant, wrote only a limited number of short stories about the zhiqing experience, and imbued her main characters – for example, Li Juntang in her novella *The Mountain Flowers Have Bloomed Quietly* (*dazixiang qiaoqiaode kaile*) – with a strong sense of responsibility and selfless devotion to the development of the local community.

Zhang. He appreciates Zhang's passionate adherence to the revolutionary idealism but also suggests that Zhang's stringent ideology and practices paradoxically lead to the zhiqing's loss of faith. Nevertheless, when many zhiqing were laughing and celebrating the collapse of the farm, the protagonist ("I"), a zhiqing, asks: "Naïve idealism certainly brings about trauma, but do we have to dismiss the idealism itself – the lofty pursuit, flags, and clatter of hoofs – and erase them from our life?" The question is the answer to itself, which is a clear "no."

Guo Xiaodong presents the same pattern of literary memory with some differences. Guo's extended family had an extraordinary pedigree, which, after 1949, turned into curses (Guo 2010). In his adolescent years, Guo Xiaodong had a strong sense of sin: "I always lived in a sense of guilt. From the bottom of my heart, I felt ashamed of not being part of the new society, not being part of the working-class people. Since I was 15, I had been self-consciously categorizing myself as an 'outcast'" (Guo 2015, 1). Meanwhile, he felt that all the discriminations and miseries of his family were justified by the class theory that the exploited class has the right to use violence to overthrow the exploiting class. He began to loathe his family and decided to use political performance to prove his revolutionary spirit. Guo went to Hainan voluntarily and performed well in work and politics. He was even recommended as a model "child who can be educated" to get into a college but was returned to his farm due to his black chushen. After these repeated frustrations, Guo Xiaodong changed his political habitus and now expresses an outright condemnation of the send-down program as a complete catastrophe (Nanfangwang 2014).

Guo's habitus change went further than Han Shaogong's. Idealism fades away from his literary memory. Guo recognizes the zhiqing's worthiness but not because of their devotion to a social–political cause. Instead, he emphasizes the intrinsic goodness in their nature, despite their life being twisted by politics and history. In his zhiqing trilogy (*The Chinese Zhiqing Tribe*, *The Exile Youths*, and *Dancing in a Dark Night*), the zhiqing characters are neither heroes nor villains. Rather, they are respectable ordinary people with merits and flaws. Some are outcasts at the bottom of society, who still manage to maintain dignity through their effort to eke out a living.

Zhang Kangkang, a Hangzhou zhiqing to Heilongjiang, differed from all other aspirants in that she explicitly demanded the zhiqing to reflect on their own problems instead of detaching themselves from the program. A bad-chushen youth but an enthusiastic activist, Zhang Kangkang was first sent down to Deqing, a county close to Hangzhou, but felt such adjacency did not prove her revolutionary spirit. She then applied to Heilongjiang, a place then regarded by Hangzhou people as the least livable – cold as hell, awful food (in southerners' views), and thousands of kilometers from home. In Heilongjiang, Zhang Kangkang's active political performance paid off. She soon became a staff member of the propaganda system and left the field for good. In 1975, she published her first novel, *The Dividing Line* (*fenjiexian*), a piece of propaganda work, but publishing a novel as a zhiqing was a rare achievement. In 1977, she was recommended to study at the Heilongjiang School of Arts, where she experienced a dramatic political awakening (Zhang 1998a, 277):

I spent most of my time in the school library. I also went to Beijing many times to watch the "internal movies" and pro-democracy big-character posters on Xidan Democracy Wall. It was the peak moment of the thought liberation movement, and China was about to experience a dramatic transition. In agony and delight, I reflected on my past. Thoughts surged like waves. The confusion that had tangled my mind for a long time was suddenly cleared up.

Zhang Kangkang's habitus change might be the most thorough among all the writers discussed here. Her fiction presents an unusually censorious pattern. In the 1980s, when most literary works depicted zhiqing as innocent victims, she revealed the murky and even cruel aspect of the zhiqing's behavior. For example, in *The White Poppy* (*baiyingsu*, 1980), the zhiqing protagonist ("I") borrows money from an *erlaogai* (released prisoners who stayed and worked on the farm) but does not pay him back because erlaogai are usually considered as "class enemies" and do not deserve respect. Finally, when "I" sees a letter from his son, who begs for money, "I" decides to sell my watch and give the erlaogai the money "I" owe. Nevertheless, "Lionhead," another zhiqing, robs and kills the erlaogai without scruple.

The themes of moral flaws, guilt, and repentance culminate in her most sophisticated work on zhiqing, *The Invisible Companion* (1986), which reflects on the contradiction between the imperfect human nature and the unrealistic expectation in the official ideology that the youths should be selfless and honest. The female protagonist Xiao Xiao loathes lies and dishonesty but somewhat unconsciously produces political lies in her propaganda work.

Xiao Xiao and Chen Xu, two zhiqing on a Heilongjiang farm, decided to flee to Hangzhou, their hometown, to secure a verification letter to clear Chen's history as a Red Guard. Yet, the letter did not work as well as they expected. Chen was still perceived as a trouble-maker on the farm. Soon they got married and had a baby. But the arrival of the baby put stress on their life, and, moreover, Xiao did not have enough milk to feed the baby. They had to send the baby back to Hangzhou. Later, Xiao found out that Chen was unbearably deceptive and calculating, while she still believed that one should neither lie nor deceive others. After a series of conflicts and quarrels, Xiao decided to divorce him.

After their divorce, Xiao moved to another farm. The new head of the farm, an "iron girl," demonstrated her revolutionary spirit by using manual labor instead of machines. Xiao was gradually involved in writing false propaganda stories for the farm and alienated herself from the rest of the zhiqing. She also discovered that everyone was deceiving others to some extent. Later, she bumped into Chen, who decided to use a fabricated report of physical exam to return to Hangzhou. A Synopsis of Zhang Kangkang's *The Invisible Companion* (1986)

Zhang's other, less well-known short story, "Never Confess" (1987), depicts an even grimmer image. All the zhiqing characters in the novel have flaws: adultery, bribery, theft, betrayal, corruption, and so on. Years after the send-down program ended, when those former zhiqing gathered together for a reunion, no one shows any desire to repent. At the end of the story, Zhang raises a bigger question about the institutional conditions for their repentance:

In all these years, have our souls ever relaxed? No one can be at ease when facing the past. When we gather together, every pair of eyes can see an inglorious past self. It is just that no one talks about it.

History cannot shoulder all the responsibilities.

Who has the courage to interrogate yourself?

Nevertheless, even if we confess, who can be the priest listening to our confession?

This ends the story abruptly and ambiguously, deviating from the main plot of the story. The "priest" does not refer to any character in the story. In an interview, Zhang elaborated her intended meaning that the radical Maoist political system and the zhiqing themselves were reinforcing each other: "Even if I made mistakes, the priest is sinful (the priest is the incarnation of truth, will of the god, and power of the church). In this sense, 'never confess' is a defiance to the absolute power" (Beijing Wanbao 2010). In other words, the zhiqing must repent, but the demand for repentance should also be directed toward the system. The system and the people are just two items in a single vicious circle.

Political Condemnation and Cautious Distance: Withdrawers

Some writers developed the "withdrawer" habitus of keeping a cautious and suspicious distance from politics. Their habitus has two dimensions, resentment and apathy, one of which may override the other in certain situations. Their literary memory, therefore, demonstrates two different patterns. First, when resentment rules, the writers intend to expose pains and traumas. This pattern prevails in the novels in the late 1970s and early 1980s, as part of the "scar literature," when the political revelation function of literature was encouraged.

Ye Xin's early works represent this pattern. With a bad chushen of "landlord," Ye could not join the Red Guards in the Cultural Revolution. He idled at home, reading, listening to music, and wandering, and developed a typical "withdrawer" habitus. In his sent-down years, he was quite sincere about working at first, but soon became disillusioned and frustrated by the villagers' unwelcome attitude and the extremely poor living conditions in the countryside. He began writing to escape the hopeless boredom and despair.

In a remote mountain village in Guizhou, Ke Bizhou, a Shanghai zhiqing with deep melancholy caused by his bad chushen, encounters Du Jianchun, an outgoing female zhiqing with red chushen, who is enthusiastic about the revolutionary cause of the send-down program. The affection between the two young zhiqing, however, is dampened by the huge gap in their chushen and corresponding worldviews.

Ke Bizhou becomes even more despondent when he is badly beaten by other zhiqing. He falls off a cliff but is saved by a local girl Shao Yurong, with whom he falls in love. Shao and her family take care of Ke and help him rebuild his self-esteem. Later, Ke successfully sells bamboo in the village to outside factories and buys the village's first electricity generator. He also publishes an essay in a newspaper. While Ke enjoys the overdue admiration from the villagers and his fellow zhiqing, Du Jianchun falls from grace because her father is purged. She loses the opportunity to enter college and accidentally offends a local cadre, whose husband, a hooligan, beats her up and destroys her belongings in revenge. Shao Yurong reports the beating to the authorities, but the hooligan kills Shao in retaliation. In despondency and fury, Ke buries Shao. Later, he saves Du from an attempt at suicide and helps her restore her faith in life. Yet, Ke tries to distance himself from her because he worries that once her father's problem is cleared, the gap in their class statuses would be an obstacle of their relationship.

Ke's worry becomes a reality as the Cultural Revolution ends, when Du's father is rehabilitated. Du's mother and brother oppose their relationship. When Ke visits his family in Shanghai, Du's family persuades Ke to leave her. As Ke is boarding a train to return to the village, Du jumps on the train to follow Ke, after a quarrel with her family. A synopsis of Ye Xin's *The Wasted Years* (1982)

One can hardly find a better case than *The Wasted Years* to illustrate how zhiqing writers' habitus shapes their literary memory. The centrality of chushen in this novel reflects Ye Xin's own and other zhiqing's life experiences in the Mao era. In 1978, he heard a story of a failed love relationship: two zhiqing fell in love, but the young man with good chushen was forced by his father to break up with the girl, who had bad chushen. The story reminded him of his bad-chushen classmates' trauma: being beaten up by the Red Guards, being denigrated by the local cadres as "dog's kid" (*gouzhuaizi*, an insulting phrase referring to bad-chushen youth), and so on. Ye Xin vowed to write a book to expose the catastrophes caused by the political class system (Ye 1999, 30–31). The novel made much bolder moves than other works in the same period. It exposed local cadres' corruption, nepotism, and the persecution and torture they committed against the zhiqing. Nevertheless, Ye Xin sheds a beam of light into this otherwise dark picture: Ke later wins local peasants' respect through his hard work and devotion to the welfare of the villagers.

Zhu Lin, with the same withdrawer habitus (Shi 2014, 308–12), shares with Ye Xin the same intention of writing: "When the send-down movement was glorified as something beautiful as a soap bubble, I felt it was not right. I wanted to tell some truth for my generation whose youthful years were wasted" (Jiefang Ribao 2010). Zhu Lin's *The Road of Life* (1979) struck readers with its exposure of sexual assault on female zhiqing, a widely known phenomenon, which, however, had rarely been touched on in literary works. The female protagonist in the novel, Juanjuan, has bad chushen and desperately wants to go to college. A local cadre uses her for the political struggle and finally rapes her. Juanjuan drowns herself. Her later novel, *The Weeping Lancang River* (1995), even centralizes the theme of sexual assault. Lianlian, the female protagonist, witnesses a rape of her friend Lulu, and later she herself is raped by a man with leprosy. The horrifying experience almost destroys her faith in human beings, but her lover Gongxian's idealism saves her from desolation. Nevertheless, when Gongxian is executed for political reasons, she succumbs to her sexual desire, lured by her political director.

Kong Jiesheng is another withdrawer. In 1966, at the age of thirteen, he was castigated by his classmates. He "felt humiliated, deeply hurt, and my whole psychological equilibrium was shaken" (Leung 1994, 68). Consequently, he decided to keep his distance from the terrifying political activities in school and on the Hainan farm where he worked (Kong 2009). Kong's *The Big Jungle* (1984) uses much symbolism to tell a story of a group of five zhiqing on a mission to explore the possibility of growing rubber trees in a big virgin forest. Only one of the zhiqing, the only female in this group, survives. The catchphrase of the novel is: "The direction is right, but the path is wrong." *The Big Jungle* can be read side by side with Liang Xiaosheng's "A Land of Wonder and Mystery." Both Liang and Kong tell stories of adventure, love, and death, against the background of terrifying natural forces. Nevertheless, Kong challenges Liang's heroic narrative by painting a gloomy picture of foolish policies, destructive development, and ideological fanaticism. This difference can be explained by the differences in their habitus.

Wang Xiaobo (1952–1997) is an outlier in this group of withdrawers in his literary style, but his literary memory still follows the other withdrawers' challenge to the state's official ideology. In the Cultural Revolution, Wang was a typical "wanderer" (xiaoyaopai) and did not participate in any political activities. The zhiqing in his works are neither victims nor heroes; instead, they pursue carnal pleasure and use their absurd behavior to defy political restrictions and surveillance. In his *The Golden Times* (1994), the female character, Chen Qingyang, is accused by the local authorities of being a "worn shoe" (poxie, meaning a married woman who commits adultery). To prove her innocence, she seeks support from Wang Er, a zhiqing in the village, but ends up having sex with him. Their relationship ironically substantiates the "worn shoe" accusation. The novel deconstructs political power through black humor and solemn caricatures. For example, when the local officials ask Wang Er to write a political confession of their crime (adultery), he writes it with such a gravitas that he provides a blow-by-blow description of their sexual intercourse. This unusual confession satisfies, mutes, and even embarrasses the officials who have an unstated purpose of probing the details of their sexual relationship. In sum, Wang's political message is conveyed in his vulgar laughter rather than tearful accusations. He ridicules the Maoist politics, debunks the pompous heroism, and liberates "humans" from the politically loaded label "zhiqing."

Yan Geling also differs from other writers in this category but does not deviate far from the withdrawers' pattern. Yan was not a zhiqing. Rather, she joined a PLA performance group as a dancer at the age of twelve and later became a journalist to report on China's war against Vietnam. Nevertheless, her political socialization formed her habitus as a "withdrawer." She grew up in a family with problematic chushen. In the first years of the Cultural Revolution, her family's house was raided, and she witnessed suicides in her family's residential compound. In the performance group, she aspired to become a good dancer but was not particularly active in politics. When reporting on the China–Vietnam war, she witnessed the brutality and horror of war and experienced a disillusionment with politics (Xia 2014).

Therefore, it was not surprising to see her works about the Cultural Revolution and other upheavals in the Mao years demonstrate a clearly negative historical evaluation. Her only work about the zhiqing generation, "Tianyu" ("Celestial Bath," 1996), a short story, was later adapted into a movie, *Xiu Xiu: The Sent Down Girl* (1998). The movie won overseas awards but was banned by China due to its exposure of political traumas and nudity. Nevertheless, the movie and short story have been widely circulated among educated audiences, including some in the zhiqing generation, who managed to watch it through VPN to bypass internet censorship. In the story, Wen Xiu, a sent-down girl to a Tibetan area, desperately tries to return to Chengdu by sleeping with various men in the local government. Her attempts fail, and she physically suffers much from repeated rapes. Lao Jin, a Tibetan man living with her, who is sexually impotent, provides her with paternalistic protection but shoots her dead, following her own willingness to commit suicide.

When apathy in the withdrawer writers' habitus rules, their literary memory paints a marginally political, or even apolitical, picture of the zhiqing characters, leaving the event largely unaddressed. Ye Xin's works since the late 1980s represent this pattern. *Karma*, a tear-jerker that later was adapted into a popular TV series, extends the zhiqing story to the next generation. During the huge wave of the zhiqing returning to home cities, five children of Shanghai zhiqing are hastily left behind in Yunnan. Years later, the children – now teenagers – come back to Shanghai to look for their parents. Their parents' life trajectories since the send-down years have diverged dramatically; most of them have their own families. The arrival of their children disturbs their life in Shanghai and eventually compels the parents to rediscover their lost conscience. The conflicts between their past and present are resolved in various ways: two children decide to return to Yunnan; one is disabled in an accident; one is involved in crime and later arrested; the other eventually reunites with his father, who clears his criminal allegation. Without a political message, *Karma* appeals to popular audiences with many clichéd, melodramatic components: pitiful children, broken families, extramarital sex, moral failures, guilt, repentance, and rediscovery. Ye Xin's most recent zhiqing-themed novel, *The Pavilion for Passersby* (*keguoting*, 2011), has a similar pattern: the past horror haunts the former zhiqing when they go on a revisiting trip to their sent-down place.

Wang Anyi presents an even more detached narrative. Wang grew up in an upper-class family. Her mother, Ru Zhijuan, was a writer and literary bureaucrat, and her father a film director. Wang went down to the countryside mainly because she became restless after idling at home for a long time rather than out of revolutionary enthusiasm. Immediately after she arrived in her sent-down place, she deeply regretted leaving home. In the remote village in Anhui, she felt isolated from urban culture and frustrated by the insurmountable barrier with the local peasants. In comparison, political discriminations and persecutions were not her concerns. When returning was impossible, she began to stay at her Shanghai home longer than she should. She confessed: "If I calculated the number of months I stayed in the countryside, I would feel embarrassed" (Leung 1994, 181).

This political apathy in her habitus has shaped her literary memory. The main characters usually remain aloof from politics and sometimes hold a cynical attitude toward the send-down program. Her early short story "A Corner of the Vast Universe" (1980) somehow followed the "scar literature" style, exposing some issues that the zhiqing encounter in the countryside, such as sexual harassment, phony activists, the "backdoor" bribery, the decline of morale, the collapse of idealism, and so on. Nevertheless, it does not contain the same angry political accusations as Zhu Lin's and Ye Xin's novels. In "The Final Stop of This Train," even such a mild political message has vanished. In *Class 69 of Middle School* (1986), a novel that features the experience and struggles of Wenwen, a female zhiqing with dubious chushen and indifference to politics, Wang rarely touches on the historical and political background.

Ah Cheng resembles Wang Anyi in his family background and habitus. His father, Zhong Dianfei, a philosophy professor, was purged as a rightist in the 1950s. Consequently, he was not allowed to participate in important political activities in his school: "Before such activities, my teacher usually called names of 30-something students and then said, 'The rest of you can go home!' What did that 'go home' mean? [It meant] you had no dignity; you were marginal." Ah Cheng stayed away from politics and spent much time reading and hanging out in Liulichang, a place in Beijing famous for antique shops. Ah Cheng's works on the zhiqing life demonstrate a mild criticism of the local politics but are most famous for their Daoist detachment. His *The King of Children* (1985) tells a story of a zhiqing-turned-village-teacher who is shocked by the school's poor condition and the illiteracy of his students. The zhiqing-teacher tries to improve the situation by abandoning the politically formulaic textbooks and using a dictionary to teach vocabulary, but the local authorities fire him for his deviance. His best-known novella, *The King of Chess* (1984), stays even further away from the politics of the send-down program and the Cultural Revolution. The whole plotline revolves around the protagonist Wang Yisheng's chess adventure and triumph, without even mild criticism of the send-down program.

In Shi Tiesheng's works, such detachment always intermingles with an idyllic nostalgia. His short story "My Remote Qingpingwan" (1983) and novella *The Story of Chadui* (1986) depict Beijing zhiqing's experience and ordinary peasants' lives in a village called Qingpingwan – literally meaning Pure and Peaceful Bend – in Shaanxi. Their life alternates between doing field labor, singing *xintianyou* (a type of local song), and occasionally attending the vagabond singers' performances. The works certainly touch on the peasants' poor living conditions and their hunger but neither raises questions about the poverty nor expresses resentment. Readers cannot find the pain and desperation in Zhu Lin's novels or the urbanites' feeling of alienation in Wang Anyi's works. Instead, as its name indicates, Qingpingwan – Pure and Peaceful Bend – serves as Shi's apolitical Shangri-la.

Was Shi Tiesheng's memory really free from pain and difficulties?

In fact, the tranquility of Qingpingwan was in stark contrast to the gloomy and frightening depiction of Beijing in his other writings. When the Cultural Revolution broke out, Shi was a student at Qinghua Affiliated School, the epicenter of the Red Guards movement in Beijing. At first, Shi enthusiastically participated in all kinds of political activities, out of his belief in the revolutionary ideology and, also, to conceal his grandmother's landlord chushen problem, which had not been discovered. Soon the activities escalated into violence. He once witnessed his friend, whose mother was captured and beaten by the Red Guards for her hidden wealth, grabbed the whip from the Red Guards and beat his mother (Shi 2010). He and other kids with not-so-red chushen were terrified and gradually stayed away from political activities (Shi 2006, 17):

I didn't know if I ought to object. But I did know I couldn't object. The effects of my objection would be like an ox objecting to pulling the plow or a horse objecting to pulling a cart. My feeling was a mixture of fear, confusion, and frustration, perhaps a little sympathy. I had fear and sympathy because my classmate was beaten for concealing his chushen. I had been worrying about my own chushen, which could be traced back to one more generation [to my grandmother]. If that were the case, I committed the same crime.

Qingpingwan, therefore, provided Shi with a haven far away from the tumultuous Beijing. Moreover, Shi Tiesheng did not stay long enough in the countryside to experience the chushen-based discriminations and the zhiqing's fierce competition for opportunities to leave the countryside, two major sources of painful memories for the zhiqing. He was seriously injured in an accident and later sent back to Beijing only about three years after his arrival. For Shi Tiesheng, the short stay in the countryside was a brief emotional escape rather than a long ordeal.

Literary Memory and Writers' Habitus

The analysis so far has shown that the variation in the authors' habitus shapes the variation in their literary memory (Table 3.1). Nevertheless, compared to the zhiqing's diverse autobiographic memories, the literary

Table 3.1. *Zhiqing writers' habitus and patterns of literary memory*

Habitus	Representative writers	Zhiqing	Send-down program	Representative works
Faithful Red	Liang Xiaosheng Zhang Chengzhi Lao Gui	Idealistic youths	Ambiguously positive	*A Land of Wonder and Mystery* *The Golden Pasture*
Aspirants	Lu Tianming Han Shaogong Guo Xiaodong	Idealistic, at least respectable youths	Negative	*The Sun over the Sangna Highland*
	Zhang Kangkang	Morally flawed youths	Negative	*Invisible Companion* *Never Confess*
Withdrawers	Ye Xin Zhu Lin Kong Jiesheng Yan Geling	Victims	Negative	*The Wasted Years* *The Weeping Lancang River* *The Big Jungle* *Celestial Bath*
	Ye Xin Wang Anyi Shi Tiesheng Ah Cheng Wang Xiaobo	Struggling ordinary people Innocent young urbanites Daoist figures Anti-heroes	Negative but downplayed	*Karma* *The Final Stop of This Train* *The Story of Chadui* *The King of Chess* *The Golden Times*

memory shows more commonality. Most of the literary works follow the pattern "good people but the bad event": a respectable image of the zhiqing and a negative view of the send-down program. Those works present the program as a catastrophe. Early works in the 1970s, such as Zhu Lin's *The Road of Life*, ritualistically use some propaganda language to cloak their criticisms, but what attracted public attention at the time was not their formulaic vocabulary but their exposure of the dark side of the program. Even Liang Xiaosheng and Zhang Chengzhi, two notable exceptions, who do not present a negative view of the program, carefully distance themselves from explicit praise of the program.

In contrast, most of the works project a positive or at least not negative image of the zhiqing as a generation who maintain their dignity, idealism, conscience, and morality despite their troubles in and after their sent-down years. In Liang Xiaosheng's novels, the main zhiqing characters are idealistic youths imbued with heroism or, after returning, urban workers with dignity. For Zhang Chengzhi, they are populist, passionate revolutionaries. Han Shaogong and Lu Tianming present their protagonists as disillusioned youths who nonetheless cherish some type of idealism. Some zhiqing protagonists are victims rather than heroes, but the victimhood also means their innocence (Zhu Lin). Sometimes, as in Ye Xin's novels, the resilient victims strive to survive and even thrive despite the calamity. The main characters in other works are innocent young urbanites (Shi Tiesheng), struggling ordinary people (Guo Xiaodong and Wang Anyi), anti-heroes (Wang Xiaobo), and those who found meanings in their non-political experience, such as the Daoist, "chess king" in Ah Cheng's story. Except for Zhang Kangkang, who demanded the morally flawed zhiqing to confess and repent, none of the writers presents a negative image of the zhiqing.

How to explain this common pattern of "good people but the bad event" and its variations, opposites, and exceptions? The common positive image of the zhiqing can be explained by this lost generation's effort to enhance their "symbolic capital" – seeking the society's recognition of their dignity despite their difficulties upon returning to cities. Ye Xin explicitly stated this purpose. His first two major works about zhiqing – *Young People of Our Generation* (1979) and *The Wasted Years* (1981) – were intended to depict a respectable image of the zhiqing generation to counter the prevalent stereotype of zhiqing as pathetic losers. The major plot line of his novels, as he summarized it, is "dejection, awakening, and striving" (Ye 1999, 47). Liang Xiaosheng also highlights the purpose of confirming the worthiness of the zhiqing generation. In his novel *A Snowstorm Is Coming Tonight*, Liang uses Cao's words to plead with readers to recognize the zhiqing's contributions and experience more than their troubles:

I hope in the future when you recall or talk with others about the ten-year history of we Corps soldiers in Beidahuang, you don't complain, don't condemn, don't laugh at us or yourself, and don't denigrate. We lost so many things, but what we gained was much more than what we lost, much heavier than what we lost.

At the time of writing, 1983, the "future" in the novel, Liang certainly already knew "what we lost" and that the "Corps soldiers" were "laughed at" and "denigrated." Yet Liang does not specify "what they gained."

The writers show varying degrees of such a desire for recognition. For example, Ye Xin, Liang Xiaosheng, and Guo Xiaodong are the ones who stress the zhiqing identity most, whereas Shi Tiesheng, Ah Cheng, and

Wang Anyi are quite detached. Therefore, it is unsurprising that Ye and Liang instead of others get the label of "zhiqing writers." Nevertheless, even those more apathetic, except for Zhang Kangkang's works, do not express an explicitly negative view of the zhiqing generation.

The writers' habitus can explain the commonality and variations in the literary memory of the zhiqing. The writers with two politically active types of habitus, "faithful red" and "aspirant," still hold on to the core of their habitus, such as political idealism and a strong sense of social responsibility, even if some of them may have changed their political views of the event. The "faithful red" writers endeavor to depict an image of idealistic zhiqing and hold an "ambiguously positive" attitude toward the send-down program and the Cultural Revolution. All the "aspirants" have changed their habitus and now condemn the program. But they still take pains to separate a positive view of zhiqing, as idealistic youths or as respectable ordinary people, from their unambiguously negative evaluation of the send-down program. The "withdrawers" have two components in their habitus: resentment and apathy. Consequently, they depict the zhiqing either as victims of the disastrous send-down program or as ordinary struggling youths without attributing their troubles to the send-down program.

Overall, twelve out of the fifteen writers have either (disillusioned) aspirant or withdrawer habitus, and this can explain the prevalence of the pattern of "good people but the bad event." Two of the writers took their habitus to its extremes, with moral accusation or sarcastic laughter, respectively. Zhang Kangkang emphasizes the moral flaws of the zhiqing and calls for their own repentance. Wang Xiaobo expresses his deeply rooted suspicion of the Maoist politics by ridiculing the political system and creating anti-hero images of the zhiqing. But both writers developed their creativity within the boundaries of their habitus: Zhang is an aspirant who went through a radical habitus change, and Wang a withdrawer, who views politics with a distant but critical eye. There is no zhiqing writer with "red indifference" habitus, probably because a privileged indifference to the harsh political reality under Mao may not be compatible with a social and literary sensibility, a basic quality for good writers.

A reader might ask if the authors' present class positions – defined as socioeconomic status – matter, since in autobiographical memories narrators' class positions shape their views of their personal past. Literary works, however, are not life stories. The writers often do not view the generation's past in light of their individual career achievements and life satisfaction. Moreover, the zhiqing writers had approximately the same class position in the 1970s and 1980s, which was much higher than the average: relatively better education, stable jobs, better incomes, and national fame, thanks to the literature market boom in the 1980s. This commonality in present class positions cannot explain the variation in the literary memory of the zhiqing generation.

The Literary Field

Some important questions, however, remain unanswered. Why literature? In other words, how and why did the literary memory become a dominant form of public memory of the zhiqing generation in the 1970s and 1980s? Also, why did the pattern of "good people but the bad event" – with its explicit criticism of the send-down program and its praise of the zhiqing – rather than other patterns become the dominant literary memory of the zhiqing generation?

The answers should be sought in the "literary field." A literary field consists of a network of people, including writers, publishers, readers, and officials as well as a network of structural things, including positions, power, resources, and institutions. The people take positions, exert influence, use resources, and negotiate with institutions (Bourdieu 1993). The literary field constantly interacts with other fields, especially the field of power and the field of economy. Its interactions with the field of power follow two logics (Bourdieu 1993). First, the logic of *heteronomy*: the literary field closely follows the rules and norms in the field of power, and thus its independence is compromised. Second, the logic of *autonomy*: the literary field tends to be separated from the fields of power and builds its own hierarchy based on its own norms.

The logic of heteronomy between the literary field and the political field was not new in the history of PRC. The affinity between literature and politics was manifested in some significant incidents, such as the political attacks on *Hairui Dismissed from Office* (*Hairui Baguan*), which triggered the Cultural Revolution. It did not stop after the Cultural Revolution. Deng Xiaoping and his cultural officials utilized the play *Listening to Thunder from Silence* (*Yuwushengchu*) to encourage the public to condemn ultra-leftism and embrace the new political agenda. Thus, exposing past traumas was not only okay but also great, as long as it helped the new regime's legitimacy. The literary field, therefore, revived and boomed in the wake of the Cultural Revolution (Siu and Stern 1983; Link 2000).

The reviving literary field was not independent of the political field. Rather, it restored the "seventeen-year" system (1949–1966), a Soviet-type literature system that dominated the literary field before the Cultural Revolution, based on the theory of socialist realism and vertical cultural administrations (Hong 2007, 187). Prominent seventeen-year cultural bureaucrats and writers, who were purged in the Cultural Revolution, reappeared as the prominent figures. Core organizations like the Writers' Association were reestablished to resume control over material and institutional resources, for example, the positions of "professional writers" or journal editors, which could provide the writers with stable salaries (Link 2000). The "socialist realism," the dominant literary theory in the seventeen-year period, remained the major principle of the field. It emphasizes the political and social functions of literature and pervasively influenced readers' expectations of literary works in the wake of the Cultural Revolution (Dong, Ding, and Wang 2005, 368–69). At the Fourth Conference of Chinese Literature and Arts Workers' Representatives in 1979, Deng Xiaoping endorsed the new slogan that literature and the arts should serve the people instead of politics, but he also emphasized that "literature and arts cannot be separate from politics" (Tao and He 2008, 30).

Meanwhile, the logic of autonomy was in play, certainly within boundaries. Some writers, scholars, and even rehabilitated literary officials advocated relative independence of literature from politics. For example, Zhou Yang, a high-ranking cultural official, argued for freedom of styles and genres in literature and the arts (Dong, Ding, and Wang 2005, 362). Political campaigns against writers did not stop – for example, the famous *Bitter Love* incident (Chan 1988), but they were much less frequent. Even when such a campaign happened, the punishment was less severe. Writers could expose the dark side of the society, especially the trauma left by the Cultural Revolution, although the exposure drew conservative critics' angry retorts. The room for literary expression, however, was still circumscribed by the logic of heteronomy because it was given by the reformist regime for its legitimacy purposes and could shrink when the opening up backfired.

Under the two logics, positions and symbolic capital were redistributed accordingly in the literary field. The triumphant "returners," writers and literary officials who had made their career before the Cultural Revolution and were purged in later political campaigns, now obtained the most important positions and honors. Those writers included two generations. Veteran writers like Ba Jin and Mao Dun, who had been involved in the left-wing literary activism before 1949, now took the key administrative positions at literary institutions. Some writers who had been active in the 1950s, such as Wang Meng and Liu Binyan, also re-emerged to center stage as cultural heroes.[6] Both groups of literary elites

---

[6] For example, the leadership of the Writers' Association in 1979, the first after the Cultural Revolution, had no one other than this group of people: Mao Dun as the chair, Ba Jin as

were eager to expose their personal trauma of being detained and persecuted in the Cultural Revolution. Even Zhou Yang, who led attacks on
intellectuals in the 1950s, now showed a surprising degree of openness,
partly due to his personal ordeal. Many of them wrote memoirs and
essays to recount and reflect on their horrifying experience in the
Cultural Revolution, one being Ba Jin's *Random Thoughts* (*suixianglu*).
Most of their retrospectives largely followed the Party's line (Meng 2009,
185), but their power and prestige in the literary field turned this trend of
exposing trauma into a new norm of the field.

The two logics, however, shared a common tenet that literature should
carry the heavy burden of answering big historical and political questions.
Even the logic of autonomy only encouraged a distance from the
propaganda-like, all-positive representation of reality. This expectation
for literature originated from the seventeen-year literature system and
continued to exist at least into the mid-1980s.

This new norm generated some political and cultural opportunities for
zhiqing-turned-writers. Their "experiential mode" of writing – telling
their own stories – was encouraged by the dominant theory of socialist
realism that emphasized the political functions of literature in exposing
trauma and reflecting on the past. The political habitus of the majority of
the zhiqing writers, who were mostly either disillusioned aspirants or
embittered withdrawers, also fit into the general intellectual atmosphere.
The literary value of their works became somewhat secondary. Literature
scholars had unanimously low opinions of the zhiqing literature and the
literature in the first several years after the Cultural Revolution in general, which ironically used a "narratology all too reminiscent of Maoist
literature" even if it attempted to stay away from the Maoist models (Chi
and Wang 2000, xxv).

Meanwhile, the heteronomous logic of the literary field's relations with
the economic field helped rather than hindered the prominence of

the first vice-chair, and most other vice-chairs were above sixty (*Wenyi Bao*, No. 11–12,
1979, page 35). The leadership of the Association for Literary and Artistic Workers had a
similar configuration: Ba Jin as the chair and, except for two (Lin Mohan and
Kangbaerhan), all were above seventy (*Wenyi Bao*, No. 11–12, 1979, page 29). The
returning "seventeen-year" writers, who were under sixty in the period, resumed their
writing with much verve. Winners of the first prizes of the National Novella Awards
(1979–1980) were all those returning seventeen-year writers, such as Wang Meng and
Zhang Yigong, who were born in the 1920s and 1930s (www.chinawriter.com.cn/zx/
2007/2007-01-08/873.html). Winners of the first Mao Dun Novel Awards (1977–1981)
were also from this group, born from the 1910s to the early 1940s, except for a few
younger ones, such as Gu Hua born in 1940 and Mo Yinfeng, born in 1938, who were
still about ten years older than the zhiqing generation (www.chinawriter.com.cn/n1/2018/
0810/c405645-30222028.html).

literature. Literary magazines, publishers, and supplements to newspapers mushroomed, largely thanks to the public's hunger for *any* unofficial cultural products after the ten-year prohibition (Link 2000; Hong 2007). Because of a shortage of serious literary products, literary magazines and publishers consciously sought amateur writers from the grassroots level through all kinds of mechanisms, including public calls for submission, literary competitions, and editors' visits to danwei to look for authors. Some of the mechanisms were the legacies from the older propaganda system, in which writing for serious publications was treated as a political task. A publisher or a magazine, mostly the prestigious ones like the People's Literature Press, sometimes sent a formal letter to a writer's danwei to request a leave of absence for a writer, who stayed in the publisher's guesthouse to revise the manuscript (Tu 2016). When Ye Xin was summoned to stay in Shanghai to revise *Stone Falcon* for the Shanghai People's Press, the Press paid him 50 yuan and some food ration tickets as subsidies (Leung 1994, 214). Major literary newspapers like *Wenxue Bao* frequently published reports to encourage local danwei to accommodate amateur writers' writing. Some danwei showed their support by penning letters to the newspaper. For example, a letter from a regional-level Party secretary in Siping, Liaoning, to *Wenxue Bao* vowed that "nurturing literary youth" was the local officials' responsibility (Wenxue Bao 1983).

This open channel for amateurs helped in the rise of the zhiqing writers, who had limited literary skills, inadequate education, and close to zero economic capital, but lots of scars to show. They made a surprise appearance in the late 1970s and early 1980s, emerging as if from nowhere – usually as an unknown returning zhiqing or factory worker or college student or young magazine editor – but suddenly publishing their stories in top-notch literary magazines, or placing novels with prominent publishers, or winning prestigious awards.

Kong Jiesheng, for example, followed this Cinderella trajectory of stardom. Kong spent six years planting and cutting rubber trees on a Hainan farm before returning to Guangzhou in 1976 and becoming a worker in a lock factory. Without formal writing training, he published his first short story, "My Marriage" (*yinyuan*), which won the prestigious National Award for Short Stories in 1978. The next year, Kong won the same award again for "Because of Her" (*yinwei youle ta*), and also published "On the Other Side of the River" (*zai xiaohe nabian*), a typical scar literature piece that triggered a nationwide controversy. In 1980, Kong was transferred from his factory to the Guangdong Writers' Association, becoming a professional writer with a salary from the Association, a job most writers would envy. In the same year, he finally received his first formal literary writing training: he attended a workshop for writers at Lu Xun Literary Institute, which many other zhiqing writers attended as well.

The older generation of writers, as victims of the ultra-left politics, sympathized with the zhiqing and offered help and patronage. Sometimes they helped clear the obstructions from conservative leaders of the young writers' local danwei. Zhu Lin's experience illustrated this intergenerational patronage. Her immersion in writing and her bold exposure of sexual assault in her writings led to her conflicts with her danwei, a children's literature press in Shanghai. When the People's Literature Press sent an official letter to her danwei to request a writing leave for her, the director of her danwei refused to let her go. Instead, he wrote to the People's Literature Press to condemn Zhu Lin for her works' political problems and her work ethic (Shi 2014, 308–12). Such a letter could have ruined the prospect of a book and even a young writer's career. Indeed, it almost did. Editors and administrators within the Press opposed the publication of the book, but the liberal-minded director, Wei Junyi, a victim of the Anti-Rightist Movement and Cultural Revolution, favored it and secured support from Mao Dun, the Zeus of Chinese literature, a survivor of the Cultural Revolution. Mao Dun liked the novel and said he hoped to "see the novel published soon" (Shi 2014, 310; Li 2015). Later, as Zhu Lin continued to have conflicts with her danwei, Wei Junyi helped her obtain a position as an editor in *Shanghai Literature*. She even visited Zhu Lin to show her support (Shi 2014, 310–11). Xiao Qian, another veteran writer, wrote the preface for Zhu Lin's later novel, *The Weeping Lancang River*, saying that the novel appealed to him because it awoke some of his painful memories of his years on the "re-education" farms.

In short, the field dynamics described above can explain why literature became the major form of public memory and why the prevalent pattern of the literary memory included an explicit criticism of the send-down program. The state wanted to use literature to expose traumas in the past to legitimize its agenda. The dominant socialist realism in the literary field led to a popular expectation for the social and political functions of literature rather than its literary values. The zhiqing writers' dispositions to write about their own stories and their limited literary skills matched this expectation. In the meantime, the booming literature market created demands for amateur writers, and the older literary elites with "scars" also helped the rise of the zhiqing writers through their patronage.

This field analysis can also explain the decline of the literary memory of the zhiqing generation. In the mid- and late 1980s, the autonomy logic was fortified in a few new trends in the literary field, such as "root-searching literature" and various other kinds of "modernisms" (Hong 2007; Berry 2017). Correspondingly, the zhiqing writers' writing styles and career paths diverged. Writers like Han Shaogong, Wang Anyi, and Zhang Chengzhi started to experiment with new styles and topics and helped define the "high-brow" taste in the literary field. They still drew on their zhiqing experience but mainly for purposes other than representing the zhiqing past. Han Shaogong, for example, called for reconnecting literature to the folk cultural traditions – the "roots" – which attempted, in an undertone, to depoliticize literature. Some of his later novels, such as *The Return* (*guiqulai*, 1985), partially draw on the zhiqing experience but mostly treat it as a vague background. By the mid-1990s, their zhiqing experience was only marginally presented or completely disappeared from their important new works (Han's *Maqiao Dictionary* [1995], Wang's *The Song of Everlasting Sorrow* [1994], and Zhang's *The History of Soul* [1991]).

Others, such as Ye Xin and Liang Xiaosheng, stuck to realism but also leaned toward a market-based popular style, as they actively sought opportunities to adapt their work into movies and TV series. They were joined by Guo Xiaodong and Deng Xian, who published their fiction and reportage in the late 1980s and 1990s. Together, they constituted the "middle-brow" zhiqing literature, which was still appealing to those readers not well equipped to read convoluted modernist novels but liked straightforward realism and dramatic plots. But even this audience was decreasing. The only zhiqing-related works that were influential outside the literary field were those adapted into TV series, such as *Karma*. The rest, including Kong Jiesheng and Ah Cheng, left the literary scene for various reasons. By the early 1990s, "zhiqing literature" had lost its popular readership and symbolic capital in the mainstream literary field. The sales and publications of zhiqing literary works sharply declined. Except for *Karma* and *The Golden Times*, no zhiqing novel after 1985 had more than 100,000 copies printed in its first edition. *The Bloody Sunset*, a market success in the second half of the 1980s, printed 40,820 copies in its first edition. This decline was part of the broader decline of literature in general as a cultural consumption.[7] In the 1990s, literature was replaced by sites of memory as the major medium, which will be discussed in Chapter 4.

---

[7] The print statistics in this chapter are collected from the copyright pages of all editions of the zhiqing novels. A limitation of these data is that many editions – especially the recent ones – do not show these print numbers. Consequently, I only use the numbers of printed copies of the first editions of the novels if they are available, and, thus, the numbers are lower than the actual prints.

Divided Reception as Recreation of Literary Memory

Literary memory goes beyond writing and producing literary texts. After literary texts are produced, they continue to generate new meanings of the past in discussions and debates in the public sphere, and, thus, provoke counter-narratives and new memories. This reception process often includes elite critics' reviews, literary prizes, public debates, readers' responses, market successes, uses of buzzwords and characters in public discourses, and so on (Griswold 1987a; Erll 2011, 154–57; Childress and Friedkin 2012).

The heyday of the literary memory of the zhiqing generation was the first half of the 1980s. The most unequivocal evidence was the number of copies printed of several representative works. The first edition of *The Wasted Years* as a book in 1982 was published by China Youth Press and printed 127,000 copies, in addition to the aforementioned 1 million copies of two issues of *Harvest*, the literary magazine that originally published the novel. Even Ye Xin's less well-known novel *Our Generation of Youth* (1980, China Youth Press) had 150,000 copies printed and Zhu Lin's *The Road of Life* (1979, People's Literature Press) 100,000. The zhiqing literary works also performed well in major literary awards. Out of twenty-five short stories that won the first National Best Short Stories Awards in 1978, sponsored by *The People's Literature* journal and selected by readers, three were zhiqing stories. In each year after that until 1984, one or two zhiqing stories won the award.

Even in these peak years, however, critics gave mixed reviews. The reviews sometimes were less about the literary value than about how to remember the past. This emphasis indicated the expectations of literature for its political and social functions and also suggested that the literary memory continued to be produced in the reception process. For example, a 1983 *Beijing Youth Daily* review of *The Wasted Years* perfectly foreshadowed a pattern that later dominated the public memory in the 1990s, "the people but not the event": suspending historical evaluations of the program but highlighting the worthiness of the zhiqing generation (Beijing Qingnian Bao 1983):

We leave the evaluation of the send-down program to history. We cannot deny that millions of youths shed their tears and sweat in the vast universe of the countryside and devoted their hope and passion. The whole generation spent their best years in the countryside. The tempering experience in the countryside made them know life, people, and themselves. They have harvested their strong and rich life!

A review of Liang Xiaosheng's "A Land of Wonder and Mystery" was just as ambiguous as the story itself. With no explicit evaluation of the send-down program, it enthusiastically commended the story as "not intended to expose suffering but to reveal the lofty spirit and excellent character" (Xiao 1983). A review of the movie based on the story slightly deviated from Liang's intended meaning, but not very far. It instantiated the pattern of "good people but the bad event": after condemning the program as "wrong" and "ridiculous," it sang high praise of the zhiqing for "sacrificing their most precious years to the frontiers and the soil" (Mu 1984).

From the second half of the 1980s on, however, rave reviews became rare. Literary critics, now baptized in the new literary trends, reached a consensus that the zhiqing literature had limited literary value and that the memory of this generation represented in the literary works was problematic.

In 1998, the thirtieth anniversary of the send-down program, a few literary journals organized symposiums on the zhiqing literature. The critics went well beyond literature and ruminated on the event, the zhiqing generation, and their memory. They almost unanimously found fault with the empty idealism in some works and took issue with self-centered grievances. One of the critics contended (Shi 1998):

The zhiqing generation writers mistake a tragedy that they passively accepted for an adventure they actively initiated. Thus, from its inception, suffering is not in their ideas. Even if the setbacks in their personal experience led to resentful complaints, their awakening has not turned into a profound self-reflection of this generation themselves.

If this criticism could be attributed to the generational bias of a young intellectual (born in 1966) toward his older brothers and sisters, an equally devastating review came from a critic of the same generation. He Shaojun, a Hunan zhiqing who edited an influential collection of zhiqing novels in 1985, someone who would be a staunch supporter of the zhiqing literature, argued that works like Liang Xiaosheng's *Snowy City* represented the zhiqing generation's dilemma of being caught between their obsession with the bygone fantasy of idealism and their condemnation of the years in which politics distorted their idealism (He 1998).

Some critics suggested that the peasants in their sent-down places were ignored or became the zhiqing's "others" in those works (Zhang 1998, 36):

Perhaps the peasants' narratives were like: a weird group of people came to our places, stole our chicken, slept with our daughters, and, then, left. Perhaps to the peasants, your "suffering" does not even exist.

This criticism of the zhiqing writing's unconscious condescension out of their unawareness of their urban privileges echoed some writers' "counter-memory" writing. For example, Liu Xinglong's *The Big Tree*

Is Still Small and Li Er's *The Devils Are Coming to the Village*, written from the peasants' perspective, deliberately responded to the zhiqing literature in the 1980s. The image of zhiqing in the two novels was a group of irresponsible young urbanites, who created disturbances in the country-side and left without any guilt. In fact, the wording of the title of Li Er's novel, "the devils are coming to the village" (*guizi jincun*), was used to describe the Japanese army's aggression during WWII. The analogy between the zhiqing and the "Japanese devils" was obviously a parody as well as a condemnation of the self-importance in the zhiqing literary memory.

The critics and even some writers also called for self-reflection and confession and associated the zhiqing identity with its flip side: the Red Guards. In addition to Zhang Kangkang, whose views will be discussed in detail in Chapter 4, Deng Xian also urged his fellow zhiqing to repent (Yin 2004, 82):

This generation evolved from students to the Red Guards, and then to zhiqing. Every one of us participated in [those activities]. We all should have an attitude of self-reflection, just like Hitler should not be the only one responsible for starting WWII. ... Some Red Guards beat their teachers, tortured their classmates, "smashed the four olds," disavowed their parents ... all these things were incredibly brutal.

Even Wei Junyi, the veteran writer and Zhu Lin's patron, said that none of the zhiqing writers had ever honestly written about how they turned into radical youths and did horrible things in the Cultural Revolution (Xie 1998, 54). A few critics defended the generation's dignity by commending the "spirit of the zhiqing culture," which referred to this generation's combining old and new, knowing the ordinary people's lives through living with them, and shouldering their historical responsibility (Fan 1998). This grandiose but weak voice was quickly overwhelmed by the call for self-reflection widely voiced in reviews in elite literary journals and the mass media. After the 1990s, the zhiqing literature was not even a topic of reviews and debates. It simply disappeared from top literary journals.

Outside the circle of elite literary critics, the zhiqing's own reception of the zhiqing literary works varies. The works most frequently mentioned are the ones that became popular in the 1980s plus a few in the early 1990s, especially those adapted into movies and TV series, such as *The Wasted Years*, *Snowy City*, and *Karma*. Some expressions derived from those literary works became part of the everyday vocabulary to describe certain zhiqing experiences. For example, the "wasted years" (*cuotuo-suiyue*) has been widely used to lament the zhiqing's lost years. "Karma," a Buddhist term, is also used to refer to the zhiqing's children left behind when they returned to cities. The zhiqing I encountered in my fieldwork sometimes jokingly asked each other: "Did you have a *karma* back in the countryside?" – meaning: "Did you have an abandoned child/spouse in the countryside?"

In contrast, no literary expressions with more idealistic connotations have reached the same level of popularity as the "gray" ones. Liang's *A Snowstorm Coming Is Coming Tonight* and *Snowy City* were adapted into popular TV dramas, but neither generated the kind of buzzwords that can give the public memory unambiguous slogans. As I will detail in Chapter 4, the zhiqing generation had to wait for the exhibits in the early 1990s to popularize the phrase "regretless youth" (*qingchunwuhui*) to counter the gray, melancholy "wasted years."

Later works are rarely mentioned in the interviews or during casual conversations, except for those works by the authors who acquired their reputation as "zhiqing writers" in the 1980s, such as Liang Xiaosheng, whose TV series *Zhiqing* (2012) became a topic when it came out. Zhang Kangkang was criticized by only a few who were well read. Yan Geling and Wang Xiaobo, two writers well known among younger, educated readers, are not mentioned at all. The popularity of *Karma* had an additional life-course reason: it came out at a time when many zhiqing residing outside of Shanghai sent their children back for school in Shanghai according to the 1989 children returning policy. Most of them did not have the same troubles as the zhiqing characters in the TV drama, but they share the same concerns about their returning children. Some faced new difficulties when they decided to return to Shanghai to accompany their children – a kind of difficulty that could be easily interpreted as "karma" from their past.

Cultural capital matters only in terms of familiarity with the literary works. Some of my interviewees are avid readers with higher cultural capital. They obviously read the novels: they can accurately describe the novels and make specific comments. Their views, however, vary. Mr. Gang, a bookstore owner, who pulled a few zhiqing-related novels from the bookshelf in his living room while we were talking, disliked Liang's new TV drama *Zhiqing* for its "lack of depth," which he attributed to political restrictions. Instead, he liked Jia Hongtu, a northeastern writer, especially his non-fiction. Mr. Kun, a poet himself, however, criticized Ye Xin's works for their "gray color" and being overly sentimental. The good works – he used He Jinzhi, a poet in the 1950s who wrote a long poem to encourage youths to march to the west, as an example – should be more "heroic" and "positive."

Some, however, have no comments to make on the zhiqing literature. Some were simply too busy to watch or read when the zhiqing novels and dramas were popular in the 1980s. As described earlier, they struggled to find jobs, worked hard to get promotions, had babies, attended evening school, and so on.

The majority of the zhiqing found themselves between two extreme groups – avid readers and non-readers – but their knowledge about the zhiqing literature was limited to the ones adapted as popular TV dramas. Many have watched TV dramas but never read the books. Here, too, the reception varies. Mrs. Xue, the zhiqing who went to Heilongjiang (Chapter 2), clearly remembered Liang Xiaosheng's *Growth Ring* (*Nianlun*) because the difficulties of returning zhiqing in the novel resonated with her experience of struggling after returning to Shanghai in the 1990s. Mrs. Wang, a Xinjiang zhiqing, however, found that the difficulties in the dramas still could not compare to hers. For Mr. Cui, whose good chushen protected him from all the troubles, watching the dramas was an eye-opening experience because, for the first time, he realized not all zhiqing were as lucky as he was. Mr. Yu did not read Ye Xin's novels, although he was an avid reader of other books, simply because they were too real, too painful: a few zhiqing on his farm had the similar karma problem. While most resonance comes from painful experience, some found the sentimental aspect of the dramas more relatable. For example, Mr. Guang, the swimming coach, liked *The Wasted Years* because he had similar complicated relations with girls on his production team.

Some of the most popular novels and dramas were common targets of criticism. The criticisms, however, were focused on the alleged bias toward zhiqing. For example, some zhiqing believed *Karma* – especially the drama based on the novel – were so popular that they perpetuated a stereotype of zhiqing as spineless urbanites with loose morals. Mr. Qian (Chapter 1) attributed this "gray" representation of the past to the embittered writers' bad chushen and their corresponding resentment toward the state and the Party, a "lay" theory similar to the analysis presented in this chapter. In contrast, Qian preferred Liang's works, which, in his words, showed "positive energy," despite his reservations about Liang's pompousness.

The reception correlates with zhiqing readers' habitus. The ones with black-chushen habitus, including withdrawers and aspirants who experienced habitus change, tend to lean toward the "gray" – trauma-exposing – literary memory, while those with the red-chushen habitus – if there is no habitus change – tend to have affinity with the works with more heroic and idealistic elements.

Nevertheless, in contrast to the elite critics, none of my ordinary zhiqing interviewees cares about the literary values of the works. They view the literary works and the popular cultural products adapted from the works as a medium of memory. None of them ever mentioned the necessity for self-reflection in literary representations of their generation past, let alone public atonement. Despite their varying views of the send-down program, the ordinary zhiqing do not question themselves. For many zhiqing still suffering from the aftermath of the program in the 1980s and 1990s, the demand for self-criticism and even public repentance was unpleasant, moralist, if not offensive. For this reason, Zhang Kangkang's works are particularly unpopular, if not infamous, especially among Zhang's fellow zhiqing to the Heilongjiang Corps. On a few different occasions, I heard the Corps zhiqing vehemently attacking her views. Self-critical voices have been limited to the intellectuals' circle. This reception is more in line with the intended meanings of the writers, reproducing the public memory pattern of "good people but the bad event," while only elite readers and critics tend to be critical of both the event and the zhiqing themselves.

4 Regretless Youth and Long Live Youth!
Exhibits and Museums as Sites of Memory

In the late 1980s and early 1990s, a new medium of public memory of the zhiqing generation – exhibits – emerged on the cultural scene. After the first one, "Souls Tied to the Black Soil" (*hunxi heitudi*, hereafter, "Souls"), was held in Beijing in 1990, similar exhibits appeared in other major cities, including Guangzhou, Chengdu, and Nanjing, and attracted enthusiastic audiences and media attention. About twenty years later, more than twenty zhiqing-themed museums started to appear around the country. The exhibits and museums display sepia photos, old mugs with political slogans, patched uniforms, and plows. The word "youth" (*qingchun*) features prominently in slogans and titles of the exhibits: "Regretless Youth," for example, as the title of an exhibit in Chengdu, and "Long Live Youth!" as the inscription on a wall in a museum in Dafeng, Jiangsu.

This new medium of public memory can certainly be explained by the zhiqing's nostalgia related to their life course. When the exhibits opened in the late 1980s and early 1990s, most zhiqing had reached early middle age, mid-30s to early 40s, the first period when "nostalgia-proneness" peaks – about ten years from early adulthood and twenty years from adolescence (Havlena and Holak 1991). After being a "lost generation" for almost a decade, many settled into jobs, got married, and had children, entering a relatively stable stage of life. It was a good time for them to breathe a brief sigh of relief, look back at their past, give themselves a pat on the back, and, sometimes, teach their children the value of hard work by telling their parents' "back-then" stories. When museums were built in the late 2000s, this generation was approaching or had reached retirement age (above 55) and felt increasingly bewildered amidst the whirlwind of social change in China, and, thus, had excessive nostalgia for their simple life in the countryside.

Nevertheless, many in this generation could not afford the luxury of nostalgia. In 1989, when the first exhibit was initiated, the children return policy began another period of ordeals for many former zhiqing, this time, ironically, in their hometowns. In the late 1990s, many former zhiqing were laid off ("*xiagang*," literally, "down from the post") at the age of 40-something, during the massive SOE reform (Hung and Chiu 2003; Qian and Hodson 2011). They used a dark-humor saying to summarize their life courses twisted by the capricious policy changes as "three downs": "Mao Zedong commanded us to go *down* to the country-side [*xiaxiang*], Deng Xiaoping told us to jump *down* into the sea [*xiahai*, doing business]; Jiang Zeming ordered us to come *down* from the post [*xiagang*]." In Shanghai, when the museums were being planned and built in the 2000s, hundreds of zhiqing regularly petitioned and protested to demand that the government adjust their pensions and healthcare policies. Thus, the increasing disparity in the same generation and the gap between the settled and unsettled lives accentuate a crucial issue: How to present the zhiqing as a generation and the send-down program as the event that shaped this generation's fate in various ways.

Moreover, exhibits and museums need space, land, items to display, maintenance, personnel, visitors, and revenues to remain open either temporarily or, for museums, permanently. While literary works sell copies to earn some returns, most exhibits and museums cost money instead of making money. The limited revenues from admissions to museums may never cover their initial investment in construction and high maintenance costs, and many of the zhiqing museums do not even charge admission fees. Thus, compared to literature, exhibits and museums need more material resources, institutional support, and significant amounts of funds. How and where did the zhiqing exhibits and museums get all these resources? Who initiated the idea, made plans, mobilized resources, held the exhibits, and built the museums?

The physical existence of exhibits and museums also indicates a political puzzle. The "Souls" exhibit, for instance, was held in the Chinese Revolutionary Museum, one of the most prominent national museums in China, which was located right by Tiananmen Square. The exhibit took place only one year after the Tiananmen protest in 1989 and attracted tens of thousands of visitors. The combination of "Tiananmen Square" and "a large crowd" was politically sensitive enough to be on the authorities' radar. Certainly, not every exhibit or museum got on the central state's nerves like the "Souls," but their temporary or permanent presence would be impossible without the central and local governments' political endorsements and land use permissions. Why, then, did the Chinese government allow exhibits and museums on such a controversial topic?

The answers to these questions rest on the processes that happen in a "memory field," a field specifically devoted to mnemonic practices revolving around a certain group's past or an event. Like other fields

(Bourdieu 1993), the memory field consists of agents, positions, capitals, and their mutual interactions. The agents in the memory field include individuals, groups, associations, and organizations who play the role of "memory entrepreneurs" (for example, preservers, historians, promoters, advocates). They organize regular public activities, such as commemorative gatherings, anniversary ceremonies, mourning, and so on, and engage in production of cultural objects, including books, movies, memorials, museums, and exhibits. The literature field in the 1980s temporarily functioned as a memory field, but it was not dedicated to the zhiqing generation and soon disengaged itself from the zhiqing memory. It was not until the late 1980s and early 1990s that the memory field of zhiqing emerged in the major entrepreneurs' work to organize the exhibits.

The memory field overlaps and tangles with the field of politics, but politics work in more nuanced ways than many observers of authoritarianism would assume. To scrutinize state–society interactions revolving around exhibits and museums requires a subtler examination of the overlapping area of the memory and political fields, including the key memory entrepreneurs' positions and their relations with the central and local governments. As Kirk Denton argues in his study of contemporary Chinese museums, "the CCP exerts a profound influence over the memoryscape and mediascape of China, and to dismiss this state presence as nothing but propaganda is to fail to understand the complexity of the state/people relationship" (Denton 2014, 4). Such a field analysis should be connected to a meticulous investigation of the memory patterns represented in the exhibits and panels. For example, how did the government–entrepreneur relationship shape the content and form of the exhibits? How did the entrepreneurs plan to present the troubled intersections between the zhiqing and the event, given the historical controversy over the event?

The exhibits and museums mark a turn in the public memory of the zhiqing generation, from public discourses and narratives to "sites of memory" (lieux de mémoire), "where memory crystallizes and secretes itself" in material forms (Nora 1989, 7). When groups build museums to preserve their memory, the memory is "seized" by "history," by which Nora means intellectual production, reconstruction, and representation of the past. Nora's controversial distinction between history and memory aside, the exhibits and museums function as the zhiqing generation's "sites of memory." Through those sites, the zhiqing generation seeks public recognition, constructs and reinforces their identity, counters the oblivion about their history in the mainstream public discourses, and preserves materials about their past – in other words, enhances their symbolic capital by mobilizing material and institutional resources. In this chapter, I examine the complex social–political processes revolving around the sites of memory. Let me start with the first significant exhibit: "Souls Tied to the Black Soil."

"People but Not the Event": The "Souls" Exhibit

The "Souls Tied to the Black Soil" exhibit opened in November 1990. Its popularity exceeded the organizers' expectations. On the first day alone, 15,000 people visited. In the following two weeks, altogether 95,000 visitors crowded the main showroom. Many used the exhibit as a reunion occasion. Even before its opening, people gathered outside the museum and tried to find each other by holding cardboard signs with numbers of their regiments and companies. They exclaimed, hugged, shook hands, and patted each other on the shoulders. On the last day, December 9, when the exhibit was about to close at 4 PM, the visitors refused to leave. Many were still talking, hugging, and crying. The museum had to extend the hours and sell more tickets to allow new visitors to flood in. Finally, at 7 PM, the door was closed. The organizers cheered, jumped up and down, and threw "snow" – white artificial materials – into the air to celebrate the success (Xu 2014).

The communal exuberance around the exhibit, however, could easily veil the difficult issues the organizers had to confront. The most important is to square the zhiqing's nostalgia with the controversies over the send-down program and the Cultural Revolution. The solution the "Souls" exhibit offered was a pattern of "people but not the event."

The exhibit started with a passage that described the send-down program as "a vigorous campaign 20 years ago," which gathered "a crowd of people whose blood was boiling and whose hearts rose and fell like waves." The next passage directly addressed the core of the difficult past the zhiqing generation had to face:

Some people say: "Let the history evaluate the historical achievements and mistakes, the right and the wrong."

We say: "Let us evaluate those things that belong to us."

We will not regret our youth spent in Beidahuang. We do not have to take pride in what we have done. We will not beg for other people's sympathy and pity.

We contributed our youth to Beidahuang. And Beidahuang rewards us decently, including not only the pasture and abundance in the "Great Storehouse North," but also a type of spirit of resilience, endurance, pursuit, and diligence. That is the "Spirit of Beidahuang!

This passage suspended the historical evaluation of the program by offering to "let the history evaluate" – in which "history" is used as a subject, a personalized actor who can "evaluate" and "judge." While the tough job of evaluating an event was left to the vague and even nonexistent subject "history," "those things that belong to us" were not. It was "our" job to evaluate our past. In other words, we *owned* our history. The evaluation of "ourselves" was positive. The heroic, idealistic, diligent, and resilient zhiqing personified the "spirit of Beidahuang," placing themselves at the center of this narrative, with the send-down program as a vague background.

The rest of the exhibit followed from this opening frame. The poor living conditions in Beidahuang were presented – for example, the shabby huts the zhiqing lived in and the severe weather in winter – but mainly as an object that the zhiqing were determined to conquer: "Beidahuang! We will conquer you! We can conquer you!" The main characters of this drama were the "Corps soldiers" who "had the morning sun in their chest" (*xiongyou zhaoyang*), advanced to the wilderness, overcame difficulties, and turned it into a storehouse of grains.

At some points, the narrative almost touched on the political aspect but soon dodged away from it. It displayed Chairman Mao's badges, red flags, uniforms, and even a petition written in a zhiqing's blood, which read "All for Chairman Mao!" Another display in the exhibit presented a story of a sick zhiqing who did not ask for leave because of the shortage of labor and the stringent discipline: "Arthritis, nephritis, menstrual period, high fever, shivering, and dysentery – (we) didn't report. Didn't report." Whether the exhibit was praising this as a heroic deed or condemning it as an act of stupidity encouraged by an inconsiderate institution remained unknown. Several pictures even depicted the "struggle" (public humiliation) sessions, political campaigns, and some ideologically loaded but practically ineffective ways of production (e.g., "sickles will beat harvesters"). The problems were described as symptoms of "ultra-leftism," an official term that referred to the political ideology of the Cultural Revolution.

At one point, the exhibit depicted the huge wave of the zhiqing's return to cities. The zhiqing's pursuits, read the narrative, "have been intertwined with this or that thing which violated the laws of historical development." This brief comment, however, did not specify what "this or that thing" meant. The zhiqing were also analogized to Sisyphus – they "have sacrificed their sweat and blood but did somewhat useless things." This gray passage ended in several vague lines that fostered ambiguity by playing on punctuation:

Ended.

Ended!

Ended?

All these "gray" depictions, however, made up only a small proportion of the exhibit and were embedded in a teleological narrative: after a zigzagging course, this generation cherished special feelings for the nation and the people, which were regarded as one of the gains from their sent-down experience.

Overall, the main narrative of the "Souls" exhibit followed the pattern of "people but not the event." Compared to the diverse autobiographical memories, this pattern excluded outright complaints about the program, explicit adherence to Maoism, and many other narratives. Compared to the pattern of "good people but the bad event" in the literary memory, this pattern has no explicit evaluation of the program. It detached the participants from the controversial event by highlighting their heroism, sacrifice, and contributions. Where the event was described, the narrative was hesitant and ambiguous, hinting at the producers' clear awareness of the controversies over the event and their reluctance to take sides. Even when the exhibit seemed to present implicit criticisms, it did not go beyond the official rhetoric about the Cultural Revolution in which "ultra-leftism" took the blame, whereas the Party–state's legitimacy remained intact. It was the "people" – the zhiqing, with the identity of "Corps soldiers" – but not the event at the center of this pattern.

The Production of the "Souls" Exhibit

The "people but not the event" pattern was a result of a cultural production process. The process started with a group of Heilongjiang Corps zhiqing, the major memory entrepreneurs, whose class positions, habitus, and connections shaped the content and form of the exhibit. Shi Xiaoyan, a former zhiqing in the Heilongjiang Corps, played a vital role in this process. In December 1988, on a business trip to Harbin, Shi met some local officials, also Beidahuang zhiqing, and came up with the idea of editing a book of memoirs, which later became *Winds and Clouds in the Great Northern Wilderness (Beidahuang fengyun lu)*. The purpose of the book was to "look back at the sweat and blood in our youth and to look for the old comrades-in-arms," especially when many of them had already become "backbones of the society" and "famous people in their professions" (Chun 2009, 11–12). The idea of an exhibit emerged later in the process of collecting memoirs. In other words, since its inception, the book of memoirs and the exhibit were not intended to express the struggling zhiqing's anxiety and grievances but to confirm the achievements of the "backbones" of the society.

Life course factors mattered here, but they played into the disparity of class positions instead of the universal psychology of nostalgia. The major "memory entrepreneurs" were those zhiqing whose confidence was bolstered by their first sweet smell of career success. Shi Xiaoyan, for example, served as the vice-head of the Social Reform Bureau, under the Party's Central Political Reform Study Office, a ministry-level advisory agency, which was led by Bao Tong, General Secretary Zhao Ziyang's Chief of Staff. Before entering the office, Shi had worked in a few government bureaus in Beijing and had been chief editor of a magazine and a newspaper.

Other key entrepreneurs – members of the "editorial committee" – had equally impressive positions and achievements. The other chief editor was Jiang Kun, a comedian who was already a household name in the 1980s. Among the thirty-five "standing editors," there were thirteen middle- to high-ranking officials, eight managers or executives, and thirteen journalists or writers; only two were low-ranking staff members in government bureaus. A few of them later became important figures in the political and economic fields: Jiang Daming, then the vice-head of the Organization Department of the Central Youth League, who later became the governor of Shandong Province; Zhu Shenwen, then the head secretary of Harbin Municipal Government, who later became vice-mayor of Harbin; and Zhou Yupeng, then the chief of Luwan District in Shanghai, who later became the vice-mayor of Shanghai. In the business sector were Zhu Xiaohua, the vice-head of the People's Bank's Shanghai branch, who later became the chairman of China Everbright Group, a state-owned financial corporation; and Li Xiaohua, a successful businessman who donated several hundred thousand yuan to the book and the exhibit. In the culture sector, there was Zhao Yan, another famous comedian; Jia Hongtu, a writer and the vice-chief-editor of the *Harbin Daily*; Liang Xiaosheng, Lu Xing'er, and Zhang Kangkang, three writers; and a few other journalists and editors affiliated with major newspapers, magazines, and publishing houses (Bianjibu 1990).

The elite members of this committee managed to mobilize resources and support from different sources, most importantly, the state's endorsement. Shi Xiaoyan persuaded China Youth Press, a publisher affiliated with the Youth League Central Committee, to publish the book of memoirs and another book with the Corps zhiqing's names and danwei. Shi's position certainly helped: he was a standing member of the Youth League Central Committee.

The final call for contributions to the book of memoirs came out in the April 21 issue of the *People's Daily*, the Communist Party's mouthpiece. The call did not appear in the classifieds section but on the normal page of "Culture and Sports," in the size of a normal report, which indicated endorsement from the government. The call had an emotional subtitle: "Tears and Blood. Tragic and Soul-Stirring. Winds and Rains. Thoughts and Feelings" and an beseeching title: "My comrades-in-arms of the Beidahuang Corps, where are you?"

The call, however, came at a bad time. It was right after Hu Yaobang's death and in the middle of the students' protest in Beijing, which became known as the "Tiananmen protest." Several weeks later, the government brutally suppressed the protest. Bao Tong, Shi's direct supervisor, was arrested, and his superior Zhao Ziyang was detained. Consequently, the Office was disbanded, and Shi Xiaoyan lost his position. The publishing plan was delayed.

Despite the political upheaval, the memory entrepreneurs still managed to obtain additional endorsements from the agricultural reclamation (*nongken*) system. The reclamation system oversaw some of the biggest farms in China, including those that used to be the Production and Construction Corps, a major type of sent-down place. The founder of the reclamation system was General Wang Zhen, then vice-chairman of PRC, who still had informal but indisputable authority over the system.

In a 1990 speech, Wang Zhen attempted to make a strong case for the reclamation system as an emblem of the superiority of socialism over capitalism and as a citadel against "bourgeois liberalization" (Wang 1990). He emphasized that the spirit of "plain life and hard work" (*jianku fendou*) was the honorable tradition of the reclamation and an asset for the whole country. This "great spirit of Beidahuang" perfectly fit the post-Tiananmen ideological agenda of the Party: to counter the "Western capitalist countries' intention of changing China peacefully," which was blamed for the Tiananmen protest, and to strengthen patriotic and Communist education. The rhetorical emphasis also quietly moved from the forcible migration of the zhiqing to the reclamation, a grand, heroic project. Thus, Wang Zhen's articulation and endorsement opened an opportunity for the otherwise sensitive theme of the exhibit.

To respond to the opportunity, the major memory entrepreneurs dealt with the framing issue with great political delicacy. When the preparation committee met to discuss it, they were engaged in a "serious debate" about the theme and tone (Chun 2009). The record available now does not specify the debate, but one might get a rough idea from the organizers who attended the meeting. There were two famous writers with dramatically different opinions, as discussed in Chapter 3. Liang Xiaosheng, who was responsible for drafting the descriptions, unambiguously praised the zhiqing's idealism and holding an ambiguously positive attitude about the send-down program. Zhang Kangkang held critical views of the send-down program and even the zhiqing themselves. Shi Xiaoyan was somewhere in between, holding an "in-Party reformist" view. In an interview with an academic journal after the exhibit, Shi said that the exhibit was intended to highlight this generation's sacrifice for the nation, their achievements, and their virtues despite the Cultural Revolution – a view consistent with the pattern of "good people but the bad event" (Fang 1991).

The key memory entrepreneurs eventually reached a consensus, perhaps except for Zhang Kangkang, who was not involved in later activities or any zhiqing-related activities. The final framing further toned down Shi's criticism of the Cultural Revolution. It suspended the controversies of the program but emphasized the zhiqing's beautiful youth, their contribution, and the "spirit of Beidahuang" they upheld. Huang Xiaodong, a curator of the Revolutionary Museum, stated in his proposal to the museum that the exhibit was "a dedication to the pioneers who reclaimed the wilderness in Beidahuang." The ultimate purpose was to "carry on the spirit of Beidahuang." The proposal did not mention the zhiqing's involvement in the Cultural Revolution or the historical evaluations of the send-down program.

This framing served as the lowest common denominator of various political views of the key parties involved in the exhibit. It satisfied the zhiqing winners' desire to celebrate their hard-won personal success in their careers. It was congruent with the reclamation system's guiding ideology of reclamation, the "spirit of Beidahuang." It pleased the central state, because it was as politically ambiguous as possible and as uplifting as desired. Thus, despite its potential controversies, it operated within a safety zone and offered something useful for the post-Tiananmen agenda of propaganda.

The Beidahuang reclamation also had their economic incentives. Through the book and exhibit, it wanted to utilize the connections with the zhiqing elite to expand their business. An important event in the production process was a gathering ("Symposium on Reviving the Reclamation Economy in Beidahuang") sponsored by the Reclamation Bureau and the book organization committee in December 1989 at a resort next to Tai Lake in Jiangsu. All the invited zhiqing were unsurprisingly cultural, political, or economic elites. At the symposium, the zhiqing offered their opinions and suggestions on how to "revive the Beidahuang economy." Some businessmen had even prepared specific plans for further collaboration with the Reclamation Bureau. The high point of the gathering came at the banquet. The zhiqing guests engaged in an exuberant drinking competition and a pop-up concert, and spontaneously performed the old songs and dances (Chun 2009, 19–24).

The book of memoirs consists of 193 stories written by Beidahuang zhiqing from various cities. It claimed to be following an egalitarian principle. The order of the memoirs follows the Chinese *bihua* (number of strokes). Nevertheless, what made the book and exhibit politically possible was not egalitarianism but the major entrepreneurs' class positions and corresponding resources and power. They managed to navigate the state system to secure political endorsement and even logistical support, including things as trivial as a conference room provided by the Central Youth League and as big as the venue for the exhibit, which was obtained through Huang Xiaodong, a curator of the museum, also a former zhiqing (Chun 2009; Xu 2014).

This institutional endorsement and ideological affinity, however, did not mean a trouble-free exhibit. Two days before the scheduled opening date, the organizers were told by the police that they needed an approval letter from a government office above the ministry level. Also, the police received reports that the exhibit would gather "a large number" of zhiqing with "flags" and "banners" in "Tiananmen Square" – a terrible combination of people, items, and place, which reminded the authorities of the protest a year before in the same place. In the evening, Shi Xiaoyan rushed to a high-ranking official's house and managed to get an approval letter. The next morning, Jiang Kun went to the Beijing Public Security Bureau to show the letter and explain the exhibit to the police officers. The police accepted the letter but still insisted on deploying a few officers at the museum to monitor the situation. The day before the exhibit, Wang Zhen's secretary came to do a final walkthrough of the exhibit and suggested a revision: the tone of the story of the martyrs was so tragic that their sacrifice could be mistaken for accidents; it needed to be more heroic. The organizers followed the "suggestions" and revised the panels overnight.

Reception of the "Souls" Exhibit

The intended message of presenting the people but not the event, however, received mixed responses.[1] Some shared with the memory entrepreneurs the pride in the zhiqing's contributions and resilience. An anonymous visitor commented in a spirited tone:

---

[1] Chun Ming's *Beidahuang: Post-Zhiqing Times* (Chun 2009, 115–29), a book by the memory entrepreneurs that describes the whole process of the exhibits, records eighty-two of the comments visitors left in the exhibit's comment book. Sixty of them are relevant to the purpose of the research.

The biggest happiness of life is to make contributions instead of making demands. History will not forget the contributions made by all the zhiqing who have shed their blood and sweat in Beidahuang and other frontiers in our motherland. Their indelible achievements have constituted the foundation of the mansion of the Republic.

Such pride, however, could only barely overshadow the discrimination they had painfully felt after their zhiqing years. A comment left by "Hong from 16th Regiment" read: "Look back at the past! [We must] let the people in the society know that we zhiqing had worked hard and shed lots of sweat. Don't discriminate against this generation!" Another comment by "Li Dongmin, the same generation," who might be a zhiqing sent down to another place, was even more emotional: "Don't say we have nothing! Don't say we are worth nothing! We are in the same generation. We are making history!"

Some comments simply expressed their nostalgia for their youth. Two zhiqing from Division 4, Regiment 41 said: "We will never forget the years in Beidahuang since our youth was sacrificed for the land of black soil. Indeed, 'souls tied to the black soil'!" Three other zhiqing said: "We gave our best years to Beidahuang, and Beidahuang will give us eternal memory."

Only a few visitors explicitly commented on the send-down program, and all those comments were negative. One read: "[The event was] a tragedy for the historical period, and a wrong path for China!" Another visitor, who identified himself or herself as "fellow traveler," meaning he or she might be a zhiqing but not to the Corps, separated their personal experience from history:

Experience is an asset for everyone's growth. But we should not forget that the zhiqing's "up to the mountains and down to the villages" was part of the Cultural Revolution. It destroyed knowledge and ruined youth, and it caused ruptures in many aspects of society.

The only Corps zhiqing critic ("Wang from No. 2 Independent Regiment and No. 15 Company") said:

If we went back to the time 20 years ago and had options, we would have never lived like this. Comrades-in-arms, do you want to go back to Beidahuang? Do you want our children to take the path we have traveled? Why?

Media reports and personal essays published after the exhibit also showed the same divergence in visitors' opinions. A former zhiqing burst into tears when he saw his poem in an informal literary magazine the zhiqing edited and circulated in the countryside. Later in the essay, he expressed his view of the generation's past in a quite defensive way (Zhang 1991, 7):

History can condemn the absurdity of the "Cultural Revolution" and the brutality of the "ultra-leftism." But history will never condemn the eternal youth and warm blood. History will not allow [people] to insensitively mock a generation of innocent, passionate, and loyal youths.

Nevertheless, a 24-year-old graduate student for master's degree reportedly questioned this self-confirming view, in a somewhat supercilious tone (Bi 1991, 35):

But they lost the things that cannot be compensated for. They need to face the fact. They must get rid of their narcissism and pride, which in fact belie their sense of inferiority, so that they can face the society, find their places, and absorb new things. Always living in the memory of the past will [make them] backward.

Note that a master's degree was a very high education level in the early 1990s, which most zhiqing did not possess. This education level may explain his sense of superiority. Other visitors saw things beyond youth and nostalgia. A visitor pointed out that outdated agricultural machinery was still used on today's reclamation farms. Another Corps zhiqing questioned if the zhiqing actually made contributions, because the farms ran at a loss in the years when zhiqing were there.

In sum, the carefully crafted framing of "people but not the event" was successful and unsuccessful at the same time. It was successful because it provided a minimum consensus on individuals without trying to reconcile different opinions about the movement. Many would like to be publicly recognized, especially in a published book and an exhibit at a prestigious venue, even if they held different opinions about the program. Nevertheless, when they attempted to confirm their dignity in their retrospective accounts of their youth, they had no available cultural vocabulary other than the propaganda-cum-cultural repertoire they grew up with. When they tried to emphasize their contributions and dignity, they still had to resort to the words, images, and practices inherited from Maoist ideology and political propaganda. Consequently, their careful compartmentalizing and passionate participation could be interpreted as the opposite: an enthusiastic endorsement of the devastating send-down program and the painful Maoist politics in general. The audience was still divided over this tension between people and the event.

"We Are Our Own Monuments!": The "Regretless Youth" Exhibit

This discrepancy between intended and received meanings was also evident in the public debates over another exhibit, "The Regretless Youth: Retrospective Exhibit of the Chengdu Zhiqing Who Went to

Yunnan," which was held in Chengdu on June 8, 1991. On the same day, a book of memoirs with the same title was released.[2]

When the organizers were discussing the theme and framing of the book and exhibit, like the "Souls" organizers, they had a debate and finally agreed on "regretless youth" because, as Ling Xian, a leading organizer, explained (Benshu Bianweihui 1991, 108):

The life in the frontiers had a huge impact on everyone. But everyone has a different opinion of the life there. Nevertheless, regardless of different feelings and thoughts, we can view this problem from the perspective of confirming our values. We have built our character in the tough life in the frontiers. In later lives, with this experience, no other difficulties can crash us.

This framing resembled the "people-but-not-the-event" pattern of the "Souls" exhibit – highlighting the individuals' values, youth, and character, and downplaying controversies of the event. The beginning passage of the exhibit started this framing in an uplifting tone:

We once shared the same red soil and green rubber trees, the same loyalty to the country, the same loneliness and homesickness, the same contemplation and impetuosity, and the same hunger and abundance.
There is nothing to regret about our youth! There is nothing to lament about our youth!
We are our own monuments!

Nevertheless, the exhibit had a subtly "grayer" tone than that of "Souls." The opening message contained some words with negative connotations, such as "impetuosity" and "hunger." In other sections of the exhibit, there was a discernible melancholy. In the section "Leaving Chengdu for Yunnan" there was this statement: "We had the poetic, youthful years but suddenly started a life that was not so poetic." In the section "Labor": "In those bittersweet days, there were the losses that we could not get back and the gains we would never lose." In "Study": "We were a group of orphans abandoned by the abundant human culture, pursuing our intellectual home."

The most obvious tone change came in the section "Return," which presented pictures of the Yunnan petition and protest, including the famous picture of the zhiqing kneeling down to demand to go home. The caption reads: "In 1979, history was not stubborn anymore." Again,

---

[2] The phrase "regretless youth" first became associated with the zhiqing experience in a piece in *Winds and Clouds in Beidahuang*, the book of memoirs that led to the "Souls" exhibit, but it was rarely noticed by the public. It was the Chengdu exhibit that popularized the phrase. Much of the material about the Regretless Youth comes from a self-published book by the organizers of the exhibit (Benshu Bianweihui 1991).

as in "Souls," the personalized "history" took the position of the subject in the sentence to avoid specifying who did what and who should be responsible. The passage also quoted Fyodor Dostoevsky's *Crime and Punishment*: "It is not before you I am kneeling, but before all the suffering of mankind." Another bold presentation was a group of female youths who had been in Yunnan for only ten days but were burned to death in a fire. Compared to the martyrs in the "Souls" exhibit, the girls were simply victims of an accident, not sacrificed for a grand cause.

These "gray" parts reflected the views of at least one of the organizers, Deng Xian, a Chengdu-based writer. He went to Yunnan to collect materials for the exhibit and came across records of the ten female fire victims. He managed to find some of their fellow zhiqing in the same company (military unit), who, Deng expected, would provide information about the girls. But the zhiqing could only recall seven of the victims' names and a surname of another zhiqing, of which they were not entirely sure, let alone other information.

Their shocking oblivion made Deng question the title phrase: Would the girls who died in the fire say "regretless youth"? He decided to include the story in the exhibit to remind visitors of the damages the send-down program inflicted on youths. He also added a description to the picture: "When these female zhiqing lost their lives in the accidental fire, they had spent only ten days on the farm. A peach tree now is blossoming at the place where they fell" (Deng 2009, 1–3). The incident made a significant impact on Deng Xian. It appeared in his first reportage book on zhiqing: *The Dream of Chinese Zhiqing* (1992). Once he was giving a talk on the book, and when he talked about the incident, he suddenly wept in front of the audience (Zhang 2010).

Deng's advocacy for including the fire incident in the exhibit was not an impulsive action. Instead, it was a result of his longtime thoughts about the send-down program, especially after his typical "aspirant" habitus changed at some moments of awakening. In his adolescent years, Deng suffered much from his black family background: his grandfather was a big capitalist, and his father was a Nationalist Army soldier who fought in Myanmar during WWII. Before being sent down to Yunnan, he was expelled from an elite youth ping-pong team in Chengdu due to his bad family background, although he was a talented player and had won several titles. Deng was determined to "choose his road" through his active work and political performance. As a model "child who can be educated," he received much honor, took the position of political director, and even joined the Party. Nonetheless, he got a reality check in 1973, when his admission offer for a Chengdu athletic college was rescinded. The reason was simple: as he was told by the Corps authorities, his bad chushen. Moreover, he was told, "Your family had too many college graduates, and now we need to let the children of the poor and lower-middle peasants go to college." Deng felt that "all my hard work was in vain due to my destiny as a slave-like child or a person from the 'Untouchable' class with the original sin." In 1977, Deng finally changed his fate by passing the newly resumed gaokao and got into Yunnan University, where he was disillusioned with the political ideology of the Mao years and the change in his habitus was completed (Zhang 2010).

Nonetheless, the other organizers dismissed Deng's disapproval of the catchphrase "the regretless youth," and the final version of the exhibit significantly toned down Deng's voice of criticism. The exhibit stopped short of an unambiguous accusation of the movement. Instead, it put a "red" cover on the "gray" content.

The "red" cover had its real-world consequences. It dissipated the government's worry about the political sensitivity of the exhibit. For the government officials who either did not examine the exhibit carefully or did not bother to read the content, the title was what they wanted. Important officials sent inscriptions to show their endorsement. Yang Rudai, then the Party secretary of Sichuan, wrote: "Carry forward the revolutionary spirit of living plainly and working hard and make new contributions to the Reform and Opening." Nie Ronggui, then the vice-secretary of Sichuan, wrote: "[Carry forward the spirit of] pioneering and hard work to revive the Chinese nation." Kang Zhenghuang, the vice-chair of the People's Congress in Sichuan, simply replicated Yang's inscription, changing only one word.

Regretless or Regretful?

The visitors, however, had more divided opinions than the officials. Some of the comments left at the exhibit echoed the intended meanings of self-confirmation and kept silent on the program. Many such comments came from those who identified themselves as Yunnan Corps zhiqing. A comment from "Old Ma" from the Yunnan Corps highlighted the personality gains for the zhiqing from the tough years:

The regretless youth!
  When my friends and I were only teenagers, we packed our bags to go to Mengding, a place far away from home. Mengding, my second hometown! You nurtured me! The memorable red soil and subtropical sunshine taught me the meaning of life. Those memorable years built my character and prepared me to bravely shoulder my responsibility and face reality in today's life and work.

Similarly, another Corps zhiqing (Qin Luying) said: "Because [we] had the experience of the tough life in the past, we have the love for today's happy life. We should not, must not, and will not regret!" Other positive comments came from those who identified themselves as chadui zhiqing and proudly used "we" to show their solidarity with the Corps zhiqing: "I was not in the same [battlefield] trench but was your comrade-in-arms. Today I share with you the same pride: I have no regret for my [zhiqing] past, which made us a mature generation." Two chadui zhiqing (named Zhou Ming'en and Zeng Qinrui) who went to Xichang made a grandiose claim that "we used our regretless youth to build an eternal monument in history!"

Many other comments followed the "good-people-but-a-bad-event" pattern. A visitor who identified as an "old-three-class" zhiqing commented: "We are a generation who have been hoodwinked. But we used our blood and tears to write regretless youth and life." Another former zhiqing, now a college teacher, wrote a poem as a comment:

> This was an asset for a person
> But it was a tragedy for history
> We rejected the mediocre and pale life
> But we also loathed the life that we could not choose

One visitor focused on the picture of the kneeling protest and praised the bravery of those zhiqing petitioners:

Who said those on their knees could not represent a kind of spirit? We believe the petition represented a great spirit of our nation – ordinary people must not be insulted! This exhibit was a generation's cry out, a blood-and-tears accusation of the false, ugly, and evil; [the protesters] represent the true, virtuous, and beautiful! Salute to the brave people!

Some visitors went even further to criticize the exhibit for not being critical enough. One "retail zhiqing" (chadui) lamented: "Regret or no regret! You certainly know it. Why still paint the reality with a romantic color? In fact, back then, we all were hoodwinked victims." Another said: "Since then, this generation of Chinese has fallen into a mud hole. What else could we say? In addition to blood and tears, there were grievances and complaints. This was a shame instead of the glory of the Chinese nation!" A Corps zhiqing (Xie Xiang) even raised the demand for compensation: "What should I tell my offspring? Another send-down program? When [we] spent the youthful years in the barren valley, what were the ultimate political and economic values of our life? In addition to 'no regret,' whom should we ask for compensation for our economic and political losses?"

Visitors from other, often younger, generations echoed these negative comments but sometimes provoked defensive reactions from the zhiqing with bruised pride. A visitor seemed to unnerve the zhiqing by saying: "A deceived generation! Pathetic!" With hurt feelings, a self-identified zhiqing replied: "You're pathetic! We feel fulfilled!"

The comments on the other extreme of the narrative – positive about both the program and the zhiqing – were very few. Among the 201 recorded comments, only 2 had explicitly positive views of the send-down program. Even a formal letter from the Yunnan Reclamation Bureau refrained from giving explicit evaluations of the program. The letter read: the exhibit and the book "not only present your indelible memory of your life but also treat that life as the starting point of your journey, the foundation of your career, and the sources of energy to keep yourselves motivated and hard-working." The letter ended with praise of the Yunnan zhiqing's contributions to the development of the frontiers and encouraged them to make further contributions to the "modernization" project.

When the phrase "regretless youth" traveled beyond the immediate context and into wider public discourses, its original meaning was depleted. The phrase became something with a life of its own, a buzz-word that stood for an entirely positive view of the zhiqing generation *and* an entirely positive view of the send-down program. Its subtle separation of the people from the event was ignored; its relatively "grayer" representation was forgotten. Instead, the public opinions reattached the zhiqing to the program. The zhiqing's self-approval of their "youth" was reinterpreted as a praise of the send-down program.

The word "regretless" infuriated many who thought of "zhiqing" and "Red Guards" as two sides of the single coin. Having no regret about their "youth" meant having no regret about their destructive behaviors in the Cultural Revolution. Writer Li Rui regarded those who chanted "regretless youth" as pitiful because "what is pitiful about those who sank into degradation is not the degradation itself but ... that they show off the degradation as if it is romance and idealism." Their idealism, Li Rui believed, was simply destructive fanaticism based on class struggle and blind loyalty (Li 1993).

Zhang Kangkang led the public attacks on the phrase. Her criticism corroborated her literary memory (Chapter 3), especially her demand for the zhiqing's self-reflection and repentance. In an influential article, "The Years That Cannot Be Comforted" (Zhang 1998b), she started with the preference of the "old three classes" to use "we" instead "I" and regarded this preference as a cultural mentality impacted by a "totalitarian state." If the zhiqing generation liked to use "we," Zhang claimed, then let "us" shoulder the responsibilities for "our" mistakes and evil-doings, because the "old three classes" were also Red Guards. Zhang continued her accusation by listing the atrocities the Red Guards committed: raiding homes, destroying antiques, beating teachers, propagating the "bloodline theory," and, when they were zhiqing, engaging in cutthroat competition for desirable opportunities by selling out their friends. Very few of them, Zhang said, chose to repent sincerely, while most freed themselves from their responsibilities by attributing their wrongdoings to the "times" and "leaders."

Even "idealism," Zhang believed, was just an empty slogan because, first, the idealism had already collapsed when the revolution was dead, and, second, many in this generation had been struggling for survival and had no capacity or freedom to be "idealistic." Therefore, with all these troubles, flaws, and even guilt:

What is the point of talking about "regretless youth"? How can a person or a generation use such an empty and flamboyant slogan to erase their lost and wasted lifetime, meanwhile feigning happiness? This is what is really pitiful about our generation.

The solution? Zhang seemed to suggest that the zhiqing should walk out of the shadow of the "old three classes" and become independent individuals to face the new, changing society.

One may challenge Zhang Kangkang's broad moral accusations by pointing out that not all zhiqing were Red Guards. Even among the Red Guards, there were mindless followers and sincere idealists who did not commit violence. Nevertheless, Zhang's point flew in the face of the memory pattern of "people but not the event" by reminding the vocal zhiqing of their unsavory past they had been trying to forget or hide.

Outside of this circle of elite intellectuals, however, the phrase "regretless youth" was widely used, with approving connotations, to describe some zhiqing's sacrifice and contributions. A few reports on the old model zhiqing in the 1950s, such as Xing Yanzi, used "regretless youth" as their titles (Guan 1992; Zhong and Yao 1997). Neither the writers of the reports nor the model zhiqing themselves seemed to know the carefully crafted subtleties underneath the heroic title or the debates over it.

The Heihe Museum

The pattern of "people but not the event" appeared in most of the zhiqing museums, which emerged in the cultural scene in the late 2000s. The Zhiqing Museum in Heihe, Heilongjiang, is one of the earliest and largest. The museum is located in Aihui, a district under Heihe, a city on the west bank of Heilongjiang River (Amur River). Painted red, the museum consists of two components, a triangular

Figure 4.1 A statue in front of the Zhiqing Museum in
Heihe, Heilongjiang. Photo taken by the author

exhibition hall and a square hall, which together constitute a shape
signifying a plow, a common tool for reclamation. Outside the museum,
there is a realistic statue of six zhiqing, identifiable as two zhiqing arriving
with luggage, two with rifles on patrol, one female zhiqing teaching kids
by a school desk, and one with a scythe in his hand working in the field
(Figure 4.1).

The museum hosts only one permanent exhibit, which was started in
2009 and revised and revamped in 2015. The most significant revision
was to centralize Xi Jinping's zhiqing experience in the new exhibit.
When I first visited the museum in 2013, Xi had just become the new
leader. The museum management added to the ending part of the
exhibit, on the wall near the exit of the museum, a glass panel with Xi's
words about his zhiqing experience and a picture of his revisit to his sent-
down place Liangjiahe. It was clearly a temporary add-on, a swift tribute
to the new leadership.

When I visited the museum again in 2017, Xi's images and words had
already been moved to the beginning of the exhibit. The exhibit now

starts with a short video clip from China Central Television's (CCTV) report on Xi's revisit to Liangjiahe, his sent-down place, projected on a giant panorama screen. The passage about his sent-down experience, which used to be on the glass panel, now is printed in a seven-meter-long red panel, above which there is a life-size picture of Xi with the peasants in Liangjiahe. Later in the exhibit, Xi's zhiqing experience is presented in three panels, while each of the other Politburo standing committee members gets only one.

The revisions, however, do not alter the whole exhibit's pattern of representations. The old preface by Liu Donghui, former Party vice-secretary of Heilongjiang, resembles the new one. Both emphasize the contributions and sacrifice the zhiqing generation made to the development of the frontiers and the country. The new preface, though, has a more enthusiastic tone:

When their motherland needed them most, this generation of passionate youth indomitably went to the countryside without hesitation. They sacrificed their youth, shouldered their historical responsibility, and made outstanding contributions. Meanwhile, they tempered themselves and raised themselves to a higher level. ... After they returned to cities, they used the spirit of "plain living and hard work," which was nurtured in the vast universe [of the countryside], to advance their career again. They have become the backbone of the dream of the great revival of the Chinese nation. They share the same fate with the Republic. History will not forget them. The people will not forget them.

In contrast, the send-down program is hastily described as "an important part of the history of the Republic" and a "migration with an unprecedented large scale."

Many symbols and words in the exhibit keep reminding visitors of the zhiqing's positive qualities and contributions. The section "The Shining Youth" emphasizes the zhiqing's contributions to the construction projects in the frontiers, including an all-female team specializing in building bridges and other physically demanding work. The section "Defending the Border and Reclaiming the Frontier" praises the zhiqing's semi-military role in national defense, including serving as first-aid teams for troops in the conflict with the Soviet Union. Other sections highlight the zhiqing's instrumental roles as schoolteachers and "barefoot doctors" (the grassroots-level physicians who received basic medical training and practiced in rural areas). A special tribute is paid to those martyrs who died in firefighting and other efforts to save "state assets," including Jin Xunhua, a household name in the 1960s. Jin's undershirt and other items are on display. The panorama video at the entrance also features a female zhiqing whose face was disfigured during firefighting.

The exhibit, in both versions, contains a few "gray" panels and stories. For example, some zhiqing were persecuted for misspeaking a politically taboo word, misplacing the portrait of Chairman Mao, and circulating banned books. A small plate presents a story of two zhiqing who fell in love but were publicly humiliated and then committed suicide. The Yunnan protest is also included in both versions. Nevertheless, the representation of those experiences does not go beyond the scope in the "Souls" and "Regretless Youth" exhibits.

After briefly tiptoeing around the controversial part, the exhibit quickly strides across the past travails to embrace the present. The restrained "gray" story is woven into a teleological narrative with a focus on correcting past wrongs, such as Deng Xiaoping's decision to allow zhiqing to return to cities and Hu Yaobang's role in implementing the policy.

Production and Reception of the Heihe Museum

The narrative pattern in the Heihe Museum resulted from the negotiation among many actors in the newly formed memory field of the zhiqing generation. The memory field started with the process of organizing the exhibits in the 1990s, and the entrepreneurs and groups involved in the exhibits continued to devote other zhiqing-related memory work. The narrative pattern directly represents the schema of perceptions of two major memory entrepreneurs, who initiated, shaped, and managed the museum. One of them, Mr. Shu, grew up in a Beijing official's family with his father as a rightist.[3] In 1969, Shu was sent down to Heilongjiang and performed well in work and politics and was recommended as a model kejiaozinv for college. Later, Shu took various positions in local governments in Heilongjiang. Overall, Shu was a typical "aspirant," whose effort has been decently rewarded by the state, although he is grumpy about his slow promotion, taking it as a sign of lack of appreciation for his work. Before being involved in the zhiqing museum, Shu had directed a few large-scale projects, including a reservoir and the Aihui Museum.

During our interview in 2013, Shu enthusiastically praised the zhiqing generation as the "strongest generation" because "we know Chinese society better than those in the Propaganda Department and ... you professors." He believed that the zhiqing generation endured the difficulties and became the major "stabilizing force" that maintained the order of society. Shu proudly claimed that during the Tiananmen incident in 1989 not a single zhiqing took to the street: "Those who were involved [in the Tiananmen movement] were those who passed the

---

[3] Interview with Mr. Shu (pseudonym), October 15, 2013.

exams to get into colleges and who knew nothing about Chinese society." His dismissal of college education, however, contradicted his statement of the purpose of the museum: to preserve the history of this generation to educate the public, who, in his opinion, had "low cultural quality" (*wenhua suzhi di*) – meaning they were uneducated.

Shu cannot block out the personal trauma caused by his family tragedy and the "bitter memories" of the generation but frames the difficult past as "lessons learned from the Cultural Revolution." He believes overexposing the painful past, such as rapes of female zhiqing, is pointless because those incidents were not in the "mainstream." In doing so, Shu aligns the museum with the present official ideology. Shu is also strategic enough not to show in the exhibit his anti-intellectualism and ultra-nationalism, which are privately well known in the zhiqing circle. This strategic aspect is manifested in his purposeful framing of "people but not the event": "We didn't say it [the send-down program] was good or bad, and so you won't be able to criticize us."

Another major memory entrepreneur, Mr. Zhong, a former official in the Antique and Culture Bureau, is an interpersonally mild person, but he shares Mr. Shu's views. The two key memory entrepreneurs' framing ideas were represented in *The Outline of the Exhibit*, a planning document for building the museum, and they resonated with many other zhiqing. The function of the document was to lay out the guiding ideas and construction plan of the museum to obtain permission from the government. It makes it clear that the exhibit is intended to, in the words of Li Changchun, then the head of the Party's propaganda system, "discover and propagate [emotionally] moving figures and deeds among the zhiqing in order to uphold the true sentiments in human society." And Li praises the zhiqing generation "as a special generation who made outstanding contributions to socialist development." Negotiations and compromise, however, were still inevitable and represented in the revisions of the document. The original *Outline* listed "resistance" (*kangzheng*) as one of the keywords to convey the idea of resisting the "ultra-leftism." But it was changed to "emotional attachment" (*qingjie*) in the actual exhibit. The original *Outline* has a section on "The Absurd Politics" (*huangtang de zhengzhi*), which does not appear in the final exhibit.

Building a museum needs substantive institutional support much more than changing phrases. While words are cheap, money, land, and other scarce resources are not. The local government in Heihe did not lend its support at the beginning, due to its political risk and uncertain revenues – "Who would be interested in coming to Heihe, a remote city on the border with Russia, to visit a museum about … zhiqing?" To persuade the local government, Shu and Zhong managed to find a powerful patron, Gong Xinhan, then the vice-head of the Central

Propaganda Department. After Jin Xunhua died, Gong, then a reporter, wrote about Jin's heroic deeds. Under the auspices of Gong, the museum secured the permission from the local government and was given land adjacent to the Aihui History Museum, a key local tourist attraction. Nevertheless, according to Zhong, the Heihe government provided only limited funds for the museum, an indication of the government's ambivalence and suspicion. Attendance in the first several years was low.

The financial situation significantly improved after the museum successfully obtained "state-designated museum" status. Since then, it has been supported by funds from the central government.[4] The local government's attitude changed correspondingly. At the time of my first visit in 2013, the museum was included in Heihe's comprehensive tourism development strategic initiative. The museum and government also drew a grandiose plan called "Beidahuang Zhiqing Cultural Enterprise Park," which aimed to expand the museum to a compound composed of a square, an outside performance area, a garden, a senior retirement home, an arts center, a beach, and other recreational facilities. The total investment in the park will be 332,710,000 yuan (Heilongjiang Cultural Industry Platform 2017).

The local government's strategic initiative makes economic sense. The City of Heihe boasts some major tourist attractions in its territory, including forests, mountains, volcanic crater lakes, and a cross-border itinerary to the Far Eastern district of Russia. In 1858, Russia pressed the Qing to sign a treaty to gain a large territory on the northern bank of the Amur river. The Chinese government and people regarded the Aihui Treaty as a national humiliation. The Aihui Museum is now a major tourist spot as well as a base for "patriotic education," particularly about the history of the Aihui Treaty. The zhiqing museum, located in the Aihui historical district, could be a valuable addition to the city's tourism resources.

The museum also relied heavily on various zhiqing associations, which mushroomed in the new millennium (see Chapters 5 and 6), for their ideas, items, funds, and visitors. In its planning stage, the museum staff got in touch with some former zhiqing who went to Heilongjiang and now were major memory entrepreneurs in the main source cities like Beijing and Shanghai. Together they set up a few "workstations" in major cities to coordinate fundraising, collect items, and organize events. Private business owners and ordinary zhiqing donated much money to keep the museum open. Some zhiqing-turned-journalists helped publicize the plan.

The group dynamics among the memory entrepreneurs reinforced the designed pattern of "people but not the event." In 2007, at the pilot stage

---

[4] Field notes, October 15, 2013.

of this project, I attended one of the meetings of the Shanghai workstation. The attendees included a designer, a curator, some key members of the workstation, and the coordinators of the major divisions and regiments. Much of the discussion focused on technical issues, such as division of labor, items to collect, and technology used in the exhibit. But framing was also the focal point. An organizer stressed that the exhibit must demonstrate the zhiqing's contributions to the construction of Beidahuang and their outstanding achievements after their zhiqing years, for example, a scientist who was a member of China's Antarctic exploration team. The idea was supported by all the attendees. Nevertheless, the unimportant members of the generation were deliberately ignored. An attendee stood up and said that the exhibit should include a description of the zhiqing's present lives, especially those whose living conditions were not so satisfying. He was interrupted by another attendee, who said that presenting those things was not necessary. The topic quickly passed.

During the casual conversations over lunch, their opinions were more diverse. Moderate complaints about Beidahuang were voiced. One of the attendees said that Beidahuang did nurture people but cannot make people stay, meaning that the place did not provide outsiders with enough opportunities to advance their career. Another person gave an example of this statement: the farms tended to recommend those middle school graduates among the zhiqing to college because they wanted to keep the better-educated high school graduates as teachers at the farms' own schools. Mild debates also occurred. When one of them praised the zhiqing for bringing "culture" to the peasants, another disagreed: "the peasants had their own cultures and probably didn't need us."

After lunch, a female zhiqing, Ms. Wang, expressed her curiosity about my research. She was surprised by a (then) young PhD student's interest in their often-neglected experience. But she also doubted: "What is the use of your research?" My explanation – it was a study of history and personal experience – did not seem to convince her. She also said that the topic was so politically sensitive that it would be hard to do this research. Later, she used her finger to point to the people in the room and said: "All the people you see here today were better off. The ones with unsatisfying living conditions simply don't come to activities like this. They feel ashamed."[5]

Despite the doubts and complaints and other diverse opinions voiced in the private conversations, this group formed a speech norm in their

---

[5] Field notes, June 17, 2007.

deliberations that suppressed controversies over the program but exalted their own contributions. The members' relatively higher-class positions released them from day-to-day worries about pensions, healthcare, and hukou, which were still troubling many of their fellow zhiqing.

Unsurprisingly, most visitors to the Heihe Museum are zhiqing on their revisiting or tourism trips. There is no visitors' book available at the museum, but some visitors have left their comments in various online spaces. On an online forum called "Old Zhiqing Bar," some zhiqing netizens believe the preface fairly recognizes the zhiqing's contributions to the rural areas. Others, however, do not buy into such glorious rhetoric. They call attention to the huge cost of the zhqing's minor, questionable "contributions" (Baidu 2010). Those comments demonstrate a similar pattern of reactions to other exhibits: a mixture of nostalgia, sorrow, pride, and criticism of the send-down program. The Zhang Kangkang style of self-reflection is absent. The reason is obvious: the zhiqing visitors who bother to travel all the way from Shanghai or Beijing to the northeastern corner of China want to seek confirmation and recognition of their worthiness rather than reflecting on their flaws.

When the museum emerged from its small frontier cocoon, it faced more critical opinions from more diverse audiences. In 2015, the museum secured a place in the National Stadium (the "Bird's Nest") to hold a semi-permanent exhibit. For a small, local museum, hosting its exhibit in such a spotlight place was a great achievement. I visited the exhibit on June 9, 2018, and noticed three differences between the Heihe Museum and the Bird's Nest exhibit. First, the exhibit had a significantly more positive tone than when it was at the Heihe Museum. The "bitter memories" section had completely disappeared. Second, the exhibit began with a picture of Mao Zedong seeing off his son Mao Anying to the countryside in 1946. One might question the relevance of this anachronistic image because even the broadest definition of the send-down program does not extend to the period before 1949; thus, by any means, Mao Anying was not a zhiqing. But the exhibit justified its choice in a passage in a label below the picture: Mao's idea that intellectuals must be united with the workers and peasants was the theoretical foundation of the send-down program. Therefore, Mao Anying, who studied and worked with ordinary people, should count as an "educated youth." Third, probably most expected, even within the limited space, the exhibit managed to devote many panels to the top leaders. The gigantic, life-size picture of Xi's visit to Liangjiahe took up a whole panel in a central spot, in addition to two other red panels containing his photographs and words.

The Bird's Nest exhibit provoked public controversies. He Weifang, a law professor at Peking University, commented on his social media that the exhibit "turned crimes into great achievements." He also hinted that the exhibit had the obvious intention to curry favor with the top leadership by sacralizing Xi's zhiqing experience. His attack brought a response from Pan Zhonglin, who moved from Heihe to Beijing to manage the exhibit. Pan claimed that the exhibit was "objective" because it was in line with the Party Central and conveyed "positive energy." In threatening language, Pan suspected that He Weifang harbored evil intentions, dissatisfaction with the Party, and hatred toward the zhiqing (Xu 2015).

He Weifang fired back. In an online post, He revealed his zhiqing identity: he happened to have been sent down to Sunwu, a place in the Heihe region. He said he and his fellow zhiqing in Heihe wasted their best years in the countryside when the American astronomers landed on the moon. The exhibit, He believed, tended to ignore this fact and glorified the program as a great movement. The exhibit's self-compliments on the zhiqing's resilience and the "zhiqing spirit" were nothing more than a case of "Stockholm Syndrome" (He 2016). His comments were echoed by some former zhiqing, who claimed that "[it is important] to remember but never sing its praise," and attacked by others, who repeated Pan's words (Yu 2015). This brief feud again accentuates a crucial struggle over meanings of the past: the effort to detach a heroic generation, including the top leaders, from the controversial event is met with the public's re-attaching the zhiqing back to the event.

The Theory of "Survival on the Surface": Dafeng Zhiqing Museum

Another major zhiqing museum, the Dafeng Shanghai Zhiqing Museum, resembles the Heihe Museum in many ways. The Dafeng Museum is located on Haifeng Farm, in Jiangsu Province, but administratively one of Shanghai's exclaves. In the 1950s, Shanghai obtained a large piece of wasteland from Jiangsu to build the "Shanghai Farm" to relocate about ten thousand social outcasts, including demobilized Nationalist Army soldiers, beggars, gangsters, prostitutes, and so on. In 1968, the farm began to receive zhiqing from Shanghai. In 1972, a large part of the land containing the Shanghai Farm merged into the new "Haifeng Farm" with its name combining "Shang*hai*" and "Da*feng*." The new Haifeng Farm received younger zhiqing from Shanghai during the Cultural Revolution. In the early 1980s, the older Shanghai zhiqing who went to Xinjiang before the Cultural Revolution were arranged to migrate from there to Dafeng after the Aksu incident (Xu 2021).

The museum was built on the original site of Haifeng Farm's headquarters, Yuanhua. It now consists of a brand-new, gigantic exhibition hall, an old museum compound, an outdoor film studio site with huts and barns from the 1950s, and other facilities like a hotel and some restaurants. At the time of my visit (2013), the main exhibit was hosted in the old museum compound. The narrative pattern of the exhibit is almost identical to that of other museums and exhibits, with a minor difference: the Haifeng exhibit features Li Yuanchao, then the vice-president of China, who worked as a zhiqing in Dafeng from 1968 to 1972. The exhibit includes a panel of his biography and picture and a panel with the pictures of his visit to Dafeng in 2012. A panel captioned "What does Dafeng mean to the young people?" also presents his four statements of the meaning of the zhiqing experience: first, in their sent-down years, the zhiqing transformed themselves from students to workers; second, they kept studying in addition to the strenuous field work; third, they knew how the ordinary people lived at the bottom rung of Chinese society and what poverty meant; fourth, they formed the habit of "eating bitterness" and built their resilient character to meet the challenges in later life.

In contrast to the reluctant local government in Heihe, the Dafeng local officials took the initiative and dominated the whole process of building the museum. The key memory entrepreneurs were non-zhiqing government officials, who were more interested in revenues and concerned with political sensitivities. In 2007, Mr. Lian, an official in the Propaganda Department of Dafeng, was assigned the job of finding local social and cultural connections to the outside world and mobilizing resources to develop the local economy. Lian came up with the idea of building a zhiqing museum in the old headquarters of Haifeng Farm, which could serve as a place for the Shanghai zhiqing to revisit and gather. Without much planning or funding (the government only provided 80,000 yuan), the museum was quickly set up.

Despite its hasty production, Lian and other local officials had a clear framing of the museum, which resembled the Heihe Museum administrators'. Lian articulated this framing in his theory of "survival on the surface," which analogized the museum to a green:

We should be satisfied with a green. We don't want to dig deep because we all know that there are broken stones underneath the green. So, our job is to make the green more beautiful. People who come here can have a place to stay, eat, and have fun. ... After all, [the send-down program] is a scar on the body of the Communist Party. You don't want to peel it off to expose the bloody flesh. If you do that, it is impossible to do [the museum]. ... If [we make the museum] happier, brighter, and healthier, the scar left by history doesn't ache anymore. Do not do research; do not dig deep; only talk about sentiments; only talk about "long live youth!"

Figure 4.2 "Long Live Youth!" in Haifeng Zhiqing Museum. Photo by the author

It is hard for anyone to disagree with "Long Live Youth!" The slogan is also inscribed in a stela in the main square of the compound (Figure 4.2). Next to the stela is a piece of white relief of zhiqing against a burgundy background. The relief shares with the Heihe statue a straightforward, realistic style, depicting the zhiqing's various jobs: teaching, field labor, and providing medical services. The inscription reads: "In the mid-20th century, 84,807 Shanghai zhiqing sacrificed their youth here and turned the mudflats and wastelands into a modern farm." This statement is a brief but typical version of the "people but not the event" pattern: it emphasizes the youths' sacrifice but does not mention the send-down program at all.

Li Yuanchao's name constantly came up during my visit in 2013, when Li was at the peak of his political career. He had just taken his new position of vice-president after serving as the head of the Organization Department, a powerful position in charge of promotion and personnel within the Party. Li paid a visit to the museum and emotionally recounted his zhiqing experience. He lingered there for so long that his planned time had to be extended from half an hour to three hours. After his visit, Li sent the museum a letter, which is on display now.

Li's unusual enthusiasm for his zhiqing past encouraged the local government, who saw the potential political opportunity and took swift action. The Dafeng government quickly approved a much larger budget to expand the museum from the old buildings and the film base to a compound with a new, fancy-looking building. Nevertheless, Mr. Lian again showed his political savviness by persuading the local government not to get overexcited, since Li then was not a member of the Politburo Standing Committee and his political future was uncertain. Consequently, Li's portrait did not appear at the beginning of the exhibit. Instead, it is in the middle, in three panels, still conspicuous but less central. With the wisdom of hindsight, Lian was right: Li's career has been slowly skidding to a halt since 2013.

Youth in a Graveyard: Haiwanyuan

The Shanghai Zhiqing Square and Museum in Haiwanyuan (hereafter, Haiwanyuan), located in Fengxian, a suburb town in Shanghai, is one of the largest museum compounds for zhiqing. The museum, the center of the compound, presents not only a framing similar to that of the Heihe and Dafeng museums but also some of the same pictures and similar items. A visitor who has been to other museums may find it repetitive.

Nevertheless, Haiwanyuan has a distinctive component: the Zhiqing Commemoration Wall, a black-marble wall inscribed with many zhiqing's names and a few images. The wall might remind a Western visitor of the Vietnam Veterans Memorial (VVM), but most of the zhiqing whose names are on the wall are still alive. It is technically impossible to include all the Shanghai zhiqing (more than 1 million). Whoever registered early got their signatures on the wall. I found some of my informants' names on the Wall, and some of them happily told me: "My name is on the Wall!"

Unlike the VVM, which says nothing about the war, the Zhiqing Commemoration Wall imposes a narrative pattern on observers: "people but not the event." The wall features a preface by Ye Xin and a concluding passage from a history book by Gu Hongzhang, a former official in the Zhiqing Work Office in the State Council. Ye Xin's preface says little more than "the zhiqing movement is a period of history." When it contends that "[we] need to have careful self-reflection," it does not specify what should be reflected on. Gu's conclusion takes a more upbeat and self-confirmatory turn but still remains ambivalent about the program: "That period of extraordinary and ordinary history was the misfortune and pride of our generation. The difficult life favored us with priceless assets: courage, dedication, perseverance, and pursuit."

A pathway along the wall is inscribed with footprints of some famous zhiqing, including those who "made it" in their later lives, active memory entrepreneurs, model zhiqing, heroes, and so on. The producers quietly demonstrate their courage by including Ding Huimin and Ouyang Lian, who respectively led the protests in Yunnan and Xinjiang and remained figures on the watchlists of the authorities. But no description of who they are and what they did accompanies the footprints.

The pattern of "people but not the event" in the Haiwanyuan compound was by design, not by accident. Mr. Wu, the founder of Haiwanyuan, stated in our interview that the compound is intended to only preserve history instead of evaluating the send-down program. But he also says that the producers tried to avoid as many negative aspects as possible unless some of the negative, "gray" events could not be avoided in a historical narrative, for example, protests included in the exhibit and the protest leaders in the footprint paths. Even so, the gray side is presented in a matter-of-fact way without historical evaluations. This way of dealing with the politically sensitive past was okayed by National Security.[6] Mr. Guo, the major designer of the exhibit, articulates the intentional framing:[7]

The most important thing about the exhibit is whether [the visitors] want to air their grievances or feel they want to live a better life after seeing this exhibit. [Our purpose] is to present more positive things and not to reveal too many negative things.

What surprises every new visitor is the location of the museum and wall: it is in a huge graveyard, owned and administered by a private company with the same name, Haiwanyuan. The museum compound, according to Mr. Wu, is part of the company's "corporate social responsibility" program, which is intended to demonstrate its devotion to social welfare and public culture. The program began with a collective burial ceremony for some zhiqing who had passed away but could not afford expensive graves. Their ashes were put into urns and buried underneath a raised flower bed properly named "Commemoration of Youth" (qing-chun ji). The burial and urns are free of charge. For such a corporate culture program, too much emphasis on the controversies over the event should be avoided at all costs. What matters for the company is also the people, the aging zhiqing who are their potential customers, instead of the event.

The Shanghai zhiqing with whom I talked have mixed reactions to the company's involvement and the location of the museum. Some feel awkward about remembering their youth in a graveyard, which reminds them of death, an unpleasant topic for the aging zhiqing. Some are

---

[6] Interview with Mr. Wu, July 2, 2014.   [7] Interview with Mr. Guo, July 8, 2014.

suspicious of the company's motives. But over the years of my fieldwork, the suspicious voice is getting weaker, mostly because of the company's continuous devotion to the maintenance and expansion of the compound. Haiwanyuan has become the most important site of zhiqing memory in Shanghai, where various zhiqing associations regularly hold their activities and even pay one-day leisure visits.

A typical trip to Haiwanyuan, as I observed as a participant on several such trips, is more like a pastoral outing than a collective mourning. The location – a graveyard – is not as gloomy as it sounds. It is right by a bay with beautiful sea views. The graveyard is well maintained, and some spots are even picturesque, especially the "Commemoration of Youth" wreath and flower bed, the zhiqing wall, and an old locomotive named "Youth Train." The company provides regular shuttles to take mourners from various spots in downtown Shanghai to the graveyard, but the zhiqing often prefer hiring coach buses with a reasonable shared cost for each person (30–50 yuan). On the bus, the zhiqing sing old songs, tell jokes, and share snacks. Sometimes they are mobilized to attend a ceremony organized by the museum or other formal associations. But they are apparently more interested in using such occasions as opportunities for reunion. At those ceremonies, they talk with each other in loud voices and cannot wait for the ceremonies to finish so that they can start their own leisure activities. Taking a stroll among the graves on a sunny day is pleasant; taking pictures before the quaint locomotive is also a common nostalgic practice. Around the graveyard, there are some places for lunch and tea. During these activities, one often does not hear serious discussions about the send-down program as a historical event. It is the "people" – the pleasant and satisfying zhiqing who are also the graveyard company's target consumers – but not the event forty years ago at the heart of those one-day trips.

The Missing "People"

Every exhibit or museum of the zhiqing generation walks a symbolic and political tightrope. It is not random that *all* the exhibits and museums of zhiqing share a pattern of "people but not the event," which highlights the zhiqing's youth, contributions, and positive qualities but avoids an explicit evaluation of the send-down program. This pattern is accepted by various involved parties as a lowest common denominator for various views of the past. For the memory entrepreneurs, this pattern confirms their personal success, minimizes internal disagreements, and builds common ground with the state. For the state, it upholds the moral and political values attached to the send-down program – such as the spirit of "plain life and hard work" and the young intellectuals' integration into the workers and peasants – but shuns an admittance of its failure. For ordinary zhiqing, it recognizes their contributions, exalts their youthful passions, and protects their self-dignity from the controversies over the event. For local governments and involved companies, this pattern dovetails with their need for revenues and prevents potential political backlashes.

Nevertheless, missing from the pattern of "people but not the event" are those still suffering from the detrimental impacts of the program and those demanding their pensions and benefits. Winners dominate the stories on the panels. For example, half of the exhibit panels at the Heihe Museum feature high-ranking officials, entrepreneurs, university professors, famous writers, actors, and so on. At one point, the exhibit mentions the massive layoffs in the 1990s and even tells stories of two laid-off workers. Nevertheless, the stories are about their successful effort to start their own businesses after being laid off. The purpose is not to expose their difficulties but to praise their resilience: "[they] use the spirit of tenacious struggle, which was formed in Beidahuang, to ride the big wave of the Reform and Open-Up and to restart their career." They were also winners or "wave riders." Missing from this celebratory narrative are the people drowned in the waves.

Almost all founders, managers, and curators of the museums claim that the primary function of museums is to "preserve history" objectively. But this claim contradicts their practices. In what sense is showing winners' success in the *present* a "history"? If it is, then why is there no "history" of the zhiqing whose life is still being troubled by the history? This question may sound naïve to all the memory entrepreneurs: if they do present those people, there would be no exhibits or museums at all. The state may allow limited presentations of the painful past in a correctly framed, teleological narrative, for ideological and revenue purposes. The state will not allow any attempt to link the difficult present to the difficult past. No memory entrepreneurs are stupid enough to try to cross that line.

Also missing from this pattern are the "people" as pre-lives of the zhiqing, at least for some of them, the Red Guards. In most zhiqing museums, a few Red Guard armbands are quietly sitting in the glass display cases, without descriptions. Only one of the museums, a private one, located in a museum compound in Shanghai, uses a whole floor of its two-story building to exhibit items from the Red Guard movement. In a private conversation, the founder told me that his real purpose was to have a museum of the Cultural Revolution in the disguise of a "zhiqing museum." The museum owner, however, passed away before accomplishing his goals. The almost complete omission of the Red Guards from most of the museums shows that "generation" is a Janus-faced social construction. After critics like Zhang Kangkang and Deng Xian quit the memory work, no site of memory touches on this side of their generational history. This absence, however, still occasionally provokes strong criticisms from intellectuals like He Weifang. Therefore, the exhibits and museums do not solve all these convoluted problems of memory. For them, as Mr. Lian aptly summarizes, the best practice is to "survive on the surface."

5 Nostalgia, Resistance, and the Pursuit of Happiness
Generation and Memory in Groups

A vast universe to make a big difference!

A truncated version of Mao's "highest directive" for the send-down program was inscribed in the granite pedestal of a black, iron statue of a group of zhiqing in the center of "Zhiqing Square." The eight Chinese characters, emblazoned in gold, were glinting under the scorching sun. The heat, unusual in June in the northeastern city of Jiagedaqi, did not prevent hundreds of zhiqing from flooding into the square, waving red flags with their associations' names while one of them played "The Sun Is the Reddest and Chairman Mao Is the Dearest!" on a saxophone. The saxophone player wore an old-style military uniform, which was used by the Red Guards as their identity symbol in the Cultural Revolution, and two other zhiqing even held up a flag with Mao's portrait and their team's name: "The Team for Mao Zedong's Thoughts and Songs."

This gathering was the culmination of an eleven-day trip to revisit Heilongjiang, where some of the travelers had gone down as zhiqing about forty years earlier. I followed them throughout the trip and, for most of the nights, slept on a train without showers but with clogged toilets. The scene described above seemed to perpetuate a stereotype of this generation of "Chairman Mao's children." The trip was more complex than just this red image. However, what mattered to outsiders *was* the image. A few onlookers watched from afar. The younger ones smiled with contemptuous amusement, while the older ones frowned. Most passersby, however, only cursorily glanced at this lively scene before they disappeared in the traffic.

"Being happy alone is not as good as being happy together!"

Another slogan in another zhiqing gathering. The slogan was displayed on an electronic screen over a stage in a huge ballroom within a restaurant, and the gathering was a banquet with about 200 zhiqing, sitting around 20 round tables. No red flags; no Mao songs; no revolutionary symbols; no one wore uniforms. The zhiqing voluntarily jumped onto the

174

stage to perform songs and dances. Sometimes, even two groups went on the stage simultaneously and triggered a wave of laughter across the ballroom, and one of the groups joyfully retreated. Some could not even wait until their turn to perform onstage. Two women at my table stood up and danced to the tunes being played up on the stage, whirling around the room and earning cheers and applause. Men engaged in fierce drinking competitions, even if many of them apparently were already intoxicated.

Loud conversations, singing, and laughter in the ballroom attracted attention from other rooms in the restaurant. Some people curiously peeked in. When I left the restaurant, I overheard the following conversation between two people outside:

"Oh, they are really happy and crazy! What danwei is this?"

"They are zhiqing, not in the same danwei. You don't know zhiqing? Up to the mountains and down to the villages? No? You are too young!"

"Okay. Whatever. Who cares!"

During the banquet, a man who sat next to me said: "Look at us! We are just old children! We don't want to waste time on thinking and talking about the past. We just want to live every day in the present happily!" In an activity for reunion and memory, forgetting the past ironically became the key to enjoying the present.

These two episodes represent two ways in which the zhiqing generation comes to terms with their past in commemorative and reunion activities. One imbued the zhiqing's activity with a nostalgia for China's socialist past, whereas the other only pursued their happiness in the present. Since the 2000s, when many members of this generation retired and had much time to seek each other out, such group activities have become ubiquitous and frequent. During my fieldwork in Shanghai, I attended two or three such activities every week and probably missed many others.

A typical zhiqing group includes those who went down to the same county or province. They have forty to sixty regular members and hold regular activities like reunion banquets, revisits to their sent-down places, and sightseeing trips. The past several years, however, saw many cross-regional groups like the first one that opens this chapter. They venture out into the larger society to hold large-scale, multi-day trips and festivals with formal performances and rituals. Nobody knows how many small or large zhiqing groups are out there. But they have gone well beyond the nostalgic and nervous reunions held once every five or ten years (Vinitzky-Seroussi 1998). They are socially and politically complex. Some of my informants, quite cynically, describe the zhiqing group activities now as a "*jianghu*," a term that literally means "rivers and lakes" and usually refers to an informal sector of society with a complex nexus of feuds, alliances, interests, and politics.

Memory at this level is neither autobiographical memory nor public memory. It is a special type of group culture (Fine 2012, 36), an amalgam of knowledge, beliefs, representations, ritual processes, and narratives and views of the past embedded and expressed in face-to-face interactions within a group (Turner 1969; Durkheim 1995 [1912]). Group memory can take the form of rituals, somewhat formal activities like ceremonies, commemorations, artistic performances, and gatherings, or "communicative memory," the non-institutional, everyday communications about the past in face-to-face interactions (Assmann 1995).

A particular challenge for commemorative groups like the zhiqing's is how to keep the members together as a group, on the one hand, and how to deal with the potential conflicts caused by diverse views of a controversial historical event, on the other. In those constant and complex interactions, the zhiqing groups work out various patterns of memory as solutions to the problem. Memory entrepreneurs' views of the past significantly shape those patterns, but they often have to negotiate with group members to maintain the interaction order among them (Goffman 1983; Fine 2012).

In this chapter, I present several groups' patterns of memory, which are manifested in their narratives, symbols, rituals, speech norms, and other mnemonic practices. I explain the variations, paradoxes, and commonalities in their group memories by the interplay between several factors: major memory entrepreneurs' class positions and habitus, internal interaction dynamics, and the memory field's relations with the political system and the market.

Birds of a Feather: The Socialist Nostalgia

The thick mist that shrouded Longhua Martyrs' Cemetery in Shanghai gradually cleared when the sun rose at seven in the morning. A small crowd of people at the gate of the cemetery were shaking hands and chatting with each other, and many pulled out and displayed red flags for photos. The long, impressive names of groups on the flags revealed their identity: for example, "The Chinese People's Liberation Army Shenyang Military District Heilongjiang Production and Construction Corp/No. X Division, No. Y Regiment Shanghai Zhiqing Association." Others unloaded wreaths and floral baskets from their vehicles. They gathered at the cemetery to attend a reburial ritual of a zhiqing martyr's ashes. The zhiqing martyr died only one year after he went to Heilongjiang when he tried to salvage some properties of the Corps from a fire that destroyed his regiment's cafeteria. The Corps bestowed the official title of "martyr" upon him, but, for various reasons, his ashes did not come back home to Shanghai until then, December 1, 2013.

After about an hour of greetings and picture-taking, the crowd was arranged by several zhiqing with "staff" badges into two lines of people, who carried an ash casket, a wreath, a floral basket, and flags and quietly marched into the cemetery. A thin man in his sixties strode briskly in the front of the lines. He gave out instructions through a megaphone in a military manner: "Slow down! Stop! Attention!" Some zhiqing quietly held a few long banners with slogans:

Bitter sacrifice strengthens bold resolve, which dares to make sun and moon shine in new skies.

Heroes are the backbone of the nation; zhiqing are the pioneers of the times!

The burial ritual was held in the main hall of the cemetery. It started with a short speech given by a representative of the zhiqing association of the martyr's regiment. He praised the martyr for his sacrifice in protecting "state properties" and exalted the martyr as the pride of "Shanghai zhiqing and Shanghai people." "Now you are home," said the representative, "rest in peace!"

The key part of the ritual was the speech by Mr. Zeng, whose life story was presented in Chapter 1, the chief editor of *The Zhiqing Bulletin*, a self-published magazine, and the head of an informal group of zhiqing who gathered around this magazine. This group, which I call "Black Soil," organized the reburial ritual. Some key members of Black Soil contacted the Civil Affairs Bureau in Shanghai and managed to find a space in Longhua Cemetery for the ash casket.

In his speech, Zeng exalted the martyr's heroic deeds but went off his script, which I had obtained before the ritual, to say:

What kind of spirit was that? It was the heroic spirit of "fearing neither hardship nor death." It was the great spirit of "all for the people and the revolution," inspired by the great leader Mao Zedong. ... Without the sacrifice of the revolutionary martyrs, there would not have been our new China. Without the sacrifice and fearless striving of the zhiqing and other people in their generation, there would not be China's status today, as the second-biggest economy and a nation standing out in the world! The zhiqing stand side by side with the Red Army, the Eighth Route Army, and the New Fourth Army as national heroes of China, who deserve our highest respect.

To an outside observer, such an exaltation was farfetched, even if eulogies usually overstate the deeds of the deceased. In anachronistic Maoist language, the eulogy linked a person's salvaging properties from a cafeteria to China's rise as a superpower. This kind of rhetoric is unusual in today's China. After the Cultural Revolution, the dominant public opinions reversed Communist heroism and prized human lives rather than "state properties." Most people today would say that it was pointless, if not downright foolish, to sacrifice a young life for some pots, pans, and food.

However strange the reburial ritual seemed to outsiders, everyone in the hall kept silent and appeared serious. It was a Durkheimian moment of ritual and solidarity for Black Soil. The loss of a member gathers other members together to mourn, and the commemorative rite reconfirms and strengthens the community in the face of death (Durkheim 1995 [1912]). The group needs the memory of a hero and a defining event like the reburial to keep their history alive and to cement their ties (Fine 2013). The memory pattern that Black Soil follows is to praise both the zhiqing generation and the send-down program – or the socialist past of China in general. I term this pattern of memory as "*socialist nostalgia.*" It dismisses the public controversies over the program by forming consensus among group members. It is not a natural outcome but a result of the interplay between the group's history, its members' social features and life trajectories, and the key memory entrepreneurs' class positions and habitus.

The group started as a newsletter-like, self-published magazine, *The Zhiqing Bulletin*, which originated in the Shanghai zhiqing's collective effort to help build the Heihe Museum (Chapter 4). The magazine was warmly welcomed by the zhiqing and later became the official newsletter of the Research Association, a government-endorsed organization, discussed later in this chapter. As the chief editor, Mr. Zeng entered the Association leadership. He instilled his Maoist views of the past into the magazine and gradually irritated other zhiqing leaders in the Association. They also had been wrangling with Zeng over some administrative and financial issues. Finally, the leadership decided to expel Zeng from the Association. Zeng gathered a group of like-minded rebels to form a separate group and started a new magazine with the same name, *The Zhiqing Bulletin*.

Black Soil group has a simple structure: a single leader, Zeng, and some active memory entrepreneurs run the group. Zeng's vision of the group is clear: a community based on the shared faith in socialism, if not Maoism. The group members agree to his vision but do not go to the same extreme as he does.

Zeng likes to give long speeches on the political significance of the send-down program. His eulogy at the Longhua reburial ritual was an example: it was much longer than others' and filled with explicit Maoist vocabulary. On another occasion, a press conference for the commemoration of Mao's 120th birthday, Zeng's speech that praised the send-down program as a necessary and successful policy was so prolonged that the audience at the press conference began to chat with each other and generated audible murmurs. A woman who sat in the front row said to Zeng, "Lao Zeng, let's finish it up!" But Zeng went on for a few more minutes and then stopped. Other volunteers raised several practical concerns, such as inadequate time for rehearsal, the performers' lack of training, and so on. Zeng brushed aside all the concerns without offering practical solutions except for vague instructions like "then tell them to practice more." Visibly frustrated and even annoyed, the two volunteers in charge of organizing the performance stopped talking, shook their heads, and began to sigh.

I had heard Zeng making the same speech on other occasions, including my interview with him, an editorial board meeting of *The Zhiqing Bulletin* magazine, on a train trip to Heilongjiang, and so on. Sometimes his big talk hijacked those meetings intended to discuss how to get things done. The core members of the group often murmured, "There he goes again," politely attempted to switch the topic ("Zeng laoshi, what you say is important but why don't we get back to X"), and even bluntly told him to stop. Zeng did not appear offended when he was interrupted, and, quite remarkably, continued to talk.

Sometimes the core members complained about things more important than his "big-talk" style. For example, Ms. Su, who oversaw accounting and day-to-day office work, said that Zeng had "zero ability" to manage a group. He made empty promises to outsiders without thinking about whether the magazine had resources to fulfill his promises. He mismanaged several train trips and almost broke down before other members came to his rescue by solving practical problems. He rarely cared about daily work on the magazine and never made it clear what he wanted to do. These complaints were not just from Ms. Su, but also came from several people close to Zeng. For example, one day I went to the magazine's office and saw another core member scolding a volunteer for distributing too many copies of the magazine to a certain zhiqing group. The volunteer, also a zhiqing, defended himself: "That was what Zeng laoshi told me to do!" The staff immediately responded: "Come on, you take Zeng laoshi's words seriously?" Ms. Su shook her head with a wry smile on her face. The conversation puzzled the volunteer, who naturally believed Zeng was the group leader.

Nevertheless, the puzzle is this: Why would the group members still bear with and follow Zeng, even if they are clearly annoyed by his work style? The first explanation is that "birds of a feather flock together": the homogeneity of the members in terms of their chushen, their corresponding life experience, and political views. The majority of the members are zhiqing to the Heilongjiang Corps, which carefully vetted the zhiqing's chushen, and therefore many, if not most, had red chushen. Those with red chushen in the Mao years are more likely to have a positive memory of the send-down program (Chapters 1 and 2). The voluntary feature of the group also strengthens this homogeneity: those who disagree with Zeng would have left or would not have joined in. Their constant complaints about Zeng, which seem to signal internal conflicts, are about his management rather than his political and historical views. This consensus is ingrained in the group's history: the core members were those ideological rebels who followed Zeng and left the "mainstream" Research Association.

Second, Zeng's devotion to the memory work of zhiqing wins respect from group members and even many outsiders, who may not entirely agree with his political views but share the zhiqing generational identity. The same group members who were annoyed by his long speeches also enthusiastically praise his passion and devotion. My observation of Zeng substantiates such compliments. Being one of the oldest zhiqing (born in 1947), Zeng treats his zhiqing work as a full-time job – in fact, more than a full-time job because he works seven days a week without breaks. Group members often receive his calls late at night. During the train trip that will be described in Chapter 6, Zeng wore a crewneck, white T-shirt, a worn and cheap dress shirt with its buttons open, stayed in the overcrowded train as other members did, and worked until midnight every day. A veteran memory entrepreneur outside the group once said, after bashing Zeng as "a crazy old Red Guard," that "at least Lao Zeng is doing a lot of things for the zhiqing generation."

Black Soil became a small associational basis for various people with similar political views but with few other channels to express their opinions. In the scene described at the beginning of this chapter, for example, some "red" groups were attracted by Black Soil and Mr. Zeng, joined the train trip Black Soil organized, and displayed their political views and styles publicly. Some groups and people bring in financial and institutional support. For example, Zeng has developed close relationships with a few marginal state organizations, such as the "Yan'an Spirit Research Association," whose members are mostly retired generals, former officials, and their family members, and "the Association for Developing Northeastern Economy and Culture," a liaison association between the Northeastern reclamation system and social elites in Shanghai. These organizations endorse and co-sponsor Black Soil's activities and help enhance the group's legitimacy. The "Yan'an Spirit" collaborates with Black Soil mainly for ideological purposes: to uphold revolutionary values, which they believe have already been lost in today's China. For the "Northeastern Economy," the purpose is obviously pragmatic: to take advantage of zhiqing's resources and connections to expand the market for the reclamation system. A few important activities by Black Soil were funded by Mr. Zhao, a wealthy businessman, not a zhiqing but a son of a former high-ranking official. Mr. Zhao owns a company that runs several openly left-wing, if not Maoist, websites and WeChat public accounts. In sum, Black Soil benefits from its position in the overlapping area between the memory field and the political field. The institutional and political support it garners comes from the conservative wing of the Party–state, which implicitly or explicitly eschews Deng's reform-and-open agenda in favor of Mao's policies and corresponding moral-political values.

With outside support, mainly Mr. Zhao's funding, Black Soil organized several large-scale activities, such as the commemoration of Mao's 120th birthday in December 2013. Zeng invited other zhiqing groups in Shanghai to participate in the commemoration symposium and a gala performance. The invited groups managed to persuade Zeng to avoid Cultural Revolution songs in the performance. But Zeng still made the symposium, the spotlight event of the commemoration, an "all-red" panel: the speakers included several famous zhiqing heroes and models, including Dong Jiagen, Zhang Ren, Yang Yongqing, Zhu Kejia, and so on. With a great sense of honor and nostalgic emotions, the model zhiqing recounted their interactions with Mao and emotionally expressed their admiration. Dong Jiagen said: "No leader in the world is greater than Chairman Mao." Xu Jianchun said: "The moment when I lit a cigarette for Mao was the most memorable moment in my life." Zhang Ren might be the most restrained and critical member of this group. She talked about how she was shocked by the Great Leap Famine when she went down to the countryside in the 1950s: Many families did not even have people strong enough to bury the corpses. Even so, Zhang said Mao's idea that educated youths must integrate with workers and peasants remains correct and inspiring. "I don't deny his and the Party's mistakes," Zhang said, "but the essence of his thoughts is still correct." When the model zhiqing told their stories, a big screen in the hall displayed the photos of their meeting with Mao.

After the symposium, there was an exhibit with a seemingly artistic title: "Stories of Youth: An Exhibit of Zhiqing's Works of Calligraphy, Painting, and Photography." Mao was not in the title but in the exhibit: a big gypsum bust of Mao with a red sentence inscribed in the pedestal, "Wish Chairman Mao Infinite Longevity!"; a colored poster of Mao receiving Red Guards at Tiananmen; a silk-knitted portrait of Mao; several posters with Mao's highest directives; calligraphic works of Mao's poems; and a whole section titled "The Monument in Our Heart and the Glorious Path."

When the model zhiqing and participants walked into the exhibit room, they surrounded the Mao bust to take several photos. Several zhiqing even engaged in verbal conflicts with each other when they fought for better positions in front of the bust. A few of them, who were also core members of Black Soil, wore quasi-military caps with red stars and were eager to take photos with the model zhiqing. The model zhiqing, no longer household names in the twenty-first century, smiled and enjoyed the rare stardom.

The Rightful Resistance

On an afternoon in April 2013, eight former zhiqing in green military uniforms with "Little Red Books" (*Chairman Mao's Quotations*) in hand danced to "Sailing the Seas Depends on the Helmsman," a song popular in the Cultural Revolution. The dance was also a typical "loyalty dance," which, as the name suggests, Chinese in the Cultural Revolution used to express their loyalty to Mao and the Party. The dance had simple body movements: waving the Little Red Books, opening their arms, and stomping their feet. The dancers and the audience certainly knew the lyrics and the melody of the song all too well:

> Fish cannot leave water
> Melons cannot leave the vines
> The revolutionary masses cannot leave the Communist Party
> The Mao Zedong Thought is the sun that never sets

A cursory observer might have believed this dance was just another performance by some "old Red Guards" who expressed their yearning for the good old days in the Cultural Revolution. All the elements of the dance – costume, song, age, and body movements – seemed to substantiate this speculation.

This impression, however, was wrong.

A moment later, another group of former zhiqing danced and sang another "red song," "We Walk on the Great Road," but they changed the lyrics to convey a message that was more "black" than "red":

> We were young and handsome in the Sixties
> Wearing red flowers on our chests, we marched to the west
> We answered the Party's call

Sacrificed our youth to the development of the frontiers
Now there is a reform, and there is an open-up
White-haired, we zhiqing come back!
No healthcare, low income
How can we live out an old age peacefully and happily?

One who stayed long enough would see more performances with "red" form but "black" content. For example, the lyrics of "Solidarity Is Power" were changed to "We must strive for our healthcare / Which is a benefit we are supposed to have / For our survival, for our rights / We won't give in until we succeed!" Another song recounted their suffering in Xinjiang: "In the remote Xinjiang / I was only fifteen, sixteen years old / Got up when roosters crowed and returned when ghosts roared / Nobody cared for me / The endless years of difficulties and ordeals / The unbearable labor but I earned only three or five or eight yuan / Only a corn bun for every meal / No meat for months."[1]

Compared to Black Soil's reburial of a fallen hero, this performance was filled with trauma, resentment, and defiance. It was one of the numerous activities held by the "Xinjiang group."[2] Members of this group were among the approximately 97,000 Shanghai secondary school graduates mobilized to migrate to the Xinjiang Production and Construction Corps in the first half of the 1960s (Xu 2021). In 1979, when most zhiqing in other places began to return to their home cities, the Xinjiang Reclamation claimed that the Shanghai zhiqing in Xinjiang were farmworkers and that the zhiqing-related policies did not apply to them. The infuriated zhiqing petitioned the local and central Reclamation administrations to demand to go home. After a few rounds of failed negotiations and conflicts, the petition escalated into a hunger strike in Aksu at the end of 1980. The local authorities conceded to the mounting grievances and released hukou and other documents to the zhiqing. Nevertheless, the central government decided to suppress the strike and arrested the leaders. In the aftermath of this protest, in 1981, the State Council issued No. 91 Document to allow some Xinjiang zhiqing to return to Shanghai or Haifeng but to keep most of them in Xinjiang (Kraus 2017; Yi 2018).

In the 1990s and early 2000s, those who remained in Xinjiang returned to Shanghai after they retired. Upon their arrival, they found a significant gap between their Xinjiang pensions and healthcare benefits

---

[1] In the first year in Xinjiang, the Shanghai zhiqing's wage was 3 yuan a month; then 5 yuan per month in the second year, and 8 yuan in the third year.
[2] The Xinjiang Group's leader Zhang Weimin wanted to be named in this book, but I chose to anonymize other groups' names for safety purposes.

and the Shanghai average benefits. Adding to their sense of unfairness and anger was the differential treatment among the Shanghai zhiqing. Some other Shanghai zhiqing stayed in Shanghai without documents but, after they had petitioned for two decades, were granted hukou, received subsidies of 369 yuan per month, and later enjoyed the same pensions and healthcare as the Shanghai retirees. The retirees complained that rule-abiding people like themselves were treated worse than the rule-breaking "369ers." Some petitioned the Shanghai government and the Corps, demanding adjustments of their pensions and healthcare up to Shanghai's level. Their demands were summed up in a single slogan: "Same city same policies." To respond to their grievances, the Shanghai government and the Corps made incremental changes in policies, such as the gradual increase of health insurance coverage. But the Xinjiang group remained unsatisfied because the welfare benefits still did not reach Shanghai's level. They were joined by more Xinjiang zhiqing, and the petitioners' crowd outside the Shanghai municipal government and the Labor Bureau grew so rapidly that it agitated the state. In 2011, Zhang Weimin, the Xinjiang group leader, received a three-year probationary sentence (Xu inpress).

The performance was part of the Xinjiang group's fiftieth anniversary of their going to Xinjiang in 1963. It certainly had no institutional sponsorship; in fact, they were lucky to find a place, since many restaurants were told by the local authorities not to host this openly defiant event. Five years later, the Xinjiang group held another ceremony to celebrate the fifty-fifth anniversary of their going to Xinjiang with almost identical performances. The only difference was the more celebratory mood since the Shanghai government had raised the Xinjiang zhiqing's healthcare to almost the same level as that of the Shanghai residents with hukou, although pensions were not changed. At the end of the activity, Zhang Weimin was honored. She received a silk banner with compliments: "A model for old zhiqing, and a pioneer of the lawful pursuit of rights!" Except for the change of "fiftieth" to the "fifty-fifth" anniversary, the background tarpaulin on the stage remained the same, with Hu Yaobang's inscriptions hung on both sides: "[The Xinjiang zhiqing's] Historical contributions remain as long as the Tomur Peak exists / New achievements are alive as long as the Tarim River flows."

Some of the songs and narratives they performed in the commemorative activities were used in their protests. For example, "Back to Hometown" (with the music of a song "Tears Behind the Bars" [*tiechuang lei*] of the 1980s, by Chi Zhiqiang) was sung in their very first petition in 2003:

Why do we have no healthcare or pension?
The hometown life is beautiful except we do not have anything to
   rely on.
Whenever we recall you, Huangpu River,
We have lots of songs to sing for you.
Our song is soaked in blood and tears,
Flowing in the cycle of months and years.

Video recordings of their protest showed that the white-haired elderlies sang these songs in front of the Labor Bureau or Corps office, sometimes under the scorching sun or in chilly winter winds. Slogans like "Don't forget our contributions!" or "We want to live!" reinforced the emotional power of this narrative.

The songs, dances, and words presented a pattern of group memory that the loyal and idealistic youths became pitiful victims of the government's unfair policies. They portrayed themselves as idealistic young people who had "answered the call of the Party" to develop the frontiers but suffered much from the horrifying living conditions in Xinjiang, including starvation, low income, and laborious work. They regarded their suffering as their sacrifice for and contributions to the country, which, however, were not appreciated. This pattern of group memory used the Party–state's political vocabulary, leaders' endorsement, and the officially sanctioned political–moral values to justify their demands.

Nevertheless, underneath this publicly expressed memory was the members' diverse autobiographical memories expressed on "backstage" occasions, such as private conversations and interviews (Goffman 1959). While some of them had views of the past in line with the group memory, many did not. Mr. Zhou, with good chushen, expressed nostalgia for the Mao era but strong disdain for Deng and the current government. Mr. Xiang, with bad chushen, in contrast, told a life story without heroic words like "contributions" and "sacrifice" but with disillusionment with the indoctrination he received in his formative years.

Even the group leader, Zhang Weimin, also had autobiographical memory significantly different from the group memory. Zhang had a black chushen due to her father's three-year imprisonment in the 1950s. Zhang went to Xinjiang in 1963 with revolutionary ideals to develop the frontiers and a naïve belief in the recruiters' depiction of the material abundance in Xinjiang. A typical aspirant, she kept this idealism throughout her life in Xinjiang. Even right before she returned to Shanghai in the early 1980s, she was still one of the most hardworking in her danwei. In cotton harvesting seasons, Zhang set the alarm for herself to get up in the early morning, but her husband turned off the alarm to let her sleep.

Zhang's life after the Aksu incident was a constant shuttling back and forth between Xinjiang and Shanghai. She and her husband first returned to Shanghai but could not register their hukou. They made a hard living by setting up a korona game table in the neighborhood, until a few years later when, under the pressure of the street administration, they returned to Xinjiang. But her husband soon was upset with the lack of opportunities in Xinjiang and decided to go back to Shanghai and illegally stayed there. She later joined her husband in Shanghai in the 1990s. During this tedious and cumbersome process of interacting with the state, Zhang gradually lost her faith in the old ideology and viewed voluntarily going to Xinjiang as an action of naïveté and stupidity. She channeled her political energy to activism, first fighting for the 369ers (her husband was a 369er) and then for the Xinjiang retirees.

Nevertheless, her negative private view of the send-down program and the government was not reflected in the group's discourses and narratives in public settings which Goffman called "front stage" (Goffman 1959). The group memory of the Xinjiang group presented in their activities was a typical strategy of "rightful resistance" (O'Brien 1996), which adopted the dominant ideology and vocabulary of patriotism and collectivism to demonstrate how the government betrayed and mistreated the loyal children of the Party. In contrast to Black Soil members, the Xinjiang group members did not share a common adherence to a set of substantive values. Rather, they used an ideologically "correct" story of sacrifice, patriotism, and loyalty to solve the practical problems of healthcare and pensions and, meanwhile, refrained from expressing their personal views on public occasions.

Pleasant Present, Forgotten Past

The "socialist nostalgia" and "rightful resistance" patterns, however, do not work for most groups and associations whose members are "birds of a different feather." Most groups do not pursue a strategic goal, let alone protests. Their challenge is to maintain what Erving Goffman terms "interaction order" among members with diverse political views, backgrounds, and present situations and facilitate the survival and operation of the group (Goffman 1983; Fine 2012, 45). Their solution is the memory pattern of "people but not the event" – the one that prevails the zhiqing museums and exhibits. A minor difference is that the group memories amplify the apolitical feature in the groups' collective pursuit of happiness in their present life, which also means forgetting the troubled event, since the thorny questions about the event may divide the group and ruin the happiness.

"Long Live Youth!"

"Long live youth! Long live life!" A group of former zhiqing held their hands together, raised them up, and chanted, following Mr. Fan's orders, "Hands up! Down! Chant!" Despite the light rain and the wet ground, they walked out of a restaurant with light-hearted laughter and paraded past the gaze of curious bystanders. A member of the group was videotaping the brief procession and would add it to a DVD that recorded the reunion, to be distributed to the group a few months later. Like many other zhiqing reunions, this one included a prolonged lunch, a few brief speeches by members, and some small rituals like the "Long live youth!" parade. This "Anhui Group" consisted of forty to sixty former zhiqing who went down to the same commune in Anhui Province.

Their slogan "Long Live Youth" may sound like wishful thinking to outsiders, especially chanted by a group of people in their sixties, but it represents this group's memory pattern. It carries the imprints from their upbringing and conveys their hope for pleasure in the present. "Long Live Youth" was originally the title of Wang Meng's popular 1953 novel of Beijing high school students' life, a natural choice made by Mr. Fan, the group leader who was also an avid reader of novels. "Long Live" (*wansui*) was also one of the most frequently used phrases in the Cultural Revolution, as in "Long Live Chairman Mao." While its ideological implications have faded into history, the slogan permeates this generation's unconscious vocabulary so widely and deeply that it functions as a go-to phrase to express their hope for rejuvenation. More importantly, "Long Live Youth," as discussed in Chapter 4, is also part of the pattern of "people but not the event": not to talk about the send-down program but to remember a generation's collective "youth," with its implications of beauty and energy.

This emphasis on youth comes naturally from the group's initial purpose. Most group members went to the same middle school, and those who went to other schools were from the same district in Shanghai. After returning to Shanghai, some of them still live in the same neighborhood or adjacent areas, while others scattered for work and life and occasionally return for reunion activities. Many activities of the Anhui group are not unlike normal reunions, typical "autobiographical occasions" (Vinitzky-Seroussi 1998). Members of the group exchange their life stories, present self-images to an audience who know part of their past and present, and probe others' whereabouts: "I retired from the China Ocean Shipping years ago, and, no, I didn't change my job"; "Have you heard of Lao Zhang's divorce? No? That was quite a drama!"; "Do you remember the tall and muscular kid in the neighborhood? Yes, he also went down to our commune. Where is he now?"

There are also mutual compliments with passive-aggressive comparisons and competitions:

"You're so well-to-do now! No mortgage, better benefits, and everything!"

"No, actually, I've been just muddling along [*hunrizi*] in these years."

"Muddling along? You've been muddling better than I have! You're a *chu*-level official now."

"Come on! Your retirement salaries are higher than mine, aren't they?"

Ten years ago, three core members of the group, including Mr. Fan, wrote and published a memoir. In the process of collecting materials for their writing, they got in touch with many fellow zhiqing who had already lost contact. They started the regular reunion activities, including parties, tours, and even a long trip to revisit their sent-down commune. Later, the core members of the group, especially Fan, intended to "upgrade" these reunions by adding more of what he called "culture" to the activity. For example, for a reunion I attended, they made a standing banner, arranged a few brief but formal speeches, showed a DVD of their previous activities, and even came up with a plan to lay themselves down on a green to form the Chinese characters "zhiqing," which was canceled due to the rain. Fan ran a small studio for video advertisement and, thus, recorded all the reunion activities and made them into a few DVDs. They invited me to be present for some of the activities with a clearly stated purpose of using my identity as a professor to make their activities more "upscale." Their group memory sometimes even became "memory of a memory" – videos and blog writings about their previous commemorations.

Missing from the group memory was an evaluation of the send-down program. This did not mean that their conversations were completely apolitical. They often aired their dissatisfactions with the present society and government, such as officials' corruption, moral degradation, and so on. But they were less opinionated about the send-down program. They often emphasized happiness in the present rather than talking about the past. One of them said in a gathering, "Why do we have to think about those big issues? Being happy is the most important thing for us! Don't think about the things in the past!" The comment sounded odd at an activity that was supposed to remember rather than forget the past. But it was nodded to and echoed by others.

This collective silence about the past was broken by two "breaching experiments" (Garfinkel 1967, 36–43), the actions to break the unspoken rules of interactions to reveal those rules. One of the experiments was artificial and the other natural. I conducted the artificial one. Over an afternoon tea chat, I asked them to comment on the "regretless youth" phrase. Ma, a female zhiqing, immediately said:

The "regretless youth" phrase didn't make much sense because we can only talk about "regret" when we made our own decisions and then regretted our wrong decisions. But back then, we had no other choice but had to go down. You tell me it was "regretful" or "regretless"? [It would be better to say] back then we were "choiceless" (wunai)!

Other people nodded and agreed. The conversation then turned into an expression of grievances about their past suffering, which was not heard in their other activities. At another dinner, about a year later, I raised the topic of the Cultural Revolution, and the members told me of the violent conflicts at their school, including the students' beating and torturing each other and Beijing students coming to the school to instigate chaos. Most of them, however, were too young to join any of the activities, were bystanders, or stayed home to avoid the trouble.

All these conversations, however, would not have happened if I did not raise the issue. They usually ended the conversations with sighs and comments that "there is no use to talk about these issues" or "let bygones be bygones," followed by a unanimous re-emphasizing of the importance of "happiness in the present."

The "natural breaching experiment" was done by a marginal member, Mr. Shu, whose life story was presented in Chapter 3: he grew up in a high-ranking official family and has confidence in his knowledge and cultural tastes. Shu only occasionally participated in group activities but became more active recently because of *my* presence. A professor's genuine interest in those otherwise "eating-and-drinking" (chichihehe) occasions, as he figured, may say something about the importance of those activities. Thus, he decided to turn those trivial occasions into more meaningful ones by bringing up serious topics related to the history and politics of the send-down program.

Nevertheless, his well-meaning effort often fell on deaf ears. Over a dinner, for example, Shu wanted to launch a grand topic about history and politics. He even printed out and passed around handouts of his essay to other people at the table. Other members kept polite but wry smiles and talked about his essay for a few minutes before they switched to another topic. On group gatherings, when he stood up and made a speech, the other members simply ignored him and continued talking and laughing. Behind his back, Mr. Fan derided Shu's enthusiasm for academic discussions as something unfit for the group gatherings and his pursuit of "sociology" as a useless, amateurish pursuit.

The group members' middle-class incomes and adequate living conditions also buffer the impacts of the program on their life. Most of them have at least average pensions (4,000–7,000 yuan), plus rent incomes, no mortgage, Shanghai hukou, and the corresponding Shanghai privilege of better benefits and healthcare. Some have upper-middle-class jobs and incomes, for example, one is a retired banker. But they are neither too rich nor too poor, just well-to-do enough to afford the expenses of regular activities and to feel comfortable among other zhiqing with similar socioeconomic status. None of the regular members of the group can be categorized as "upper class" or "lower class." Their upper-class fellow zhiqing attended one or two events but did not come back, due to their difficulties in finding social equals. For example, a woman from a high-ranking family, who graduated from the same middle school and went down to the same county, did not join any of the activities. Her social circle, according to my interview with her, consists of those within the same class, for example, the daughter of Ke Qingshi, the former mayor of Shanghai. Their lower- and working-class fellow zhiqing also rarely attend. They cannot afford the shared expenses (usually 100 to 150 yuan per person, and sometimes more if a trip is involved). They may feel even more humiliated when the organizers waive their payment. None of the group members has ever joined the crowd of protesters outside the Labor Bureau.

The Anhui group is among the countless groups of zhiqing who went down to the same commune, county, regiment, and even company (military unit in a Corps) or village and now hold regular reunions and fun activities. The group's shared past in the countryside and corresponding interpersonal connections developed since their childhood constitute the basis of their interactions today. Their memory is more "inward" – focusing on their group's shared history – than "outward" – focusing on their generation's past. For a group like this, the political aspect of the send-down program is more an occasional topic over an afternoon tea than something with painful lingering effects on their daily livelihood.

The Pursuit of Happiness

The sky is crystal-clear after storms.
The road is particularly wide and flat after paths with thorny bushes.
Holding our hands together to enjoy the beautiful twilight.
Difficulties yesterday and tranquility today are both the spectacular
  sceneries of life.
Waves and spindrifts from the Yangtze River and Yellow River
Are remembering our lyrical youth.

About eighty former zhiqing, standing in a rather crowded activity room of a community center in Shanghai, sang the song "Our Shared Name: Zhiqing." The elderly amateur singers took pains to sing in tune but still made the conductor, Ms. Li, a fashionably dressed musician, also a former zhiqing, stop from time to time to correct their mistakes. At the audition before the rehearsal, Ms. Li had already expressed her frustration to the organizers of the choir that she could not bear the members' lack of basic music training. But she was hushed by the organizers and reminded that "we are here for fun instead of for a competition."

The rehearsal is one of the many activities held by the "Zhiqing Commune" (hereafter, the Commune), an association of zhiqing with more than 200 regular members. The name Commune is reminiscent of the politically charged "People's Commune," but, as the head of the association, Mr. Ming, emphasized at the beginning of the rehearsal, the name is to stress their "togetherness" rather than its political implication. He concluded his brief speech by chanting the Commune's slogan: "Being happy alone is not as good as being happy together!"

This "being happy together" slogan was fully played out at the dinner after the rehearsal. More than 100 singers and association members attended the meal. I was invited to the dinner and was seated at a table with the major organizers: Mr. Ming, the head and donor; the music director, Ms. Li; and a few leaders of the small groups in the association. Just after a couple of rounds of toasts and drinks, two zhiqing from our table stood up and began singing the Korean-language songs they learned during their sent-down years in the Yanbian Korean Ethnic Prefecture in Jilin. The cheerful mood quickly spread to the whole room. People applauded and cheered to the rhythm, and about ten women and men darted across the room to our table and gathered around the two singers, singing and dancing. The people at our table were besieged by waving arms and loud singing and were infected by the exuberance. Even the conductor Li, who appeared a bit grumpy in the rehearsal, was now laughing and cheering, ignoring the obviously out-of-tune singing.

The Commune is a typical "association," a type of zhiqing group with a larger size and more diverse members. Some associations include members who went down to the same county, such as the "Wannan Zhiqing Friendship Association," the same region, like the "Jiangxi Xiajiang Zhiqing Friendship Association," or the same province, such as the "Inner Mongolia Zhiqing Friendship Association." But the ambitious ones like the "Commune" accept zhiqing from different regions. The associations' structures – the division of labor and the power hierarchy, for instance – are more complex than those of reunion groups. In the Commune, for example, there are about twenty regular staff members volunteering to serve in several departments, including website management, a literary group, a choir, a newsletter/magazine, and so on.

Their commemorative activities, thus, are not "reunions" among old friends but gatherings with strangers whom they probably have never met before but with whom they share the same generational experience. In those activities, "generation" is a culturally and socially constructed identity rather than part of a cognitive framework for memory (Eyerman and Turner 1998; Edmunds and Turner 2002). A particular challenge the associations face is the greater diversity in the members' autobiographical memories than that in small groups. The Commune's choir is a miniature of such diversity. In the choir, there are mainly three groups of people who went down to different places: the Heilongjiang Corps, a county in Jiangxi, and the Yanbian Korean Ethnic Prefecture. While the Yanbian people are mostly jolly dancers uninterested in political discussions, some of the Heilongjiang Corps have left-leaning political views no different from those of the Black Soil zhiqing. Most of the Jiangxi chadui zhiqing condemn the send-down program as well as the Cultural Revolution. Besides these groups, there are also random, ungrouped zhiqing with various views of the past. Moreover, not every zhiqing joins the associations to talk about the past. Their motives can be as diverse as in other human associations, including fun, fame, social interactions, low-cost tourism, and even dating and sex.

Thus, a key problem every such association faces is to keep the members involved in the association activities without evoking their disagreements on the past, at least publicly. In this choir, a practical problem is to sing a song acceptable to all of them. "Sailing the Seas Depends on the Helmsman" would never work. The pattern of "people but not the event" fits the need to deal with this level of diversity, the difficulty of consensus, and a lack of previous ties (Fine 2012, 45). It is ambivalent and minimalist enough to serve as the lowest common denominator of various points of view. After all, who does not want to be regarded as a worthy, respectable person? Who does not aspire to a pleasant life in the present, despite a difficult past?

Take the song "Our Shared Name: Zhiqing," for instance. It was composed and written by two members of the association and has been widely circulated in the field of Shanghai zhiqing. Its lyrics recognize the past difficulties ("the path with thorny bushes") but contains neither complaints nor praises, that is, no evaluation of the event at all. What brought the thorny bushes to the paths? No answers. The difficulties are also redeemed in today's "tranquility" under the "crystal clear sky" – neither success nor suffering, simply tranquility. At the center is the "shared name" zhiqing – a generational identity given by the "times" they have lived through. It is the people but not the event emphasized in this pattern. This ambiguity is acceptable to zhiqing with all kinds of views of the past: difficulties mentioned, "lyrical youth" remembered, hope remaining for the "twilight" years ahead, and their generational identity centralized, and they are not as radical as the Maoist songs or as melancholic as laments about their present misery.

The Commune's other practices also follow the same pattern, with more stress on the pursuit of happiness in the present. "Being happy together" has already become the Commune's official slogan, chanted in gatherings, printed on banners, and repeated on WeChat. For those zhiqing who did not want to bother themselves with past pains, such a phrase with communal and pleasant messages is a perfect justification of their focus on the present rather than the past.

Every member I met at the Commune emphasized the group's solidarity and pleasure. Mr. Ming, leader of this group, contributed much to this solidarity. He has donated a significant amount of money to the Commune. In addition, he built a small resort in Hunan and rented a piece of land and a villa in a place near Shanghai and invited the members to take turns spending group vacations there. He did not show commercial interest in the activities. Long before the zhiqing activities began, he had already sold his businesses and lived mostly on his dividends and income from dealing in luxury furniture. When asked about his motives for organizing and funding zhiqing activities, he only mentioned "happiness" and repeated his mantra: "Being happy alone is not as good as being happy together." His selfless contribution won him many sincere admirers within and outside the association. In a few activities, I heard the members half-jokingly singing a song with changed lyrics (rhymed in Chinese):

> Ming, Ming, we love you!
> Like mice love rice!

This song was usually followed by a burst of laughter and applause, with Ming himself blushing.

Their past pain was certainly not entirely erased. Nevertheless, even if it was remembered in forms of cultural objects like memoirs, the public activities still maintained the same atmosphere of pleasure and solidarity. In 2013 and 2014, the Commune devoted much time to a collective book of memoirs on the zhiqing's experience of returning to Shanghai. In June, when the book was published, the Commune held a ceremony and banquet to celebrate its publication. Some key members of the editorial committee were invited to speak about the book. One of them said that "the solidarity of the group came from our shared experience of the painful youth," but he immediately continued to express his excitement about the book, praised the authors' contributions, and confirmed the solidarity of the group. Other speakers followed suit by expressing their gratitude toward the members and emphasizing their excitement. The brief speeches were followed by a chorus (again, "Our Shared Name: Zhiqing") and a banquet, at which the participants, as usual, were drinking, singing, and dancing. This warm atmosphere was in sharp contrast to the book, in which the authors recounted their difficulties in getting back to cities in various ways, including cheating the physical checkup to get *bingtui* (sick return) and engaging in cutthroat competitions to get recommendations for college.

The Commune's apolitical face also helped its survival and operation. An association at that scale with so many regular activities is inevitably on the state's radar. At the first several large-scale gatherings, the Public Security Bureau sent officers to their venues to watch but were convinced that the gatherings were filled with "positive energy." After a few observations, the police stopped coming. Also, the Commune's "positive energy" helped it secure the venues for regular activities: for example, the choir rehearsal was held in a community center owned by the street administrations. Moreover, as in many other associations, most members of the Commune at least did not have to worry about their livelihood and could afford the regular activities. Although there are no statistics kept of the members' demographics, the head and managers' estimates, and my observations and interviews all suggest that the members have at least middle-class socioeconomic status. Such a population does not usually have desperate complaints to air publicly.

Where the State and Society Meet: The Research Association

Since the 1950s, more than a million Shanghai zhiqing have gone up to the mountains and down to the villages. They went to the rural areas and frontiers, where they built their character and contributed their youth years to the construction and development. It is always necessary to confirm and cherish the spirit of the zhiqing, such as self-reliance, self-improvement, resilience, collaboration, and selfless contribution.

This passage, on the "About" page of the website of the Association of Zhiqing Academic Research and Culture (hereafter, the "Association"), articulates the Association's official view of the send-down program and the zhiqing: keeping silent on the program but confirming the "spirit" of the zhiqing.

The Association's close affinity with the state's view comes as no surprise. It is the only zhiqing group in Shanghai with legal registration, which is impossible to acquire if the organization has no governmental blessing. The Association was founded in 2011 by a group of former zhiqing with higher political, cultural, and economic capital. For example, the "honorary directors" of the Association include a former vice-head of the Central Propaganda Department and a former vice-mayor of Shanghai. The founding director was also a retired official – Party secretary of a university. Among the eleven vice-heads, there were one retired official, one former editor-in-chief of a newspaper, four university professors, two famous writers, and three private business executives. The Association has also developed collaborative relations with a few local colleges, which host most of the Association's activities.

Civil society scholars would categorize the Association as a "GONGO," an oxymoron referring to a "government-organized non-governmental organization," which, through its active engagement in civil society, directs civic engagement toward the state's goals and agenda (Unger 2008). The Association's website and newsletters make it clear that its purpose is "to make sure the zhiqing research and cultural [activities] advance in the correct direction." The "correct" direction, as the first head of the Association said in its opening ceremony, means the direction defined by the Party–state's ruling ideology. The Association holds regular "political studies meetings," including talks and forums on topics the state propagates, such as President Xi's "China Dream." In a field with potential and actual political ferment resulting from contested memories and current problems, the Association functions as an institutional and ideological "stabilizer," which promotes the state's official version of the past.

Despite its quasi-official status, the Association faces the same challenges as other organizations: competing functions, members' diverse views of the past, and the key entrepreneurs' individual power and influence. The Association also uses the same memory pattern, the "people but not the event," to accommodate culturally and politically disparate members. What is distinctive in the Association, however, is that this pattern, quietly but powerfully, attempts to contain the diverse views within the political limits set by the state. It is used as a "front stage" memory, a view of the past that is ambiguous and politically "correct" enough to disseminate in official settings, such as public meetings, newsletters, and websites. Diverse individual views of the past, in contrast, are expressed in the "backstage" settings, such as in member-only meetings and communications in WeChat groups (Goffman 1959).

At the front stage, this memory pattern attempts to be compatible with another of the Association's functions – research – and highlights its apolitical dimension. Unlike numerous other associations with "research" or "culture" in their titles, the Association takes research seriously. It has undertaken a multi-year project of collecting archives in various provinces. It regularly provides funding for junior scholars' research projects. It has co-sponsored with a research university a few serious academic conferences attended by scholars from Chinese and overseas universities. The leadership attends those research activities and claims that the Association's work is intended to "preserve history and seek historical truth."

This academic neutrality, however, subtly suppresses ideological debates over the program with a tacit assertion that academic research should be devoid of political evaluations of the event. But such neutrality is far from a value-free stance because, as the ending of the "About" page emphasizes, the Association's work faithfully follows President Xi's "China Dream" agenda. Nevertheless, it does not always accomplish its mission. For example, the Association chose not to announce a conference co-sponsored by the Association and a university in Shanghai to prevent "random zhiqing" from attending the conference and making it an occasion for ideological debates. That preemptive action, however, only worked within the limits of academic neutrality the Association set for itself. It could not stop the invited scholars and artists from linking the zhiqing topic to the Cultural Revolution in their presentations. Occasionally, proposed by some influential members whose views differ from the official one, the Association also held meetings and symposiums for politically sensitive topics – for example, a symposium for a new memoir on the Yunnan zhiqing's protest in 1978 – but had to try to reframe it as an activity to assess the book's research value.

At the "backstage," the Association members constantly challenge the official memory pattern. One needs to be part of the Association to get into those backstage activities. I myself was not a member of the Association but acquired my access through my informants in the leadership. In WeChat groups, the members often debate political issues. The Association leaders implicitly or explicitly defend the official line but usually refrain from using a commanding tone, while many members openly take issue with their views. The voluntary structure of the Association certainly matters here. The leaders can hardly control any critical resources. Disgruntled members can always air their grievances and, if they disdain the leaders, can leave without notifying anyone.

The demographics of the members also place them in almost the same class positions as the leaders. The Association selectively admits those middle- to upper-middle-class zhiqing as members, especially the core members who take positions in the Association: lawyers, teachers, engineers, professors, and so on. The stated purpose is to have "high-quality" members carry out its research function, but the unstated purpose is to fend off those zhiqing with lower socioeconomic status who are more likely to have grievances and thus could create "disturbances." This selective, if not biased, admission practice, however, creates a group of rivals to the leaders who follow the official ideology. Sustained and emboldened by their cultural and economic capital, the core members are vocal and opinionated. Once there was an intense online debate, in which a few core members grilled Wan, the director of the Association, for his affirmatory remarks about policies in the Mao years. After the debate, I half-jokingly said to Mr. Zhu, one of the challengers, referring to Wan's position before his retirement: "Now you really offend Secretary Wan!" Zhu grumpily responded, without getting my joke: "I'm not afraid of him! [He is] just a retired official with no power over us. Who fears him?" Debates also break out in face-to-face situations. For example, at an annual meeting of the Association, several members in the discussion panel I attended criticized the Association leadership for logistical problems. Later, such technical discussions led to their strong condemnation of the Maoist views of the past some leaders held.

Even at front stage events, the tone of discussions sometimes deviates from the official line. When that happens, the leaders of the Association often struggle to control the interactions and bring them back to the pattern of "people but not the event." The symposium on *Memory of Life* was such an occasion. *Memory of Life* is a book that collects memoirs and materials about those zhiqing who died in Heilongjiang, their sent-down place. The chief editor, a wealthy businessman and vice-head of the Association, took pains to mobilize a team of zhiqing to collect names of the dead zhiqing and contact their relatives and friends to write memoirs. It took three years for the team to finish and publish the book. The editors invited the relatives to attend the symposium. The zhiqing in the book chiefly were not martyrs or heroes; many died in accidents or committed suicide. Such a "gray" book was a mismatch for the Association's overall upbeat stance. But the editor enjoyed a higher status and good reputation among the members and other leaders; his project was the first book devoted to the dead zhiqing and struck a chord with those who had witnessed their comrades' death. Moreover, he was wealthy enough to be a major donor to the Association and to fund the project by himself. The popular support for the book, in addition to its financial independence, made it hard for Wan, the director of the Association, to reject the plan.

Wan presided over the symposium and gave opening remarks about the significance of the book: first, to recover and preserve history; second, to carry forward the spirit of zhiqing, to live a better life today, and to "devote ourselves to the development of our second hometown and our country." Clearly following the official line that past suffering was redeemed in today's better life, Wan intended to set the tone for the symposium. The later discussions proved his effort futile. The first speaker, the chief editor, emphasized the importance of including suicide cases, which no official narratives would incorporate. Another editor echoed his comment with a more sorrowful tone: "The book is not only a commemoration of their lives but also a commemoration of our youth which has gone forever." A professor then highlighted the suicide cases and told a story of a red-chushen zhiqing who killed himself after his father was purged and interrogated. Wan, stone-faced, did not comment on the speeches and simply introduced the speakers.

It was the relatives' words that turned the atmosphere into one of sorrow and resentment. A male zhiqing to Jilin whose sister had died in Heilongjiang, said: "Who said our youth is regretless? Who said our youth is regretless? ... If you were asked to send your children to the countryside, would you say 'yes'? Of course not!" The next relative's words moved many in the room to tears:

Please allow me to call them [the deceased zhiqing] children. When they walked to heaven, they were still children. They never aged. In heaven, there was no strenuous labor, no pain, no illness, no struggle, no grievance, only happiness and laughter. They were always young. This morning, when I was in a half-awake state, I suddenly felt that my brother and his buddies were still a group of children and asked me with a smile: Do you still remember me? Do you still remember me, after forty-something years?

Right after this tear-jerking speech, another relative made a short but powerful comment: "If we want to reflect on the history of the send-down program and the Cultural Revolution, then the critical issue is that [both campaigns] ignored the value of human lives." Her remark was echoed by an officer from an association from the northeast, a former zhiqing, who choked back his tears and claimed: "The only way to revive the nation is to respect and cherish the basic rights of humans and tell the truth!"

Seeing the atmosphere turning in a direction he did not intend, Wan strategically changed his tone to say that he could be one of the dead because he also did dangerous jobs like drilling and blasting stones in a mine. But he still ended the symposium by repeating his upbeat opening remark: "To remember them is to carry forward their spirit and better construct the country." No one objected to this vague remark, and the meeting ended soon thereafter.

Groups and Memory

Groups are what Mannheim termed "generation units," which form as members of a generation respond to their common historical fate in different ways (Mannheim 1952 [1923]). What is special about group memory is that it is not a simple aggregate of individual memories. Nor is it a carbon copy of public memory. It is both and neither. It emerges from group processes, in which both individual and public memory must be embedded and realized in interactions. Such processes produce patterns of group memory, which serve as cultural mechanisms for groups to deal with the difficult past and to maintain the order of interactions among members of the group and keep the group functioning. Memory entrepreneurs lead the groups but also need to square their individual autobiographical memories with group members' social features and group processes (Table 5.1).

In Black Soil, the major entrepreneurs gather a group of like-minded people with similar chushen and experiences. This homophily among "birds of a feather" leads to a pattern of socialist nostalgia: positive views of both the zhiqing generation and the send-down program. In the Xinjiang group, despite their various views of the program, they strategically use mainstream vocabulary (sacrifice, contributions, and justice) to present a group memory of "rightful resistance" in order to

Table 5.1. *Group processes and memory patterns*

Group names	Memory entrepreneurs	Group processes	Memory pattern
Black Soil	Faithful red (Zeng)	Birds of a feather/ homophily	Socialist nostalgia
Xinjiang	Aspirant (Zhang)	Framing in activism	Rightful resistance
Anhui and Commune	Withdrawer (Fan) Aspirant (Ming)	Interaction order among diverse members	People but not the event/ pleasure in the present
Research association	Elite zhiqing with various habitus	Overlapping between state and society Interaction order among diverse members	People but not the event (front stage) Various views (backstage)

demand healthcare and pension benefits from the government. In most groups and associations, the group process revolves around maintaining interaction order among members with diverse views of the past. Thus, evaluations of the program are downplayed ("people but not the event"), and present pleasure ("being happy together") is highlighted to avoid controversies and conflicts. In the quasi-official Research Association, the group processes are divided into "front stage" ones – the activities shown to the public and the state – and the "backstage" ones. In front stage activities, the Association presents the official version of "people but not the event" – highlighting the causes the program was designed for, such as intellectuals integrating themselves with the masses, which remain at the heart of the present state's ideology, but not the event itself. At the backstage, non-state elite members of the Association may promote a less positive group memory, while the state members struggle to hold the Association together by, sometimes awkwardly, incorporating alternative memory into the official pattern.

In terms of quantities, Maoist, semi-official, and oppositional groups are rare; in fact, Black Soil and the Research Association are the only cases of their type in Shanghai, and the Xinjiang group is one of only a few cases of resistance groups. Most groups and associations in the field of Shanghai zhiqing are like the Commune and the Anhui group, who follow the "people but not the event" pattern to deal with the dual tasks of remembering the past and maintaining the interaction order. With some interesting variations, such as highlighting the pursuit of happiness, this pattern is consistent with the official view of the send-down program. This consistency, however, does not result from the groups' deliberate effort to conform to the official ideology, although they certainly know where the political limits are. Rather, it is a result of the interaction processes within the groups. This consistency also enables many groups to exist and flourish. When criticism of the program is still heard in some groups, the voice of self-criticism of the zhiqing themselves has disappeared. This trend is also evident in the activities that involve multiple groups, which will be described in Chapter 6.

6 "Comrades from Five Lakes and Four Seas!"
When Groups *Chuanlian* (Link Up)

We come from five lakes and four seas and have joined together for a common revolutionary objective.   Mao Zedong, 1944[1]

Most zhiqing today can still recall this Mao quotation, which they memorized and recited when they went out for "link-ups" (*chuanlian*) in the Cultural Revolution – to "exchange revolutionary experience" with youths in other places. Many of them point out that the zhiqing groups today bear an uncanny resemblance to the Red Guard groups: self-organized and mostly unregulated, with frequent and rowdy gatherings, big flags and banners, self-published newsletters, and so on. The zhiqing groups also participate in numerous activities similar to those of chuanlian: they travel to other cities and interact with groups from all over the country, who bear the same identity as "zhiqing generation." Those intergroup activities can happen in informal encounters between two small groups, like dinner parties, or in formal, large-scale activities that have hundreds of participants, such as public lectures, gala performances, commemorative ceremonies, visits to museums, and even week-long, out-of-town travels. The involved zhiqing do come from "five lakes and four seas." Some may travel across the country to join the activities with grandiose names like the "National Zhiqing Festival." The frequent, ubiquitous intergroup activities are the epitome of the memory field for zhiqing that has matured in the early 2000s.

If one follows the Red Guard analogy, then one thing should not be omitted: the conflicts among different factions and groups. The zhiqing groups do not get involved in violence, but arguments and skirmishes frequently happen over interpersonal issues, divided opinions of the past, and logistics of activities. The interaction order the groups carefully manage to maintain may be strained and even break down. The fragility

---

[1] Mao's 1944 essay "Serve the People." I revised part of the official translation "all corners of the country" to restore its original expression of "five lakes and four seas" (Mao 1966, 148).

of the interaction order reveals the otherwise covert fault lines of classes and political views. Moreover, market forces and state power play more extensive roles in intergroup activities than in within-group activities. Travel agencies manage venues, transportation, hotels, food, and tours for the activities. The local governments grant the groups permission or at least tacit consent to hold large-scale activities but, meanwhile, keep an eye on them due to their political sensitivity.

All these complexities, however, facilitate the dominance of the pattern "people but not the event." It meets different groups' demands and boosts and even inflates their sense of worthiness. Nevertheless, as the activities boom within the zhiqing's memory field, this prevalent pattern results in the fading cultural influence of this generation in the general public.

Youth and Happiness

The intergroup, chuanlian-like activities can date back to the 1990s when the first batch of exhibits were organized and held (Chapter 4) but did not become large scale and ubiquitous until the 2000s. The first landmark activity in Shanghai was the gala performance "My Country and I" in 2004, organized and sponsored by a zhiqing website and seven regional zhiqing associations to commemorate the thirty-fifth anniversary of the beginning of the send-down program. The statement of purpose of the gala, printed on its brochure, follows the "people but not the event" pattern:

Youth is the best period of one's life. Thirty-five years ago, this generation sacrificed their best years without hesitation. That innocence and idealism added much historical burden to our lives, and people today are still debating over it. Nevertheless, history has proved and will continue to prove that this generation is reviving after so many catastrophes because we have used our young and best years to experience life at the bottom of society and explore the essence of life.

When I started my fieldwork in 2013, gala performances had become so popular and frequent that I myself attended five large-scale galas (with more than 200 participants) in Shanghai in about two months. Other small- or large-scale intergroup activities are countless: for example, a pop-up dinner party attended by about 10 zhiqing, a banquet attended by about 600 zhiqing to release a new self-published book by a Xinjiang zhiqing, a singing-and-dancing performance in a public park, and so on.

In some activities, the expression "five lakes and four seas" has its literal connotation. For example, in an event in Suzhou with about 400 participants, I met groups from Chongqing, Fujian, Zhejiang, and

Anhui, in addition to various groups from Shanghai and Suzhou. Even a "festival" in an obscure county in Anhui attracted a group from Yunnan, who toured the country to attend several such festivals back-to-back during the entire summer. The distinctive appearance of those festivals is full of reminiscences of chuanlian: red flags with group names, old songs played loudly through portable speakers, and sometimes square dances.

Underneath this appearance, however, is a greater diversity of participants than that found in within-group activities. Most participants of the tourism festivals are predictably middle-class to lower-middle-class zhiqing who are attracted by the trips' low costs and do not care much about the correspondingly poor qualities – shared hotel rooms and bad food. But there are also people with higher class positions – lawyers, doctors, professors, officials, private entrepreneurs, and so on. The participants cover the full political spectrum in today's China, from Maoist diehards, moderately left-leaning patriots, and harsh critics of the state, to completely apolitical pleasure-seekers. Thus, facing this higher degree of diversity, the organizers and participants rely even more on the pattern of "people but not the event," with more emphasis on "pursuit of present happiness," to keep the activities going without conflicts.

In various activities, organizers frame their goals to "carry forward the spirit of zhiqing," which roughly refers to patriotism, resilience, diligence, sacrifice, and other positive traits. At the rhetorical level, no one in this generation would challenge any of the words, although they may interpret them differently. This rhetorical consensus is good enough for the large-scale activities. No one would try to tear down a banner with those words because of different interpretations. An even more ambiguous phrase is "zhiqing culture." It can be used in almost all contexts: in names of associations, tourism festivals, symposiums, research projects, and even zhiqing-related products such as a brand of liquor. It sounds politically neutral and socially decent. Compared to the flamboyant "spirit of zhiqing," it is also low key. Its ambiguity is its strength. Consequently, it becomes a "go-to" phrase.

"Youth" is a keyword to this apolitical pattern. It strikes a chord with most zhiqing who want to express their nostalgia and assure themselves and others of their vitality. In almost every activity, there is always a group of (mostly female) zhiqing, dressed in colorful gowns and silk scarves, who diligently fit themselves into the stereotype of "square-dancing mamas." They dance whenever and wherever possible: parks, squares, and even at some unlikely places and times, such as at midnight at a railway station when waiting for the train on an out-of-town trip, early morning in a peanut field on a one-day trip in a Shanghai suburb, and so on. The male zhiqing are also determined to demonstrate their prowess by heavy drinking, binge eating, and some unusual adventures: for example, on a trip to a mountainous place in Hunan, which I did not witness but saw on a video, male zhiqing stripped and jumped from a bridge into a river to engage in a swimming competition.

"Pursuit of happiness" is also highlighted. No one can reject happiness even if they may not have a consensus on the past. "Happiness" (*kaixin/ kuaile*) shows up in slogans and speeches and is also practiced by the dancing, laughing, and drinking participants. As the head of a dancing group said: "As long as you are happy and healthy now, everything is fine!" Sometimes the past was evoked to confirm the pleasure in the present. An active member of the dancing group said: "Most of us are already very content with today's life because everything today is so great compared to our lives in the countryside."

This emphasis on people, present, and pleasure is also a politically preferable option. Local governments are afraid of the political sensitivity of the activities but interested in the revenues and publicity that a "national festival of zhiqing" can bring in. Moreover, through the activities, the governments can develop sentimental connections with the former zhiqing, who may bring in outside investments and guanxi to their "second hometowns," so to speak.

Companies too are interested. The 17 million aging zhiqing is a lucrative market. Some companies sponsor zhiqing activities, woo organizers, support struggling zhiqing newsletters, and even publish their own zhiqing-related newsletters. In doing so, they want to sell serviced retirement homes, vacation condos, health products, travel packages, and even burial plots (Chapter 4). Sometimes, the companies' commercial interests converge with the local governments' interests in revenue, especially when the companies may be owned by the government. For example, Mr. Zang's "Wannan Zhiqing National Cultural Tourism Festival" brought about 200 zhiqing to Wannan, his sent-down place, a small county seat set against a backdrop of spectacular mountain scenery. The zhiqing spent money at shops, parks, hotels, and restaurants. They were also the potential clients for a real estate developer owned by the local government. At the meals, the CEO of the company toasted Zang many times, until Zang was intoxicated, and made tons of flattering comments on Zang's "contributions to his second hometown." In between compliments and toasts, the CEO was also explicit about his purpose: "We need to develop a closer collaborative relationship!" which, as he later explained, meant "please bring us more zhiqing visitors interested in our condos!" The next day, the company sent a shuttle bus to take some zhiqing to see the condos. Neither companies nor local

governments want to see political trouble. To be happy, free from alter-
cations, and spend lots of money are their expectations for the crowds
of zhiqing.

A two-day "zhiqing festival," including a gala performance and banquets, organized by Mr. Guo's association "Shencheng Zhiqing," was an
illustrative case. The event was sponsored by a company and the local
government in Huxia (pseudonym), a Shanghai suburban town. The
town developed a large resort with small cabins for Shanghai urbanites
to stay in to pick organic fruits while on vacation. For various reasons, the
resort attracted few tourists and almost went bankrupt. Mr. Guo made a
successful pitch about the festival to the financially devastated local
government. As he boasted at an internal organization committee
meeting that I attended, he told the local government that his event
would not only bring about 200 zhiqing consumers but also publicize
Huxia as a "brand" of tourism "in the whole nation." The local government then donated 20,000 yuan through its own tourism company, in
addition to offering a free performance venue and discounted cabin
hotel rooms.

The goal of this event, Guo said, was to make the zhiqing happy. The
slogan he used on the event brochure and banners was: "I feel happy
when I make you happy!" Guo also envisioned a more ambitious plan to
expand this happiness to more zhiqing by launching an "East China
League for Zhiqing Culture and Tourism," in which the constituent
regional associations rotate to hold large-scale events in various places
near Shanghai. This league will "create a platform for health and happiness and let the zhiqing enjoy the pleasure."

Underneath this all-inclusive happiness frame were the participants'
different views of the past and various purposes of joining the activity.
Inside the tent for audiences at the event venue, the "Red collector," Liu,
displayed his collection of Cultural Revolution posters, old newspapers,
pictures, and some newly made banners with old Maoist slogans, such as
"Mao's Thoughts Will Shine On Forever!" or "Learning from Lei Feng
as the Good Model!" But Liu had to compete with the zhiqing associations and groups for the limited room on the tent walls where they hung
their association red flags. Some participants, however, did not hide their
disdain for Liu's Maoist exhibit. Sitting not far from Liu's banners, a
female zhiqing told me about her family's ordeals in the Cultural
Revolution and vowed never to say, "Our youth is regretless." Another
male zhiqing I had just met at the event bemoaned that many zhiqing in
the class of 1969 like him did not receive much formal education, could
not handle computers well, and did not have well-paying jobs. More
participants, however, were exchanging gossips.

Nevertheless, all of them seemed to accept the happiness frame, the lowest common denominator of all views and thoughts. The frame was realized in the zhiqing's exuberant mass participation in collective entertainment. In almost all the zhiqing galas, the performers are zhiqing amateurs, who regularly practice and rehearse in parks, community centers, or wherever there is an open space – for example, a warehouse the "Zhiqing Square" dancing group borrows from a private entrepreneur. Some groups invite or hire professionals to teach them. Many cannot afford professional instruction and simply teach themselves by watching videos. As the foot soldiers of the zhiqing activities, they run from one activity to another and often travel outside of Shanghai, with big bags and cases of costumes, instruments, and props. For most performances, they receive only nominal compensations, for example, 100 yuan for each performer per event, with discounts or waivers for event fees and free meals and hotels. The money, however, is a "fee for hard work" (*xinkufei*), a token of appreciation with a "better-than-nothing" amount to defray some but certainly not all of the expenses. It is not about the money, as they claim. Singing and dancing are not only enjoyable hobbies but also healthy exercises. Communality is another reason for them to join the group and the zhiqing events. One of the members of the Zhiqing Square group said: "If I don't come to a rehearsal, I feel something is missing." Another member said: "I moved to a place really far away so I couldn't come every week, but I tried to come here every other week." They called the dusty, humid underground warehouse, which they borrow for their rehearsal, their "home."

Being invited to events frequently also makes the performers feel needed. This sense of self-importance and even local stardom is made possible and accentuated by the ubiquitous presence of amateur photographers at every zhiqing-related event. Many of the photographers are male zhiqing who are enthusiasts equipped with professional-grade, DSLR cameras, tele-lenses, tripods, and photographers' vests. They take pictures of the performances, comment on each other's equipment, and upload their pictures to WeChat afterward. The performers' pictures, therefore, are widely circulated online and create a sense of pride in them. The performers' eagerness for appearing in those pictures is evident. On my fieldwork trip in 2017, I brought with me a pro-grade Nikon and a tripod to record videos and take pictures to supplement fieldnotes. Consequently, some performers thought I was one of those amateur photojournalists, or at least someone who could spread their images. I was frequently asked to take their pictures, and a few of them even deliberately danced close to my camera and paused for better poses.

Happiness also comes from what I term "mass participation in collective effervescence": the informal, karaoke-style, and pop-up performances on the basis of "first to jump on the stage sings first." These raucous, hilarious moments mostly take place at dinners, after a day of activities, when the zhiqing are emboldened by alcohol. The zhiqing participants sometimes dance and sing at the table, as I described at the Commune's dinner in Chapter 5. If there is a stage or platform, a group of zhiqing dance on the stage, encouraged by the applause and laughter and joined by other half-drunken ones who make whatever body movements they can. They often ask the organizers to play specific music. Some organizers try to keep a queue of the requests, but their effort is often in vain because too many jump the queue and simply occupy the stage. But no one seems to care about order. Everyone is enjoying the effervescent anomie.

The singers and dancers often go off script and collectively enter a state of "the weirder, the better." At a dinner party during the event in Huxia, for example, a group of women was dancing on the stage with a male zhiqing singing "Wusuli River," a popular Hezhe ethnic song. But one man rose from the audience, and with his hands up and a tree twig in his mouth, walked like a duck to the stage to share the spotlight. He made the whole room burst into laughter, including the performers. The duck-walking man then hugged the singer and inserted the twig in the singer's collar. When the song approached its ending, the part with the lyrics "the people's mountains and rivers last forever," the woman dancers closely surrounded the singer and the duck-walking man in the middle and posed for the audience, who laughed and applauded crazily.

Fault Lines along Class and Ideology

The emphasis on youth and happiness, however, has its limitations. It is almost impossible to keep talking about the people without talking about the event that defined their collective fate. It is also almost impossible not to let the unhappy ones talk. The happiness frame attempts to maintain the interaction order at the expense of an open discussion of the troubled past and the troubled present. Such a discussion, however, does not go away. It is not on the "front stages" of the events, such as performances, slogans, brochures, social media reports, or even the spontaneous mass participation. Instead, it takes place on "backstages," in private conversations, discussions at banquet tables, and murmurs and gossips (Goffman 1959). Many of those discussions are filled with a strained atmosphere, sometimes with conflicts, albeit minor. The awkward interactions and conflicts make visible the cracks along the fault lines of class and ideology in the edifice of the grand, harmonious narrative of the "zhiqing generation."

Much of the tension in the intergroup activities comes from class disparity, in subtle or explicit ways, when zhiqing from different classes mingle on social occasions. For example, at many banquets, people with higher class positions are arranged at the tables closer to the central stage, and the distance to the stage signifies the status of the guests. At some events held in theaters, there is a long desk on the stage: that is where higher-status people should sit. On some occasions, because of my higher cultural capital (professor), I was invited to sit at the tables closer to the stage or the long desk on the stage. During one event, I sat at a table in the middle of forty tables, instead of a table closer to the stage, and talked to my fellow diners. But I was soon found by the organizer, who almost scolded me: "Why do you sit *here*? *We* are waiting for you!" He dragged me to a separate room where "we," the organizers and "distinguished guests," including two professors, three retired officials, a press editor, a journalist, and a few owners of local companies, were dining. After the dinner, the local merchants gave each of us in the room a "small gift": an Hermès scarf worth more than $300!

Resentment based on class sometimes breaks out. At one of the public lectures sponsored by the Research Association and open to the public, a mini-drama took place. The speaker was a Fellow of the Chinese Academy of Science, the highest possible status for a Chinese scientist. He recounted his experience as a zhiqing in Anhui and how he struggled against all the odds and became a leading neuroscientist. After his talk, a zhiqing walked to the podium, grabbed the microphone, turned to the audience, and said:

Professor X [the speaker] went to Y county as a zhiqing. I went to Y county too. He now is a famous scientist, and I learned a lot from his lecture. But I am not a famous person. I am really grassroots. Not even grassroots. I am poor. So, my question is: Why on earth are some zhiqing so poor but others so better off even if they went down to the same place? I know Professor X worked very hard. I worked hard as well! But I wasn't given any opportunity to succeed. I wasn't allowed to go to college. If I were allowed …

Before he finished his comments, Wan, the presider of the talk, interrupted him: "Okay, stop, we know what you're talking about! Thanks for your comments, but you can get off the podium now." This rude interruption was echoed by some members of the Association in the audience, who shouted: "Get off!" The person, whose name I later learned was Lou, seemed embarrassed and dropped the microphone and left the podium. Lou still suffered from the impact of the zhiqing years, for example, all kinds of diseases caused by strenuous work in the field (he coughed constantly, even in my face without covering his mouth). He said he was a smart student and hardworking zhiqing but was not allowed to go to college due to his bad chushen. He repeatedly said: "If I were given the opportunity ..." This "if ... then" story is hard to verify retrospectively, but it clearly expresses the disadvantaged zhiqing's feeling of being unfairly treated, especially when the commemorative activities highlight the winners' success.

Another female zhiqing also made her grievances known at public activities. She attended almost all the public activities I attended in the first period of my fieldwork in the fall of 2013. As soon as the speakers finished their talks, she distributed to the speakers and the audience a stack of printed documents about the unfair treatment she received in her danwei, which led to her unemployment. She demanded the government's compensation for her lost years in the countryside, which caused her low education and poor health condition. The speakers and the distinguished guests sitting on the podium were confused, annoyed, and impatient. Sometimes, the organizers tried to stop her from talking with the speakers.

Once I was introduced to her, and she believed I could somehow help her case, even if I made it clear that I was not a lawyer or an official but a useless sociologist. Her response made me amused and sympathetic at the same time: "I saw you on the stage several times, and other people told me you are a big shot. You definitely have the ability to help me!" I was amused by her overestimation of my abilities and her assumption about the space–power connection. But I was also sympathetic to her helplessness especially when her grievances were exacerbated by her witnessing the visible disparity in class positions of those who experienced the same historical event.

The tensions and conflicts over class disparity are often intertwined with political and ideological arguments over the send-down program and the Mao era. For example, at one banquet I was sitting by Mr. Zhong, a wealthy restaurant owner, who, when our conversation led to his zhiqing experience, said, "The Cultural Revolution was not a revolution but a massive crime!" This statement immediately provoked counterarguments from two people at the same table. They claimed that the GDP growth rates in the Mao years were higher than those after 1978, and that the society under Mao was more equal and less corrupted than today. They also hinted that rich people like Zhong would certainly like the corrupted present government controlled by capitalists. Zhong argued back by raising his voice and ridiculing their anachronistic views. As always, neither of the two sides of the debate could persuade the other.

Another skirmish took place between the "red," Mr. Qian, an adherent to the official ideology and even Maoism, and the "black," two members from the oppositional Xinjiang group, at a lunch party at my key informant's house. Qian said at the lunch table, apparently knowing his interlocutors were protestors:

We zhiqing did suffer a lot in the past. But we should not be too obsessed with the past and always talk about who should be responsible for our suffering. We also should stop asking for compensation for the lost years. In other words, we should not do things like petitioning.

His remarks immediately provoked the Xinjiang group's reaction. One of them fired back:

How can we not care about the past if some of us still don't have decent living conditions or basic healthcare? Why should we carry the burden of the nation instead of the nation carrying the burden for us?

The argument lasted several minutes, and the host switched the topic. But another debate emerged a few minutes later when one of the people at the table said that "the zhiqing culture is a farce since the zhiqing were poorly educated and had no culture at all." Qian reacted to the claim by saying that the zhiqing did have a spirit or a culture, which, in his understanding, was the zhiqing's "ability to carry the burden of the People's Republic regardless of whether you went down voluntarily or were forced to go down." This grand narrative provoked a new round of debate.

Later, on the bus to the subway station, one of the Xinjiang zhiqing expressed his frustration: "It is so easy for those people with everything to dismiss other people's suffering. He [Qian] demanded that we – ordinary people with nothing – understand the government. Why didn't he ask the rich people and the officials to understand us?"

An even more serious clash happened at a research lecture in 2018, given by the head of the Association, Wan, about "the Educated Youths' Up to the Mountains and Down to the Villages and Some Related Issues," an obviously broad-brush topic. As part of the Association's supervising agency's public education program, the lecture was open to the public and had been publicized on social media. About forty "*yitui*" zhiqing ("*yidi tuixiu*" zhiqing, those who retired in their sent-down provinces and returned to Shanghai with lower pensions, who protested in front of the Labor Bureau every Wednesday) learned the news of the lecture and decided to use this occasion to have their voice heard.[2]

---

[2] I was not at the site but knew about this conflict almost in real time on WeChat. Several zhiqing sent messages, pictures, voice recordings, and videos to various zhiqing chat

Before the lecture, one of the Association members saw this crowd of yitui zhiqing in a nearby subway station and warned the organizer on WeChat, but it seemed that no one knew what the yitui wanted to do and how the Association should respond to this. Thus, Wan began his lecture at the scheduled time. But he quickly noticed the murmurs from the yitui zhiqing in the audience. When the humming sound became too loud for him to continue his lecture, Wan stopped to say:

Today's lecture is a scholarly one. I just learned that the yitui zhiqing are also attending the lecture. Someone even talked with me about her son's hukou and other issues. I'm sorry, but we don't discuss those issues today. We can't solve those issues. If you come to the lecture for those purposes, please don't continue to stay here. If you raise those questions, you're disturbing our lecture, and our staff will have to ask you to leave. You can go now or anytime. But please do not disrupt our activity.

Many yitui raised their voices, and murmurs turned into shouts: "What kind of history are you researching?! Focus on the present!" or "Respect history and focus on the present!" Some yitui zhiqing even used curse words to vent their anger: "He talks about history? No, [he] simply praises the Communist Party! *Cena* ["fuck you" in Shanghai dialect]!" One of the yitui said, quite philosophically: "Our present problems are still historical problems! They are remainders of history!"

A staff member of the Association walked into the crowd and tried to persuade the zhiqing to leave peacefully: "I'm sorry, but we are not the government. We can't solve your problems." Several yitui yelled back. One of them said: "We are not disturbing anything. We don't want you to solve our problems. We want a chance to speak, to talk about our problems. You don't let us talk about our problems." Another zhiqing even stepped on to the podium to question Wan: "You're zhiqing. I'm zhiqing. Why can't you research and talk about me, talk about our problems?" Wan appeared shocked, not only by her question but also about the sudden burst of anger and shouts. A few Association members advised him to leave. Wan quickly left the room, amidst yitui zhiqing's cheers and applause. Some of them, who wore the same type of T-shirt that read "zhiqing's children wanted to go home!," occupied the stage and podium, raising their banners and signs. Others were excited by their victory and talked among themselves.

This "occupy" incident provoked a minor storm in the field of Shanghai zhiqing. While the Research Association tries to avoid the

---

groups, of which I was a member. Soon after the incident, I had conversations with the yitui and the Association members.

thorny issues of the present by hiding behind academic objectivity, the yitui zhiqing poignantly reminded the Association of the harsh reality that some of their fellow zhiqing are still suffering. In the discussions afterward, some Association members condemned the yitui zhiqing's low "*suzhi*" (quality) manifested in their rage, and emphasized that discussions should be based on "reasonable communication." The yitui zhiqing, in contrast, continued to celebrate their victory and condemned the Association's hypocritical "academic research." One remark on their WeChat group expressed a common belief among them:

So, talk about researching history. We yitui zhiqing are *living history*. One of us wanted to talk for 10 minutes but was not allowed. Why? You don't study those zhiqing who are still suffering, but you study those zhiqing with 8,000–9,000 yuan [pension] a month?

The "New Long March" along the One Belt and One Road

The closest scenario to the original meaning of chuanlian – to "exchange revolutionary experience" with the Red Guards in other places – would be an activity in which memory entrepreneurs imbue their large-scale, intergroup event with ideological doctrines to achieve belief-based solidarity among the former zhiqing. Nevertheless, just as the revolutionary fervor about chuanlian fueled only socially and economically wasteful passion in the Cultural Revolution, so too the excessive ideological meanings almost inevitably conflict with the participants' diverse purposes, the market forces, and boundaries among small groups.

The best activities in which to observe these conflicts are the trips the Maoist diehards organize. Those trips are not reunion groups' revisits to their sent-down places, where they find the huts they stayed in, hug the grandmas in the villages, and lament their lost youth. Instead, the trips are the quintessential "five-lake-four-sea" activities – large-scale, multigroup journeys to the organizing groups' sent-down places. They usually take several days to a week or even longer and attract hundreds of participants.

In the summer of 2017, I attended one such trip organized by Black Soil, touring ten places, mostly in Heilongjiang and Inner Mongolia. It lasted eleven days, and the participants slept mostly on sleeping cars on a train, when the train ran at night to the next stop. The costs were between 3,400 and 3,900 yuan, depending on whether one chose a hard bed in a cabin with six passengers or a soft bed in a train cabin with four. The prices included food, lodging, vehicles, and admission fees, and were at the market average for an eleven-day, multi-site trip. On the surface, the trip did not seem different from a normal tourist trip: participants ate arranged meals at round tables; tourist guides tried to sell local produce and souvenirs on buses; and so on.

Nevertheless, the trip was not only a tourism trip but also a "zhiqing" tour, as indicated in its name, "2017 Magical Heilongjiang Zhiqing Train Tour." Most participants were zhiqing, although some performers were not. They joined the tour as members of preexisting zhiqing friendship associations or performing groups. Black Soil was the major organizer. In a preparation meeting, Mr. Zeng, leader of Black Soil, gave the trip a grandiose official slogan, which was printed on the banner the organizers carried along the trip:

> The New Long March along the One Belt One Road
> The Zhiqing Always Follow the Party

The slogans linked the state's new initiative (One Belt One Road, President Xi Jinping's signature project that involves investment in infrastructure development in many countries) to the revolutionary heritage (the Long March). This high-flown framing was realized in the itinerary. Besides the major tourist spots along the route, the organizers arranged zhiqing-specific activities: performances at the Heilongjiang Reclamation Bureau and visits to several zhiqing-themed sites, including a co-op established by the late-model zhiqing Yang Xiaohu, the Heihe Zhiqing Museum, a village where many Shanghai zhiqing used to reside, and so on. Zeng emphasized that the officials at the highest local ranks would attend their performances to show their support. The most creative activity was that, in the Ninety-Three Reclamation Bureau, a city administered by the Reclamation system, the participants would assemble in a square to form two Chinese characters of the word "*zhiqing.*" The organizers hired a cameraman to operate a camera-equipped drone to take aerial photos of the human formation.

Zeng clearly envisioned a politically meaningful trip, almost a revolutionary pilgrimage to the sacred sites of zhiqing history, or something like a diplomat's trip where the local leaders warmly received his delegation. On the first day of the trip, when most participants were checking in to the hotel, Zeng was busy meeting with the Reclamation officials, and the pictures of their meetings were immediately uploaded to the trip's official WeChat group. The pictures exuded a sense of importance: Zeng talked with the officials in a formal, carpeted meeting room, which resembled central state leaders' meeting rooms often displayed on China's TV news.

Behind this grand façade, however, was Black Soil's purpose of gaining profits from the trip to alleviate its severe financial problem. This purpose was not stated publicly but was a tacit knowledge inside the group. Black Soil made its first trip in 2012 and realized profits on it. Encouraged by its initial success, Black Soil ran the trip again in the next year but did not recruit enough zhiqing and lost almost 60,000 yuan, a significant loss for the group. In 2015, the magazine moved to a new, more expensive office. A zhiqing-turned-merchant covered part of the rent of the new office, but Black Soil still struggled to pay most of the expenses. Black Soil then decided to revive the trip. The 2015 trip was a moderate success, but the 2016 one caused a minor loss. Despite the unpredictable chance of profits, Zeng decided to run it again in 2017. The trips' limited profits mostly came from some privileges and goodies that commercial travel agencies did not usually enjoy. For example, the staff members working for the trips were unpaid volunteers, mostly the regular Black Soil staff. Zeng also managed to persuade a few local governments to provide dinners and some local performance venues for free. Certainly, the Reclamation and the local governments had their motives. A travel agency owned by the Reclamation worked with Black Soil to run the trips. The cities where the trip stopped also liked to see a crowd of hundreds of tourists, given that those cities, except Mohe and Heihe, were not the hottest tourist attractions.

In this sense, the trip was a combination of a politically meaningful journey and a "normal," commercial tourist trip. This combination, however, created a dilemma for the organizers. If they wanted to make the "new Long March" more politically meaningful, they needed a group of like-minded people with similar political views and experience, ideally, those who went down to the Heilongjiang Corps, to have more "red" activities and visit more "red" sites. Nevertheless, this would inevitably lead to a much smaller group and fewer profits or even a loss, especially when the repeated trips they had organized may have already exhausted this pool of zhiqing. If they wanted to make higher profits, they needed to attract as many people as possible, particularly those who simply wanted a fun, low-cost, safe, well-organized trip. Meanwhile, they had to cut the activities that only make sense to people who view the trip as a pilgrimage.

Adding to their trouble was the group model of participation, that is, many zhiqing participated as members of their own small groups and associations rather than individuals. For the organizers, mobilizing groups instead of individuals was more efficient. Nevertheless, when groups mingled, the members often cared more about their own small groups than their fellow zhiqing, who shared the same generational identity but in fact were complete strangers. Complaints, skirmishes, and even fistfights broke out when groups were vying to get trivial things, such as seats at a dinner table, luggage spaces under a coach bus, and better spots for photos. Their internal solidarity was rarely extended to a strong generational identity.

Therefore, the organizers had to walk a political and logistic tightrope in balancing both ideological and economic considerations. From what I observed on the eleven-day trip, the organizers often staggered and sometimes almost fell from the tightrope.

The participants of this trip covered a wide range of zhiqing. The most conspicuous one was probably Mr. Tong, who often wore the Red Guard's green military uniform with a fist-size Chairman Mao badge on his chest and an armband that read "Chongqing Female Zhiqing Propaganda Team," the group he leads. He joked he was "Hong Changqing," the political director of the Red Women's Troops, whose stories were adapted into a model Peking Opera during the Cultural Revolution. When we met, Mr. Tong gave me his business card and a Chairman Mao badge. The back of the card read:

I went down as a zhiqing to a Sichuan county in 1964 and returned to my hometown in 1972. I retired in 2005. Since then, I have been devoted to red culture propaganda in a hotpot restaurant in Chongqing. I have distributed about 120,000 Chairman Mao badges, all out of my pocket. My vow is: To propagate red culture and work hard, until my life ends!

What was most flashy about Mr. Tong was his saxophone, which he brought with him and played Mao songs not just in performances but also when the groups were walking, eating, and waiting for buses. His conspicuous roadside performance often attracted the attention and laughter of passersby.

Many other participants were also openly Maoists, though with less ostentatious styles. They joined the trip because they found an affinity with Zeng's political views. A zhiqing from Hunan seized every opportunity, for instance, when visiting an exhibit, to attempt to convince others that many good things already existed in the Mao years and many bad things today did not exist then. Another group of people carried with them a red flag, which bore the group's name: "Red Song Choir for Mao's Thoughts."

Besides the Maoist diehards, there were two conspicuous, noisy groups. One was the "K City Zhiqing Artistic Group" (hereafter, K Group), which consisted of about thirty members. They attracted much attention because of their collective recklessness. They carried a portable loudspeaker with them, played rhythmic music, and began their "square dancing" wherever they could. At every tourist spot, they swarmed a landmark to take photos with different postures and different combinations of people, until they were shouted down by other zhiqing who had waited for minutes and became impatient. Another group is the "Q City Veterans' Artistic Group" (Q Group). The members were reserve army veterans rather than zhiqing, but they were invited by Zeng to join the trip because they could perform in various genres, from dances to songs to traditional instrumental music. Zeng also felt an affinity with their ideological stance – typical military patriotism – and certainly liked the fees they paid.

Regional zhiqing groups and associations were the majority. They often sat together on a bus, at the meal table, and throughout the whole trip. They spoke dialects other people did not understand. They always brought their associations' flags with them. Their interests in the ideology ranged greatly from enthusiastic to apolitical. Some participants, however, were real "reunion visitors" who went down to one of the stops of the train trip and had a plan to revisit some places they once lived or worked. They had smaller groups, usually fewer than ten people, and were relatively quieter, but eager to talk about their experiences in Heilongjiang when asked.

A few participants were retired officials whose official ranks were high enough for Zeng to inflate the trip's importance and to smooth the guanxi with the local governments: for example, a former central government official with the *ting* rank, a former *People's Daily* journalist, a former state-owned-enterprise CEO, and a few former Heilongjiang Reclamation retired officials. They were introduced at the performances and arranged to sit a table close to the stage. Other non-group participants ("*sanke*") included individual zhiqing, or semi-professional or amateur performers who were invited on the trip to enhance the quality of the performance.

To lead this diverse troop with 700 elderlies was obviously a tough job. Chaos erupted on the first day in the lounge of the hotel in Harbin, where the Black Soil staff and the travel agency set up a table for participants to register and check in to their hotel rooms. To save money, organizers of those zhiqing activities usually arrange for a participant to share a room with another person of the same sex. But some groups did not want to share rooms with strangers, and this sometimes would result in a member of the group using one room without a roommate, for which the organizers had to pay extra money. The staff and agents, thus, tried to persuade groups to mingle with others, but the conversations sometimes led to quarrels in loud voices, especially when the groups had just gotten off the train or plane and were tired and eager to check in. Retrospectively, this was just the beginning of a series of small and big dramas during the trip.

Zeng's strategy to manage the group, however, was relatively simple: to repeatedly emphasize the political significance of this trip and to leave the nitty-gritty to the staff. At the first meeting of the organizers, including Black Soil staff, the travel agents, leaders of various groups, and me, Zeng gave a long speech to elevate the trip to a politically significant activity that could be incorporated into the "One Belt One Road" initiative: "The key to the Belt-and-Road initiative is high-speed trains, our country's trademark technology. We travel by trains and, thus, become part of the initiative." Hearing this far-fetched connection, I immediately asked myself: How can this trip on a slow train become part of the Belt-and-Road initiative based on the modern marvel of high-speed trains? But nobody else seemed to pay attention to this discrepancy. Zeng also emphasized that the local governments were "eager to welcome our visit." After the speech, Zeng stopped talking, leaving the logistics to the staff and travel agents, without showing interest in making decisions on small things. Many logistic issues remained unresolved after the meeting ended.

This mode of management was repeated throughout the trip. The logistical work was in a permanent state of indecision and chaos. Toilets on the trains were always clogged; people were assigned to the wrong buses. Unresolved issues from yesterday piled up until the issues became emergency. The Black Soil staff was confused. The Reclamation travel agency sent three tour guides and an official on the trip, but they too seemed confused. All the staff members were busy controlling the damages caused by the accumulative effects of previous problems.

An incident that happened on the first night on the train demonstrates this chaos. Before we boarded the train, everyone on this trip was assigned a bed in a sleeping car, sharing a cabin with others. At night, hundreds of us stood in a waiting room at the Harbin Railway Station, with very few seats and with air conditioning barely functioning. After waiting for an hour, we finally boarded at 9 PM.

The chaos, however, had just begun. Many with tickets on the No. 9 car of the train found that the No. 9 car was the dining car without any sleeping cabins and, consequently, that our cabin numbers were all wrong. Nobody could explain what happened in the assignment process. Some took quick action in groups. They found an empty cabin for themselves, completely ignored their assigned number, and closed the door. This caused conflicts when others who followed the actual numbers got to their cabins and were surprised that the cabins were already occupied. Quarrels were heard everywhere. The attendants on the train ran back and forth with their uniforms soaked in sweat, trying to get people settled. Finally, Zeng worked out a solution and announced it through the PA system, but the solution required that everyone reshuffle their cabins. The train attendants simply ignored the solution and used their own way to settle the waiting passengers. One of the tour guides angrily raised her trembling voice to argue with the attendants, who also had no idea what had happened. Another tour guide, a young girl, cried, fearing her superior would blame her for creating the chaos, and her eyeliner streaking down, leaving black traces on her face. Some, however, had already settled in amidst this chaos. A few had done their tooth-brushing. Some even already had begun singing, laughing, and drinking.

The attendant first put me in an empty cabin but later relocated me to another cabin with two men already in there. One of them complained: "This tourist group sucks! Other trips are not like this. I will never take a low-cost itinerary like this again!" Clearly, he regarded the trip as one of the low-cost trips, paying no attention to the ideological meanings that Zeng took pains to attach to it. The other person, from Guangdong, also complained in a loud voice and insisted on closing the door: "Don't open the door, no matter who knocks on the door!"

The Guangdong man seemed to have the ability to predict the future because there were knocks on the door soon. He yelled, "Don't open the door!" I thought for two seconds and got up to open the door because we did not pay for the one leftover bed, and the attendant had the right to get people in. My reaction proved appropriate; two people stood outside were people I personally knew. Ms. Su, one of the Black Soil staff, and the official from the travel agency asked me if I could give my lower bed to a retired official, Liu Ju, who was too overweight to climb up to the upper bed in his cabin. I said yes, and they breathed a big sigh of relief. They held my hands to praise me for being a "high-quality" person. The praise might be exaggerated, but their expressions of relief made me guess that Liu Ju's request to swap beds was probably declined or even ignored in his own cabinet and elsewhere. Amidst this chaos, who would give their comfortable and accessible lower bed to a retired official with no actual power, whose only use was for Zeng to make connections with the local governments? Finally, I was transferred to another cabin and fell asleep quickly.

The next day, despite the widespread complaints about the misman-agement and chaotic situation the night before, Zeng remained upbeat at the daily management meeting. He said, "Last night, we had a small problem with car arrangements, but it has been solved well." Nobody at the meeting nodded. Then Zeng switched to his favorite topic: how the local government in the next stop "attaches great importance to our trip" and would receive us at the railway station. Then, again, he stopped talking and left the logistics to the staff.

Quarrels and conflicts constantly happened between staff members and participants and among participants. Once I witnessed a real fight between two Shanghai participants, a mom and a daughter, and the K Group, over seats at a dinner table. Their argument soon escalated to an exchange with curse words, in their respective dialects. Soon both sides threw chopsticks and plates at each other. Other people attempted to intervene by saying, "We're all zhiqing. Why fight? Why fight?" The intervention did not work. The conflict ended when the mom and daughter were dragged to another table with vacant seats before the performance began. Ironically enough, the program of the performance emphasized the solidarity of the zhiqing generation as well as their great contributions to Beidahuang.

Not one day of the trip went without hearing loud complaints openly aired. At the daily organizing meetings, some leaders of groups expressed their distrust in Zeng's ability to handle such issues. Some even yelled, when he was making political speeches: "Enough is enough! It's pointless to talk about those useless things!" Nevertheless, Zeng stubbornly ignored the complaints and continued his prolonged speeches.

None of Zeng political activities was altered. The essential activity for Zeng was the drone photo-taking of the "zhiqing" word assembled by human bodies in a public square in Ninety-Three Reclamation. The day before the drone photo was to be taken, I glanced at the weather app on my cell phone, which showed that the highest temperature for the next day in Ninety-Three Reclamation would be 33°C (91°F). The drone photo-taking was scheduled at 1 PM, a terrible time and temperature for elderlies to sit, stand, and perform in a public square under the hot sun. I pondered for a while whether I should do something. Many ethnographers do not intervene in the "natural" flow of interactions. But in that situation, I decided to send a message to the organization committee's WeChat group to remind them of the weather and asked Zeng if he had arranged anything to avoid possible injury. The main reason for my intervention was my concern for the elderlies' health. Another reason was more methodological: an ethnographer is not a walking camera to record interactions objectively. What matters in ethnography is *intersubjective* reality, which emerges from interactions between the researcher and the researched. I expected that my intervention might lead to some happenings that could be interesting for the research.

At the daily management meeting at night, my message was the central topic. Zeng assured us that he had already informed the Ninety-Three Reclamation Bureau, who had put a cover on the stage. Someone questioned him, "What about the audience who have to sit under the sun for three hours?" Zeng responded by promising to shorten the performance time but insisted on the audience sitting in the square.

Most people at the meeting were clearly upset, loudly airing their disagreement. The head of Q Group burst with anger: "You arrange our performance for the afternoon, under the sun, at a temperature of 33. It is unfair! Why did other groups perform indoors but we outdoors? We won't do it!" He slammed his hand on the table and stormed out of the dining car. Several others asked Zeng to cancel the performance and let the zhiqing rest, since they had been exhausted by the killing pace of the trip. Zeng did not respond. In the end, Zeng said that he would contact the Ninety-Three Bureau again to see if they had any idea how to deal with the issue.

After cursorily ending the discussion on the weather, Zeng switched to the discussion of the aerial photo-taking, the essential part of Zeng's plan since the photos could be perfect materials for his propaganda. He spent much time discussing with the Guangdong people in charge of the drone camera. The Guangdong group, however, had a disagreement among themselves about how to arrange the crowd to spell out the words. They raised their voices, switched their inarticulate Mandarin Chinese to Cantonese, which effectively fueled a raucous debate. The debate ended when one of them cursed in Cantonese and left the dining car. Others at the meeting used their hands to hold their heads and looked exhausted, bored, and frustrated. The meeting ended without a clear solution.

The grievances over the heat issue, however, fermented. The next day, a few small group leaders raised the issue again on WeChat. A doctor from Ningbo reminded Zeng of the high probability of heatstroke, given the participants' old age, hinting at a cancellation. Her message was echoed by many on WeChat and in offline conversations. Even the leader of K Group, who had been a staunch supporter of Zeng, said: "Yes, one of our members got sunstroke yesterday. I agree with the doctor." Nevertheless, Zeng sent an announcement on WeChat that the zhiqing were "required" to sit in the square to watch the performance and take the aerial photos, although the whole process would be shortened to eighty minutes. The Reclamation Bureau, he said, would put a sunscreen net above the stage.

This message infuriated many. People around me were murmuring, "He is crazy; he is crazy." A few said that they stayed in the air-conditioned restaurant where we had lunch and did not want to expose themselves to the sun. A significant number of people, urged by Zeng, still went to the square, and I followed the crowd. When we got to the square, the situation was even worse than expected. What Zeng described as a "sunscreen net" was a black, textile net hanging above the stage, while the whole audience area was exposed to the scorching sun. My cell phone app showed 33°C, exactly the highest point of the day, and the actual temperature in the square was even higher. Sweat trickled down my back; the hot air was suffocating. Seeing this, most zhiqing hid under the trees at the two sides of the stage. Only about a hundred, holding umbrellas, were sitting in front of the stage. After a few minutes, half of them ran away for shade, leaving Zeng and some other organizers to stick to their posts. Later, Zeng walked to the tree area to urge people to sit in the square, but no one responded to him; many shook their paper fans and looked elsewhere. Dead silence. Zeng appeared embarrassed and walked back to his place under the sun. The performance turned out to be terrible, too. The instruments were obviously out of tune due to the heat, and the performers looked sweaty and exhausted, and they wished to finish it as soon as possible.

When it was time for aerial photo-taking, some clouds and breezes brought the temperature down a little (to about 30°C), and the sun was less punishing. This made the assembly possible. Urged by the staff, the zhiqing stood in the shape of the two words and then walked in circles, chanting patriotic slogans, with the drone camera humming and hovering above their heads. After a hasty hour, the photo-taking finished, everyone breathed a big sigh of relief and boarded their buses. Many people on my bus said: "Fortunately, no one fell." In addition to enduring the heat, we still had to sleep in the train that night, with all the toilets clogged and the unpleasant odors spreading throughout the whole train. Dreading sleeping with sweat-soaked clothes and our sticky and smelly bodies, the zhiqing crazily looked for places to take showers, either in public baths or in hotels. I found a hotel room and asked my cabinmates to come to take baths in turn.

In contrast to this chaotic reality, the brief report written by the organizers made everything appear ironically positive:

Yesterday afternoon, the participants of this train trip toughed through the 33-degree heat and successfully held the aerial photo activity. ... The participants assembled neatly and orderly. The drone camera hovered above our heads while we are cheering. Some of us held the banner "The New Long March along the One Belt and One Road; The Zhiqing Always Follow the Party" and walked around the square for several laps. This activity symbolizes that the zhiqing activities are incorporated into the state's construction and development plan.

Zeng's ideological agenda culminated not in practice but in the report.

After the upheaval of the aerial photo-taking, all the politically meaningful activities were done with, except for an assembly in Jiagedaqi, which is described at the beginning of Chapter 5. The trip was "downgraded" into pure tourism. The level of tension greatly decreased. The fun theme took over the trip. K Group resumed their square dancing, and men gathered in groups to consume the vodka they had bought from the supermarkets in border cities. Mr. Tong still played his red songs on his saxophone, and many sang along with his tune almost half-jokingly. Tong himself even got more relaxed than ideological. For example, in the Zhalong Natural Preservation District, a habitat for red-crested cranes, he danced with other members of his group, waving his arms to imitate cranes flying, singing, "Flying, flying, and we are flying!" Many tourists were laughing at and taking photos of the silly, childish dance of this group of elderlies with Mao's image on their shirts.

Many problems on the trip probably would not have occurred on a commercial tour, for example, the aerial photo-taking in hot weather only for propaganda purposes. The organizers' ideological goals, which prioritized political activities but ignored the logistics, did not match most participants' expectations. They still viewed this trip as a commercial trip and complained about the logistics issues as though on a normal itinerary. Regular members of Black Soil privately talked about all the issues and even directly criticized Zeng. But they rarely did that in public. The reason, as my "cabinmate" Lao Zhang said, was that "we are all zhiqing and work as volunteers," and, therefore, it was hard for the fellow zhiqing volunteers to make complaints as they would do if they were traveling on a completely commercial trip. Moreover, despite all his problems, Zeng was still admired by almost every member of Black Soil for his devotion. Being one of the oldest members of the group, Zeng worked from early morning until midnight and rarely had time even to take a shower. Consequently, complaints remained unaddressed, quality of service remained bad, and most problems remained unsolved. The trip failed to meet its ideological goal, a "New Long March."

On the last night on the train, however, all the unpleasant issues seemed to be forgotten. At the routine management meeting in the dining car, the organizers thanked the train attendants and obviously forgot the clogged toilets and no running water. They also thanked the Reclamation travel agency, not mentioning the quarrels and debates with them. Other people thanked the organizers for their "effective and hard work," forgetting the complaints they had angrily made just a couple of days ago. People filled their cups with alcohol and toasted each other. A train attendant even wrote a poem to praise the zhiqing group. Many people were singing revolutionary songs from the Mao years to emphasize the solidarity among the zhiqing. Zeng got excited and claimed in a loud voice that this trip was an "extremely successful one." Yet, I saw some Black Soil members pull a wry face and even laugh out loud. Soon thereafter, the eleven-day trip ended when the train reached Harbin.

Booming Inside, Fading Outside

Underneath the enthusiasm and even frivolity in the zhiqing's frequent activities, there is an eager cry for recognition: Never forget us! In Bourdieu's terms, it is a pursuit of the generation's collective symbolic capital. Such symbolic capital may function as belated compensation for their trauma, their struggles, and the twists and turns in their life courses.

Sometimes, however, the pitch of this cry for recognition gets higher than acceptable. For example, many self-congratulating posts are widely shared by the zhiqing on WeChat, and their titles well represent their content: "The Zhiqing Generation Is the Strongest Generation in the World!"; "The Most Diligent Generation Is Now Aging!" The zhiqing activities also adopt various impressive names. "Symposium" is a quite modest name, and "summits" are ubiquitous. "National festival" is a normal name for a tourism trip, while "global zhiqing conference" is not uncommon. Commercial interests also drive some zhiqing to cross the fine line between confirmation of generational identity and inflation of self-importance. Companies involved in organizing the events use magnificent names to make the zhiqing feel good in order to sell their products, from retirement condos to low-cost tourism packages.

This booming inside the field of the zhiqing, however, is in stark contrast to a lack of attention to this generation outside their comfort zone. In public perceptions, as previous chapters have shown, the image of this generation has never been as heroic as they themselves imagine. Their performances can hardly impress the outside public. Their songs and dances are mostly from the 1950s and 1960s, with a few relatively new ones from the 1980s. Even the zhiqing themselves, who wax nostalgic about the songs they grew up with, sometimes lament that the performances are repetitive, amateurish, and uncreative. A person who attends a few such performances would see the same songs, same dances, same model Peking Operas, same qipao shows, even by the same groups of people. The audiences applaud politely, cheer lukewarmly, and can't wait for their favorite after-program part when anyone can jump onto the stage to dance and sing.

The repetitive content of their performances reinforces their public image as "Chairman Mao's children" who still seem to hold dear the red songs and dances. This image is certainly a misconception. In fact, as this book has shown, only a small proportion of this generation are Maoist diehards. Many of them, nevertheless, are caught in a dilemma of aesthetics and politics. They do not long to return to the Mao years, but they have no alternatives to express their nostalgia for their youth. The "red songs" with varying degrees of "redness" are the ones they grew up with.

A few performance organizers told me that they carefully choose those songs with ethnic melodies and some red but not Mao cult content to avoid the stereotype of Red Guards. In fact, songs like "Sailing the Seas Depends on the Helmsman" are only occasionally heard, and the most common songs are in the same vein as "Wusuli River." Nevertheless, for the younger generations who know relatively little about the nuances, all these songs are the same "old stuff."

The performances are mostly *by* the zhiqing, *of* the zhiqing, and *for* the zhiqing. In Bourdieu's terms, they are a form of "restricted cultural production" with performers and audiences being the same group of people (Bourdieu 1993). Various tourism trips based on those performances can hardly justify their prices, even if the prices are low. Take the Huxia trip as an example. For almost two full days, a participant is fully occupied with watching the zhiqing's amateurish performances and takes breaks only for meals. No sightseeing is arranged because the resort is so underdeveloped that much of the land is deserted. It is hard to expect someone from outside to pay 350 yuan for that, even if new forms of entertainment are often more expensive. In fact, in many activities, I was one of the few youngest, if not the youngest participant. Other younger outsiders were people with various commercial and professional interests, including travel agents, paid performers, sales representatives, and so on. They were more impatient than I was. A travel agent complained to me on the eleven-day "long march" trip that it was her worst experience ever. Another younger participant on the same trip, who accompanied her elderly teacher, bluntly said: "If not for my teacher, I would never travel with those old people!"

Not only performances but also other cultural objects produced and disseminated in the field of the zhiqing follow this restricted production model and have limited outside influence. A popular genre is personal memoirs. Numerous zhiqing write their memoirs in various forms: individual and collective ones, as posts on blogs and social media, self-published books without ISBNs, self-published books with purchased ISBNs,[3] and, in rare cases, officially published with legitimate presses. During my fieldwork, I received many of those individual memoirs. Some authors asked me to help publish their manuscripts. I did try to contact a few editors, but they unanimously said "no" because the topic remains politically sensitive and, more importantly, because there is no

---

[3] The ISBNs of the self-published books are purchased from either publishers or agents, but the publishers usually do not exert the same level of control over the publishing process as with books in their normal lines. The books are theoretically legitimate and can be sold in the marketplace.

market for this kind of book. In most cases, the authors pay a significant amount of money (20,000 to 40,000 yuan) to get their books published. They themselves are responsible for marketing and selling their books. One of the zhiqing I interviewed took years to write an autobiographical novel made up of three volumes as well as two other books that compile historical materials, with purchased ISBNs. As a result, he ran into financial trouble, given that he does not have good pensions and still shares a two-bedroom condo with his married son. In many activities that I attended in the five-year period, I saw him setting up a table and selling his books for 100 yuan a set. Most authors do not even try to sell their books, simply giving them away to their fellow zhiqing. No one knows for sure how many such zhiqing memoirs have been published. Many of them have obvious value for historical research, but, as cultural objects, most memoirs never go beyond the zhiqing circle.

The luckiest memoirs receive the endorsement and financial support of the local governments in their sent-down places. The cost of this endorsement, however, is censorship or self-censorship. I attended an editorial committee meeting for such a collection of memoirs by Shanghai zhiqing who went to a Division of the Xinjiang Corps. The Division leadership supported this project, and the editorial committee signed a contract with a local press in Xinjiang to publish the book. The editors emphasized that the memoirs must be filled with "positive energy" (*zhengnengliang*) to represent the spirit of the zhiqing and the Corps. Some "gray" parts of the memoirs, including representations of the harsh reality of the zhiqing life, the editors said, must be deleted or altered.

Occasionally, a cultural product – a movie or a TV series – related to zhiqing but produced by outsiders ignites exuberance within the zhiqing field, since the product signifies outside recognition. Unfortunately, such products rarely attract much outside attention. Once there was a young movie director, Mr. Lu, who became interested in the topic of the zhiqing. He managed to find investment and used his own money to produce a movie about zhiqing life. The movie did not even make it to theaters due to the lack of a market for it. Mr. Lu almost went into bankruptcy. Some zhiqing in Shanghai heard about this and decided to save Mr. Lu's film because "it is about us." Different groups and associations worked together to persuade a theater to show the film and mobilized their members to buy tickets. Nevertheless, the revenues from this mass mobilization could only cover a fraction of the investment. During the screening in Shanghai, Mr. Lu could not even afford to stay in a hotel but had to sleep on a "bed" made up of two chairs in Black Soil's office. Leaders of the groups and associations took turns to treat Lu to dinner, but that was basically all they could do for this broke director.

Some intellectuals see similar things in public memory. Yang Jian, a zhiqing-turned literary scholar, wrote in his book that ordinary zhiqing were excited about even slight public attention and, meanwhile, upset by criticism. For example, a female zhiqing responded to criticism about a TV program about zhiqing: "Don't say that! If this was wrong, then what is left for us?" (Yang 2002, 418). Nevertheless, most cultural products about zhiqing do not even draw outside criticisms. The only recent cultural product with some outside viewership is *Zhiqing*, a TV series, which, written by Liang Xiaosheng, was widely regarded as a tribute to President Xi and thus received investment from state-owned companies.

The scant outside attention should not be explained by a lack of effort on the zhiqing's end. The zhiqing groups are among the most active memory entrepreneurs in China today, and the memory field for zhiqing the most developed. For example, in addition to their active work in promoting their memory through meetings, performances, memoirs, and films, the Research Association also regularly distributes grants to PhD students and junior scholars to support projects on zhiqing. The Association also co-sponsors academic conferences and mobilizes zhiqing volunteers to participate in research projects about zhiqing. On some occasions, such as Director Lu's film promotion, different groups put aside their rivalries and work together. Moreover, without their donation, mobilization, and volunteering, there would not be zhiqing museums and memorials.

The limited outside influence has to do with its dominant pattern of "people but not the event." The more they emphasize the people – themselves – but not the event, the less likely they are to be accepted by the outside public, who would think they are narcissistic, anachronistic, and evading their responsibility for the political upheavals in the Mao years. The zhiqing, even if they disagree with this image, have very few cultural and aesthetic options to justify themselves. Their repertoire is mainly inherited from the rhetorical and artistic styles in the Mao years, which seem outdated and overpoliticized. While they are tired of being attached to the troubled identity of Red Guards and try to simply present nothing else but their "youth," the outside audience does not really care about their "youth" – "Who doesn't have youth?" – but mostly focuses on their idiosyncrasy as being "Chairman Mao's children" and reattaches them to the Red Guard and the Cultural Revolution. Thus, no matter how hard they try, they are still held hostage by their history.

Another paradox is that, when the zhiqing endeavor to show their worthiness, they consciously and unconsciously defend their "ownership" of their history and memory. They patrol the boundaries demarcated by experience and age, two factors related to temporality rather than cultural or economic capital. Their cry for recognition – "never forget us" – is often mixed with a less loud but much deeper voice that "only we can write our own history." Such defensive reactions may discourage outside interest.

This paradox is manifested in their interactions with academics, who probably have the most serious interests in their history. Overall, university-based historians in Shanghai have good relations with the Association. The historians rely on the Association's official connections with provincial archives to acquire the otherwise inaccessible materials. The historians also need the Association members' volunteer labor to read and record information from the corpus of local gazetteers and archives, a project that could otherwise cost much more money and human labor. This mass mobilization of non-academic labor for an academic purpose somehow resembles the strategy of the History Workshop Movement, which was designed to blur the boundary between academia and the public by mobilizing workers to conduct oral history interviews (Samuel 1981).

The difference, however, is that Association members have higher class positions than the workers in the History Workshop Movement. They are better educated; their lives are comfortable enough for them to regularly attend "cultural activities," such as public lectures, exhibits, symposiums, and so on. On those occasions, they participate in Q&A sessions, take pictures with famous writers and professors, and write about the activities on their WeChat. Some of them have college degrees but lack basic training in history and social science. Nevertheless, a college degree, regardless of major, is generally considered as a high cultural capital in *this* generation and, thus, gives them confidence in participating in highly specialized topics. This confidence in their cultural capital is combined with their sense of authority based on their experience of simply being zhiqing. "With experience," many claim, "I think I have the authority to speak [*fayanquan*]."

This interesting combination of cultural capital and experiential authority fully manifests itself in their interactions with young scholars working on zhiqing-related topics. The zhiqing believe that the young scholars lack experiential authority and have less authority for serious discussions, despite the younger scholars' higher cultural capital incarnated in their degrees and publications. Some zhiqing ask questions at conferences and write lengthy posts on WeChat to challenge young scholars' work. Such questions and posts usually end with paternalistic, condescending remarks that urge the young scholars to pay attention to their lived experience instead of just "numbers," which they believe are the only things the young scholars care about. The young scholars often generously smile and politely insist on the scholarly, systematic nature of their research, which goes beyond personal experience. The zhiqing fire back and question: "Without personal experience, how do you know what was going on then? By guesses?" That is usually the end of the conversation, since the scholars are not interested in giving a whole lecture on methodology.

In contrast, the zhiqing show much more respect for those professors who are former zhiqing, in other words, people with higher cultural capital and higher experiential authority. I have not seen anyone use harsh words to challenge those senior zhiqing-turned-professors as they often do to younger scholars. Nevertheless, those senior zhiqing-turned-academics try to distance themselves from the zhiqing field to avoid troubles and engage themselves in the dialogs only if necessary. Once a senior history professor openly defended his students when they were grilled by the zhiqing audience: "If people without personal experience of an event cannot research the event, then most of us [historians], especially those who study the Qing or Ming, would lose our jobs! Historical research is not like writing memoirs but follows a certain methodology that systematically examines many personal experiences as a whole!" No one challenged him. But the zhiqing audience later stood up to cite their own personal experiences to question younger scholars' research, in addition to their murmuring to express their disagreements even when the scholars were presenting: "No, this was not what happened in my county!" As on other occasions, the zhiqing kept throwing down the gauntlets, but the young historians did not bother to pick them up.

Conclusion

In Seattle in 2015, President Xi Jinping delivered a speech to an American audience, recounting the poverty he witnessed in Liangjiahe, the village he was sent down to, and his effort in leading the villagers to improve their living conditions. His dream, he said, was that the villagers "could eat meat regularly." Now, Xi said, Liangjiahe had become a miniature of China's great development in the past thirty years: the villagers had healthcare, internet connectivity, houses, and other modern conveniences (Xi 2015). An impressive story indeed. It merged the leader's personal experience with the place he labored in, and, ultimately, the nation's fate. It demonstrated the leader's confidence in leading the country from its low point decades ago to its prosperity in the present and future – a typical "China dream." More specifically, his personal experience was incorporated into the cultural justification of his signature poverty reduction plan: the leader knew poverty by living in it in his formative years and was determined to reduce such pain for the Chinese people.

Xi's life story should sound familiar to the readers who have read this far. Like many life stories presented in this book, his story consists of two components: a narrative about his *personal experience* and *historical evaluation* of the send-down program, more precisely, without explicit evaluation of the program. This pattern is not randomly chosen. In 1999, when Xi was the vice-Party secretary of Fujian Province, he wrote an inscription: "The vast universe will never be forgotten in all my life!" (*guangkuo tiandi, zhongshen nanwang*). The inscription changes Mao's original directive ("The zhiqing should go to the vast universe of the countryside, where they can make a huge difference!") to a more politically neutral but personally meaningful phrase. It does not say anything about the program (Zhang 2014). In sum, Xi's life story is a variation of the "people but not the event" pattern, with a change from the "people" – the whole generation – to one man.

Hidden beneath his silence about the program, however, is an implicitly, ambiguously positive view of the Mao era. In today's China, explicitly positive views about the traumatic events in the Mao era like the Cultural Revolution and the send-down program are not politically feasible for a leader. Leaders before Xi openly condemned the Cultural Revolution. Against this background, Xi's reluctance to criticize the political tumults of the Mao years is salient. In his famous speech of 2013, Xi emphasized it is wrong to "use the historical period after the [start of] the reform and opening-up policy to censure the period before the reform and opening-up policy" or to "use the historical period before the [start of] the reform and opening-up policy to censure the period after the reform and opening-up policy" (Li 2013). This seemingly symmetrical statement tries to hide but in consequence reveals its real emphasis in the first part: what the Party did in the Mao years was not all wrong. On many other occasions, he emphasizes the essence of the Maoist ideology, for example, "plain life and hard work" and "integrating with the ordinary people."

Foreign media tend to interpret the apotheosis of Xi in official narratives as a personality cult and compare Xi to Mao. But Xi is not Mao. He is one of "Chairman Mao's children." Xi instantiates what I call "aspirants." Due to the political problems with their families, they want to win respect from society and the Party by being more revolutionary than the revolutionary. Their pain from humiliation and persecution is suppressed – or at least significantly alleviated – by the rewards they received in the state system. No evidence shows that Xi ever experienced a habitus change in college or after the Cultural Revolution. Instead, right after he graduated from Tsinghua, he entered the military, a place least conducive to political awakening. Like other aspirants with similar life trajectories, Xi's zhiqing narrative is filled with confirmation of personal success as well as an ambiguous but positive view of the Maoist past, veiled by a seemingly neutral silence about the event.

The narrative of Xi's zhiqing years is not just his personal life story but also a result of the official cultural production. It appears in various forms of memory: news reports, books, sacred sites, and the like. Numerous Communist Party organizations have taken a "red" learning/sightseeing journey that includes Liangjiahe, the new Mecca, and Yan'an, the old Mecca, only tens of miles away. Xi's image – young, handsome, unusually sophisticated for his age – is detached from the painful history, which is vaguely presented or not presented at all. For the state's propaganda machine, Xi's life experience of fighting uphill battles and venturing to impoverished areas is an excellent story to use to educate a new generation of youths – as long as the event part of this story is not more complicated than it should be.

One thing, however, is completely absent from this official memory: many zhiqing's ongoing afflictions due to the cumulative effects of being sent down. When Xi became the highest leader, some of the protesting zhiqing hoped that Xi's coming to power would generate more attention to their troubles. This proved wishful thinking. Crackdowns continue; some problems remain unsolved. The zhiqing standing outside the Labor Bureau did not get any response from their fellow zhiqing residing inside Zhongnanhai, the Party Central's compound. One man's glory overshadows his fellow zhiqing's suffering.

Memories of the Zhiqing Generation and the Red Legacy in China

Xi's story is just one among many that this book tells. I set out to achieve three goals in this book: one empirical, to understand memories of the zhiqing generation; another theoretical, to contribute to the theoretical literature on generation and memory; and the other ethical, to contemplate some ethical–political issues of memory. Here I recapitulate my major arguments. Let me start with the first one: What does this book tell us about the memory of the zhiqing generation as a part of China's "red legacy"?

Memories start with individuals. Individual biography and history meet at autobiographical memory. Each life history of the zhiqing has two components: their views of their *personal experience* and their *historical evaluations* of the send-down program and related events. Each of the two components varies along class lines, including "class in the present" and "class in the past." The "class in the present" – the zhiqing's present class positions, measured by their economic, cultural, and social capital – shapes their memory of their *personal experience*. The higher the class position, the more likely it is that a zhiqing holds a positive view of his or her personal experience in the sent-down years and its impacts on their later life. Autobiographical memory, like Bourdieu's taste, expresses and justifies their present class positions.

Their "class in the past," including their chushen in the Mao years and their corresponding political habitus, shapes their *historical evaluations* of the program. In general, those with habitus based on "red" chushen in the Mao years are more likely to have positive evaluations of the send-down program and other Mao government policies and campaigns than those with habitus based on "black" or middle chushen. The mechanisms beneath this correlation have both realist and constructivist aspects. People with different habitus experienced the send-down program differently: for example, the faithful red viewed it as a revolutionary pilgrimage, whereas the withdrawers stayed away from political trouble and were reluctant to go down. The different experiences became the foundation of today's memory. The constructivist aspect of this mechanism is that their different habitus remains robust even today and still shapes their view of the send-down program. Their habitus may also change as a response to the dramatic social transformation in China from the Mao years to the reform period and leads to more negative historical evaluations. The aspirants are most likely to change their habitus when their active political performance was not rewarded, or when they experienced a political awakening and their pain caused by their chushen was reactivated. But those aspirants whose habitus remains unchanged – such as President Xi – tend to have positive evaluations of the send-down program because they actively internalized the official ideology in the Mao years to prove they were also revolutionary.

The literary memory emerged and boomed as a major form of public memory in the late 1970s and throughout the 1980s. The dominant pattern of memory in the literary works was "good people but the bad event!": a generally negative representation of the program accompanies a positive image of the zhiqing as heroes, strivers, and at least respectable victims. This pattern reflected this generation's desire to explain their suffering and difficulties and longing for public recognition when the society viewed the zhiqing returnees as losers. Other minor patterns also exist, for example, Liang Xiaosheng's passionate portrayals of the idealistic youths and ambiguously positive attitude toward the program. The commonality and differences in their literary memories can be explained by the types of habitus the writers have.

This general pattern of "good people but the bad event" also resulted from the dynamics in the literary field and its interactions with the fields of power and economy in the late 1970s and early 1980s. The state wanted to use literature to expose the past trauma to legitimize its current reform policies. Writers, readers, and even cultural administrators wanted to stay away from the propaganda-cum-literature in the Cultural Revolution. This trend led to an overall criticism of the program as well as the Cultural Revolution. Moreover, the hunger for literary works created unprecedented demands for new works, and the young, amateur zhiqing writers, assisted by the patronage of the older writers who shared with them suffering and trauma, quickly emerged on the literary scene. Nevertheless, the reception of the literary works was divided: while the elite critics found fault with the works' limited value and the zhiqing's self-importance, ordinary members of the generation accepted and even reproduced the intended meanings of confirming their self-importance despite their varying views of the event.

Since the 1990s, however, the prevalent pattern of public memory changed to that of "people but not the event," in which the negative evaluation of the program – the "bad event" part of the previous patter – was muted. The pattern highlights the zhiqing's youthful passion, contributions, and positive qualities but avoids an explicit evaluation of the send-down program. This pattern was presented in exhibits and museums beginning in the late 1980s and the early 1990s. The major memory entrepreneurs were a group of zhiqing elites who were eager to confirm their personal success and express their nostalgia. The "people but not the event" pattern, with its apolitical features, served as the lowest common denominator of various views of the past, accepted by memory entrepreneurs, local officials, and corporations involved in the production of the museums and exhibits. It was intended to decouple the zhiqing, with their positive qualities, from the controversy and political sensitivity of the event.

This pattern also became the most common group memory in the commemorative activities, whereas other patterns, such as Maoist nostalgia and oppositional memory, existed in only very few groups. This pattern emerged from and was reproduced in interactions within the groups. Highlighting themselves, pursuing happiness in the present, without talking about the thorny past was the best possible way to avoid debates and keep alive a communal life. This pattern was even more useful for different groups and individuals to participate in intergroup activities, in which their diverse views are always in conflict with the need for solidarity and happiness.

This pattern, however, led to paradoxical outcomes. In the intergroup activities, tensions and conflicts broke out and revealed the fault lines of class disparity and ideological differences. Outsiders often view their emphasis on themselves as narcissism and their silence on the event as a positive evaluation of the send-down program and the Cultural Revolution. Their claim to own their history alienates outsiders interested in understanding their past. Their loud voices in all the frequent, exuberant activities fail to strike a meaningful chord with the rest of the society. Two voices are missing from this chorus of self-importance: the voice of those zhiqing who still suffer from the detrimental impacts of the program, and the zhiqing's self-reflection on their moral–political responsibility for the public upheavals of the Mao years.

All these complexities of memory revolve around the intersections between personal biography and history (Mills 1959), including the tension between this generation's effort of confirming their worthiness and their difficulty in evaluating the controversial program that shaped their youth, the entanglement between the imprints from their coming-of-age experience in the Mao years and the dramatic social changes in the post-Mao years, the conflict between their collective identity as a generation and the wide disparity in their class positions within the generation. The tension, entanglement, and conflict can be explained by a few important factors and their interactions at three different levels (individual, group/community, and public): class, habitus, field, and group dynamics.

With these empirical findings, this book joins the dialog about one of the central topics in the literature on the "red legacy": How do people in the post-Mao era remember both their personal experience and their collective past in the Mao years? I contribute to our understanding of this topic by offering some new things.

First, I study memories of the zhiqing generation, one of the most important, long-lasting memory phenomena in contemporary China, which, however, has been understudied. Drawing on mountains of data collected and analyzed through multiple methods, I present a subtle, rich picture of how this generation takes pains to come to terms with their difficult past in various ways, through different forms, and in several historical periods.

Second, this book shows the dramatic variations and equally dramatic commonality in the memory and mentality of this generation of "Chairman Mao's children." The metaphor of "Mao's children" has its purpose. Like children in a family, they share some common traits but differ from each other. For all of them, the influence of their parents is lifelong and indelible. Bourdieu's habitus is a concept to theorize such influence. But their habitus is neither homogeneous nor static. Rather, their habitus formed in their various responses to the political class structure, changed at important historical moments, and varied among people who have different life courses and current class positions. Conversely, these variations are significantly reduced when autobiographical memories are expressed in public and group memories. Many memories have been marginalized, and the pattern of "people but not the event" becomes dominant not only in the official discourses but also in popular memories in exhibits, museums, and commemorative activities.

In presenting and analyzing the commonality and differences, this book draws inspirations from pioneering studies like Anita Chan's *Children of Mao: Personality Development and Political Activism in the Red Guard Generation* (1985) and Guobin Yang's *The Red Guard Generation and Political Activism in China* (2016). Even this book's title resembles Chan's. My study enjoys the privilege of time and access that these studies could not have: for example, Chan's research was conducted in the 1970s with zhiqing émigrés to Hong Kong before China opened up.

At that time, much of their memory had yet to unfold and develop. Thus, my book takes a step forward. Moreover, as both books' titles suggest, their analyses focus on "activists" and choose the "Red Guard" generation as those young people's generation identity. In contrast, my analysis expands the scope to include those less politically active members of this generation in order to present more diversity in this generation. For this purpose, the concept of "zhiqing" is a better fit than the "Red Guards." "Zhiqing" is also the identity label this generation chooses to call themselves so that they can distance themselves from the stigmatized "Red Guards." The label itself tells much about their memory and mindset.

Third, my analysis demonstrates the importance of class in explaining this generation's memory. In the context of contemporary China, "class" has deep and rich historical and political implications. It changed from a political categorization system in the Mao years to the present stratification concept primarily based on socioeconomic status. The zhiqing generation was caught between the past and the present, the new and old class systems. When they view their personal past, they tend to use today's rules of winning and losing and evaluate the past through their class positions today. When they evaluate the send-down program and the Cultural Revolution, their views are still shaped by their political class–based habitus formed in the Mao years. This paradox shows both how much Chinese society has changed from the Mao years to the present and how much the people who have lived through both eras have *not* changed.

Moreover, class tells us what the phrase "Chairman Mao's children" exactly means. Mao once asserted in his "On Practice": "In class society everyone lives as a member of a particular class, and every kind of thinking, without exception, is stamped with the brand of a class" (Mao 1965: 296). This generic statement, however, was enacted in various political practices and policies that altered and ruined millions of people's lives. My analysis here also tries to understand what this "stamp of class" (*jieji laoyin*) is and how it works: It is the class-based habitus the zhiqing generation formed in their political class positions under Mao and that it still matters today in shaping their memory and views. The caste-like political class system based on chushen was probably just one brief episode in the long history of Chinese society, but its unusual rigidity forged particularly robust habitus of a whole generation. This politically stratified habitus is the "stamp," or the "red legacy," those Chairman Mao's children carried over from the Mao era. It lasted, changed, and continues to influence their mindset and dispositions today.

Memory and Generation: Class, Group, and Field

The second goal of this book is to understand generation and memory and their implications *beyond* the zhiqing generation and China. The book adds several new, significant points to the sociological literature on this topic.

First, I go beyond the cognitive concept of "generational memory," which is narrowly defined and operationalized as the naming of events by individuals. I conceptualize memory as mnemonic practices in which members of a generation understand and reproduce meanings of their personal past and their generational experience. I identify two meaningful components of generational memory: *personal experience* and *historical evaluation*. The whole book is an effort to identify, describe, and explain the various patterns of the two components and their connections in different forms of memory. This reconceptualization also involves an explicit distinction among three different levels of "memory": individual, group/community, and public. While the dominant approach focuses on individual memory, I include all three in this book. This distinction avoids unnecessary confusion and debate about the term "memory" and facilitates an examination of qualitatively different properties of culture and social processes at different levels (Jepperson and Swidler 1994).

Second, while most existing studies are focused on *inter*-generational differences, I emphasize *intra*-generational differences of memory, including various patterns of meaning in different forms of memory at different levels. It is these intragenerational variations that make the generational memory a colorful, "high-definition" image rather than a black-and-white, low-resolution one.

Third, I do not stop at thick descriptions of the variations, a common analytical strategy in the field of the sociology of memory. Instead, I venture into the more complicated realm of explanation. The major explanatory factors I rely on are class, group dynamics, and field. While field is commonly used in studies of collective memory (Steidl 2013), class and group are less developed "independent variables" and, thus, may suggest new theoretical approaches for future research on memory.

Along this line, a major contribution of this book is to bring "class" back into the field of collective memory. The underdevelopment of class in the sociology of memory is surprising and perplexing because class is one of the essential concepts in sociology. Even in the field of memory studies, class appeared quite early. Class is the theme of the longest chapter of Maurice Halbwachs's classic *The Social Frameworks for Memory* (Halbwachs 1992), but it has been almost "forgotten." It is not in the index in several popular introductions to collective memory (Misztal 2003; Erll 2011; Olick, Vinitzky-Seroussi, and Levy 2011). Even when class is sporadically studied, the focus is primarily on memory's function in forging class identity in political activism and processes (Samuel 1981; Bauman 1982; Hobsbawm 1983; Lee 2000).

The findings in this study reconnect with Halbwachs's theoretical idea of class by drawing on Bourdieu's theory of class, including class positions and habitus. This theorization happens at different levels. In autobiographical memories at the individual level, I argue that class position shapes one's view of one's personal past and that habitus shapes one's evaluation of a historical event. At the group level, members of a generation form different groups, often along class lines, and the interactions among the groups reveal the fault lines of classes. At the public level, the key memory of entrepreneurs' class positions and habitus shapes what memories they want to present in cultural objects.

"Group," another essential concept in sociology, also remains underdeveloped in the sociology of memory. I contend that the group perspective can provide new insights into generation and memory. When members of a generation organize themselves into groups, they not only want to share their memories of their generational and personal experience but also want to keep themselves together as a group to have communal life. This dual task is especially difficult for members with diverse views of a controversial event. Consequently, "group memory" might be different from individuals' autobiographical memories because group memory emerges from interactions, including conflicts and negotiations.

Both class and group are what Mannheim terms "generation units," in which members develop distinctive *"formative tendencies and fundamental integrative attitudes*, thus identifying ourselves [themselves] with a set of collective strivings" (Mannheim 1952 [1923], 305; emphasis added). Future research may go beyond the topic of generation and memory and explore class and group in other mnemonic practices. There is a high possibility of connecting the sociology of memory to the vast literature of stratification and culture (Lizardo 2010). A cultural sociologist may have already sensed the affinity between my analysis of autobiographical memories and Michele Lamont's "symbolic boundary" theory: memory functions as the way in which people draw boundaries between themselves and others with different class positions (Lamont 1992). Group memory also paves the way for a systematic agenda of an interactionist approach to the sociology of memory, which has emerged in some of Gary Alan Fine's works on memory entrepreneurs (Fine 2001). When it is fully developed, this approach will provide a "third approach" in addition to the dichotomy between individual and "collective" memory (Olick 1999).

"People But Not the Event": The Politics and Ethics of Remembering

The analysis in this book inevitably addresses normative questions about the ethics of memory, the third goal of this book. The zhiqing's generational memory at the group and public levels gradually converges in the pattern "people but not the event." If history is a drama, this pattern casts a positive but artificial spotlight on the participants, dims the rest of the stage, and hides the controversial event in the dark. It makes the participants feel good, appreciated, and respected. These feelings are much needed, especially when the participants have suffered and are still suffering from the detrimental effects of the event.

The pattern is not idiosyncratic. It appears in other contexts where a group of people comes to terms with a controversial, detrimental event in which they were the participants. The Vietnam Veterans Memorial followed this pattern, at least as memory entrepreneurs like Jan Scruggs and designer Maya Ying Lin intended: remembering the individuals but not talking about the event (Wagner-Pacifici and Schwartz 1991; Sturken 1997). The minimalist design of the Memorial – with only names but no description of the war – was intended to decouple the veterans from the war. This decoupling was resisted by those veterans who needed a lofty design to confirm their spirit and contributions, and the state also sided with them for the ideological purpose of promoting patriotism. The resistance finally led to the addition of a national flag and a realist statue of three soldiers.

Nevertheless, if "generation" in public discourses is a socially constructed identity rather than a naturalistic concept like age cohort, then in the process of constructing a "generation," some parts of the infinite past and some people of this generation are inevitably downplayed, altered, and excluded to make the identity coherent, clean, and even glorious.

This pattern of "people but not the event" tends to inflate the positive qualities of the "people." "Remembering the people" in this pattern often means "remembering our own." "Remembering our own" often means remembering "our good side" and forgetting our bad side, which is often tied to the controversial aspect of the event (Nguyen 2016). The individuals are detached from the event to avoid ethical debates about whether the "good" individuals should shoulder at least partial responsibility for the "bad" event, such as the veterans' moral responsibility for the atrocities in the Vietnam War and the zhiqing's responsibility for the violence in the Cultural Revolution. Certainly, not all veterans or zhiqing were involved in the atrocities, but many *were*. The prevalence of this memory pattern suppresses the reasonable voices that demand at least some members of the generation to take stock of their actions in those political upheavals.

Moreover, the "people" in this pattern do not include those who still suffer the most from the aftermath. Their stories were represented in novels in the 1980s, even in idealist Liang Xiaosheng's works, but they gradually faded away, if not completely disappeared, from exhibits, museums, and group memories. Protesting groups were marginalized. The emphasis on "people" also tends to forget the zhiqing's "others," particularly those peasants in their send-down places who also bore the consequences of the failure of this program. This is a blind spot in almost all memories. Some stories of "remembering our own" do show "our bad side," but the bad side is still "*our* bad side"; the focus is still on "us" instead of "others" (Nguyen 2016).

Class distinctions are self-evident here: people with lower class positions are silenced, while winners appear in the exhibits' panels. If memory is a dialog between personal biography and history, this pattern gradually becomes a monolog. It is for only some members of the generation, those who do not have to stand outside a government bureau to petition and who are cocooned in their privileged positions in today's social hierarchy. For them, past suffering was just an impressive rags-to-riches life story they told in their WeChat posts, over dinners in upscale restaurants, and in their motivational speeches delivered to the younger generations. People in the middle feel proud of being in the same generation as the winners, and their self-significance gets inflated in those stories. Even the zhiqing with the lowest class positions still had some privileges that the peasants did not have in the Mao years, for example, the minimum education, which enabled their expressions in the public discourses. The most voiceless people from the Mao era are those who are not literate enough to talk about their suffering. The peasants' scars did not even make it to the "scar literature." Memory is as unequal as other things in society. Or, put in a more cynical way: some suffering is more equal than others.

This inequality is not only social but also political. At the top of the social hierarchy within the generation is one man. At the top of the generation's memory is also this one man's seven years as a zhiqing. Below him, the powerful and the successful in this generation use the memory to construct their uplifting, ascending life stories for the purposes of self-congratulation and political propaganda. The state is happy to see this pursuit of happiness and self-confirmation of achievements. It suppresses harsh criticism, dilutes serious self-reflection, and silences those who are still held hostage by their past.

All these political–ethical problems of memory are certainly not what Mills terms "personal troubles" pertaining to only individuals' characters and local milieus. Rather, they are "public issues," which have to do with larger political, cultural, and social structures (Mills 1959, 8). When China bid farewell to the Mao years in the late 1970s and early 1980s, there was no complete regime transition. A new regime was salvaged from the past catastrophes and only attempted to correct some of the wrongs. Serious reflections on past traumas are allowed only when they can help the new regime's legitimacy. Discussions of past events are suppressed if the events do not fit into the Party–state's official narratives.

Perhaps the best way for many who experienced the event and many who want to use their memory for various purposes is to, as the Dafeng Museum administrator says, "survive on the surface" instead of digging deep. The message, stated or tacit, is clear enough: focus on the present; be happy together; remember our own, of course, remember our good side; keep silent on the troublesome historical issues. This propensity to confirm themselves, reassure happiness, and forget the past blocks more reflexive communications. Critics and self-critics stay away from the booming zhiqing memory; only a few zhiqing-turned-intellectuals occasionally bother to engage themselves in brief public debates over the zhiqing's generational memory.

The result is a "covert silence": rather than a mere absence of sound, the silence on others' suffering and lack of self-reflection is covered and veiled by much mnemonic talk and representation (Vinitzky-Seroussi and Teeger 2010). The zhiqing's vibrant, lasting memories mute some painful ethical and political questions. This silence is unequal; this inequality is political. To study this cacophonous, deafening silence, one needs, as the great Chinese writer Lu Xun once said, to "listen to thunder in silence." I hope this book has accomplished this goal.

Appendix Methods and Data

Research Process and Theorizing

Pilot Research Stage (2007–2012)

At the pilot stage of this project (2007–2012), my collaborators (Dong Guoli and Ren Jiping) and I conducted eighteen unstructured, exploratory interviews with various kinds of zhiqing, attended a few zhiqing reunion activities, and read scholarly works, memoirs, and novels. Only five of the exploratory interviews, which were conducted at the later phase and more systematically designed, are included in the final analysis presented in this book. Four of the five interviews were conducted by Ren Jiping, under my supervision, and I conducted the other one by myself. The interviewees were recruited through snowball sampling.

My primary site was Shanghai, not just because of convenience and access, but also because Shanghai was the largest source city for cross-regional send-down (719,900, 50.5 percent), i.e., the movement from Shanghai to other places, more than half of the whole nation and more than Beijing and Tianjin – second and third largest – combined (523,600) (Gu 2009a, 261–62). Shanghai was also the city with the most vibrant memory field for zhiqing.

At this stage, I was struck by the diversity of the zhiqing's memory because it contradicted my assumption of the commonality within the generation and differences between generations. To identify the patterns of variations and find possible explanations, I came up with an "educated guess," primarily inspired by the "lay interpretations" of my interviewees. They told stories revolving around their past and present class positions and opportunities to achieve mobility, such as urban jobs, recommendations for college, Party membership, career success or failure, "going up" or "going down" in life trajectory, and so on. Moreover, they tended to evaluate their personal experience in the countryside by making a causal link between past experience and present class positions. This preliminary finding may sound commonsensical but was theoretically surprising

241

because class has been largely "forgotten" in the field of collective memory. To address this significant gap, I officially started this project.

Second Stage (2013–2017)

In the second stage, I made three methodological moves. First, I began to use the theorizing/abductive analysis in all three levels of study and found it very fruitful (Swedberg 2012, 2014; Tavory and Timmermans 2014). The theorizing agenda emphasizes discovery and uses heuristics to construct new theories. Thus, it provided me with methodological and analytical tools to develop new ideas in a constant dialog between data and theoretical hypotheses.

Second, I decided to use "sequential interviewing" as the major method of selecting interviewees (Small 2009). In this method, each interview is seen as a case instead of a response in a sample. Through "literal replication" and "theoretical replication," mechanisms are identified and tested. I also found the sequential interviewing compatible with abductive logic, although neither Small nor Swedberg has noticed their affinity. They both emphasize discovery, generating new theories, and traveling back and forth between theory and data. This combination of sequential interviewing and theorizing proved effective in refining the otherwise linear hypothesis of class and memory, generating new theory, and explaining contradictions and exceptions.

The sequential interviewing generated new findings that complicated my previous linear thinking of class and memory. I found that in each life story of a zhiqing, there are two intertwined but separate components: the story about his or her *personal experience* and *historical evaluation* of the send-down program. What I previously found was more about the correlation between class and memory of personal experience, but the correlation does not always correspond to the historical evaluation part of their life stories. I also found it difficult to conceptualize "class" in two eras – before and after 1978 – both of which this generation lived through. In the Mao years, class was very much a political concept in both ideology and practices. Their coming-of-age experience in the political class structure should matter to their memory if we followed Schuman's critical-years thesis. But the politics-based class is incompatible with the post-1978 class based on economic and cultural capitals. After comparing and testing different class theories (Wright 2005), I am convinced that a theoretical framework based on Pierre Bourdieu's theory of class can provide the best possible tool. Bourdieu's theory includes class positions and class-based habitus and, thus, enables a fine-grained description and a systematic explanation of the complex class-memory nexus in this case (see Chapters 1 and 2).

Third, I expanded the scope of research to three levels of memory: autobiographical memories through life history interviews, public memory through studying cultural objects, and group activities through participant observations. At the public and group/community levels, class and habitus remain important, especially in memory entrepreneurs' class and habitus, but they are not the only factors. They interact with several other key factors, such as cultural production, field, and group. This expansion also draws on Bourdieu's field theory and are supplemented by other socio-logical theories (Fine 2012). By the end of this stage, I had come up with explanations of most of the puzzles I discovered.

Final Stage (2017–2018)

The final stage of research (2017–2018) had much more focused goals: to test my findings in more interviews, ethnographic observations, and additional library research. I recruited interviewees through the network I had accumulated in my second stage and a WeChat public account. I conducted forty-eight life history interviews. I also did more participant observations, including the eleven-day train trip to Heilongjiang, which was tiring, eye-opening, and inspiring (Chapter 6). The findings were encouraging. In 2018, I concluded this project by conducting the last, long (four-hour) interview with a Xinjiang zhiqing protest leader.

Altogether I conducted 124 interviews, including 87 life history inter-views and 37 interviews for other purposes, such as with memory entre-preneurs involved in a variety of memory work, the Xinjiang protesters, and museum managers and curators. I also conducted 61 ethnographic observations of various activities, including performances, meetings, and trips. I collected countless unpublished personal and collective texts (unpublished memoirs and self-published magazines, for example), hun-dreds of media reports from the late 1970s until the present, archival materials in the Shanghai Municipal Archives, secondary sources, and primary images and videos.

Life History Interviews

Selecting Life History Interviews

I recruited interviewees mainly through snowball sampling or chain referral, with different key informants as entry points. The response rate was high (only five people I/my informants contacted said no). This was beyond my expectation because the rejection rate of my previous studies was around 10 percent. In selecting and analyzing interviewees, I used the "sequential interviewing" method (Small 2009). The sequential interviewing is compatible with the abductive logic, which emphasizes "a creative inferential process aimed at producing new hypotheses and theories based on surprising research evidence" by constantly traveling back and forth between theory and data (Swedberg 2014, 5; Tavory and Timmermans 2014). Each interview was analyzed in depth immediately after it was done and generated preliminary findings – for example, class. Then, I tried to find another case with identical features in all important dimensions ("literal replication") and another case differing in only one important dimension, for example, class position ("theoretical replication"). The two replications were designed to identify and test the factors and mechanisms in the preliminary findings by examining its variation along the dimensions selected. Once the major factors (class and habitus) are temporarily hypothesized, to do "literal replication" means to find a similar interviewee within each class–habitus category (for example, upper- and upper-middle class with faithful red habitus). To do "theoretical replication" means comparison across the categories. No prescribed number of interviews was given, but a rule of thumb is to have at least two interviewees in each class–habitus to satisfy the literal replication. In most cases, each category has much more than two. In this study, the minimum number of cases with two interviews in each subcategory should be twenty-four, but I ended up doing eighty-seven. The interviews stopped when the same pattern repeated itself to the point that no new findings were yielded.

The descriptive statistics of the interviewees are reported in Table A.1.

Conducting Life History Interviews

The execution of the life history interviews was semi-structured. I treated each interview as a "guided conversation," an interaction between the interviewer and interviewee for the research purpose. I had an interview outline with points and questions but adjusted it to suit conversation flow rather than mechanically following it and turning the interview into an elaborate version of a Q&A. I usually started an interview with a polite greeting, random chats, and, if I had not met the interviewee, a brief, informal introduction of myself and the research, to ease the interviewee's feelings of uncertainty and anxiety. I memorized the questions in advance. I did not have a sheet of paper in my hand so that the interviewee would feel it was more like a conversation than a formal interview. The wording of the questions was more improvised to suit the situation

Table A.1. *Descriptive statistics of interviewees*

	Category	Frequency	Percentage
Age (when sent down)	Mean=17.5, SD=1.56		
Sex	Male	63	72.4
	Female	24	27.6
Sent-down years	Before the Cultural Revolution	11	12.6
	1968–1976	76	87.4
Types of sent-down places	Production and Construction Corps (*bingtuan*)	27	31
	"Inserting to villages" (*chadui*)	53	60.9
	Farms	7	8.0
Personal experience	Positive	63	72.4
	Negative	24	27.6
Historical evaluations	Positive	15	17.2
	Positive with ambiguity	15	17.2
	Neutral/Indifferent	14	16.1
	Negative with ambiguity	5	5.7
	Negative	38	43.7
Class in the present (Continuous, 3–15)	Mean=9.77, SD=3.02		
Class in the present (Category)	Upper and upper-middle	35	40.2
	Middle	33	37.9
	Working and lower	19	21.8
Class in the past (chushen)	Good (red)	38	43.7
	Middle (ordinary)	16	18.4
	Bad (black)	33	37.9
Habitus	Faithful red	23	26.4
	Indifferent red	15	17.2
	Aspirant	27	31.0
	Withdrawer	22	25.3
Habitus change	Change	28	32.2
	No change	59	67.8

instead of following prescribed sentences. I usually let the conversation flow, practiced some control when it deviated from the theme, and, at the end of the interview, made sure all the questions were covered. After the interview, the interviewee answered a few basic questions about their demographics through a paper-copy or cellphone/online questionnaire. The interview sites were varied: the interviewees' offices, their homes, my offices in my hosting institutions, cafes, teahouses, parks, restaurants, and so on. All the interviews were recorded, with the permission of the interviewees.

This strategy of semi-structured interviews worked well. I could tell from the interviewees' body language and facial expressions that, soon after a moment of exploration, most of them talked in a comfortable and relaxed way without feeling that they were being interrogated. As the conversation progressed, most interviewees became surprisingly honest, sharing with me many things from their private life and candid opinions. For example, here's an incomplete list: the Red Guard faction conflicts, divorce, domestic violence, strained relationships, distrust of the government, illnesses, retirement salaries, explicit praise of Mao, denigration of Deng, their children's failure to find spouses, conflicts with their siblings, and, in one interview, the interviewee's unpassionate sex life with his wife. On quite a few occasions, the interviewees choked back tears and even cried. On other occasions, the interviewees were so excited that the interview ran over the scheduled time for a few hours. My only regret is having too limited space in this book to include so many rich, illuminating stories.

Every life history interview for this project consists of two major parts. The first part is mainly a retrospective account of one's life course, including one's experience before, during, and after the sent-down years. In the second part, the interviewee is asked to give his or her views and opinions about his or her sent-down experience and its aftermaths as well as his or her evaluations of the send-down program. In real-world practice, however, the distinction between the two parts is subtle. Sometimes how one talks about the zhiqing years constitutes a narrative pattern implying certain evaluative views of one's past. The main goal of the life history interview is to identify and explain such narrative patterns.

Measuring Class and Habitus

The concept of "class" used in this project includes "class in the past" and "class in the present."

The "class in the past" consists of two components: class position and habitus. Class position in the Mao years (mostly chushen) is relatively easy to operationalize: I rely on the interviewees' self-reports on their chushen. The political habitus includes two dimensions: disposition of action and schema of perception (Chapter 1). Table A.2 shows the operationalization of political habitus:

With this operationalization, I could categorize the interviewees' original habitus into four categories (see Chapter 1, Table 1.2).

I operationalize "class in the present" by drawing on Bourdieu's and other stratification scholars' theories and studies as well as historical specificities. "Class" here includes three forms of capital (economic capital, cultural capital, and social capital) with a scale of 1–5 for each (Erikson, Goldthorpe, and Portocarero 1979; Lin and Wu 2009; Bourdieu and Wacquant 2013). Using the three-capital model is better than a unitary class measurement because a single dimension overlooks

Table A.2. *Operationalization of habitus*

	Item	Conceptualization	Operationalization
A. **Dimensions of habitus** B. **Change and durability**	Disposition of action	Activeness in political participation	1. Before the Cultural Revolution: institutional roles 2. During the Cultural Revolution: the Red Guard movement 3. Voluntariness of going down 4. Political participation/ performance in the send-down years 5. Political participation after the send-down years
	Schema of perception	Adherence to the official ideology	1. Adherence to the official ideology before being sent down 2. Change or no change in the countryside; disillusionment. 3. Change or no change after the send-down years 4. Political views now: (1) about the Mao years, especially the Cultural Revolution; (2) about the current regime.

the fact that people's class experience usually develops along different dimensions (see Table A.3).

Some details of operationalization need discussion here. First, I use occupational status and skills, one of the major returns of social capital to measure social capital (Lin and Erickson 2008). This operationalization is also in line with other measurement models from different theoretical perspectives but on the same empirical topic of Chinese stratification changes (Lin and Wu 2009). Second, for each capital, I inductively glean information from interviews and existing studies to determine the number assigned to measure one's capital volume. For example, in measuring one's cultural capital, I mainly use education level but complement it by considering historical specificities and adding non-educational cultural capital. Unlike Zhou and Hou (1999), I do not merge "polytechnic" or associate degrees (*dazhuan*) into "college." The polytechnic colleges are much less selective than four-year colleges. Also, one can obtain a polytechnic diploma through evening school or other continuing education, if one's danwei recognizes it. In comparison, for

Table A.3. *Present class positions*

Rating	Economic capital	Cultural capital	Occupational authority and skill (social capital)
5	High income (above 10,000 yuan/month)	Postgraduate degree; or high-level position in a cultural occupation	High-ranking official (above *chu*); enterprise executive; private entrepreneur; high-prestige/ranking professionals
4	Mid-high income (5,000–10,000 yuan/month)	Full-time college education; or above middle-level position in a cultural occupation	Upper-middle (*chu*) official; upper-middle level manager; upper-middle-level professional jobs
3	Mid-range income (3,500–4,999 yuan/month)	Post–high school degree; or High school degree but active participation in cultural activities	Middle-level (below *chu*) official; middle-level manager; middle-skill professional; small enterprise owner
2	Lower-middle income (below 3,500 yuan/month)	High school degree; or below high school but some involvement in cultural activities	Skilled worker; low-level office work; low-level government jobs
1	Low and unstable income (below 2,000 yuan/month)	Middle school and below	Manual labor job; unstable job; underemployment job

this generation to get a formal four-year college degree, one needs to pass arguably the most difficult gaokao in history or to be recommended, either of which was much more selective, in different ways, than polytechnic degrees. Non-educational cultural capital (engagement in cultural practices and a position in a cultural institution) is added because this generation generally suffered from a lack of formal education, and, thus, using only formal education may not be differential enough. Third, the class positions here are "relative class positions" – not their positions in the national population but their positions in this generation, because, as my interviews show, what matters in their autobiographical memories is their relative class position. This is also where Bourdieu's relational conceptualization of class meets reality.[1]

---

[1] The mobility in one's class positions certainly has the same impacts on autobiographical memory: upwardly mobile people will have more positive memories about past difficulties. But I have two methodological considerations and decided on using present

The following scales of class are used to construct overall class positions as a categorical variable: (1) 11–15, Higher-class positions, including upper-middle class and upper class; (2) 8–10, Middle-class positions; (3) 3–7, Lower-class positions, including lower-middle class, working class, and lower class.[2]

Narrative Pattern Coding

To code the life stories, I use the coding frame of two parts of the story (personal experience and historical evaluation) presented in Table 1.1. The key is to code every interview as a thematic unit, that is, as a "whole" instead of looking for keywords. The negative, positive, and ambiguous views are not only from the interviewees' answers to the interviewer's questions ("What do you think of the impacts of your zhiqing experience on your later life/career?" and "What do you think of the send-down program as a historical event?") but also from nuances, details, tones, and plots of their life stories ("that was the biggest regret in my life" or "the detrimental impacts of those years have lasted so many years" or "The wrong policy made my life miserable"). The codes are quantified and input in an SPSS file.

I assess my coding reliability by having a Chinese graduate student previously unacquainted with me code twenty randomly selected subsamples for the two components. The coders (the assistant and me) are

---

class positions instead of mobility. First, if the "mobility" refers to intragenerational class mobility, then the zhiqing started their first "jobs" as peasants or farmworkers, at the same positions. Therefore, their present class position is a good measurement of mobility. Second, if the "mobility" refers to intergenerational mobility, then it would be hard to compare their parents' class positions in a political class system to their own in today's class system. For example, a person's parent was in the "capitalist" category (black category) but this person is an ordinary, middle-class office worker. It is hard to say that his or her mobility trajectory is downward or upward. Moreover, in the actual life history interviews, only very few people compare them to their parents' class status.

[2] The cut points need more justification. For the measurement of upper- and upper-middle-class status, 11 is a borderline case. But such a case has 4 on at least two of the three forms or 5 on one and two 3s of capital and, thus, qualifies as a minimum case of upper-middle-class status. The number 8 is used as the minimum case of middle-class position because it has 3 on at least two of three forms of capital. Borderline cases (10, 11, 7, and 8) are examined to see if they need adjustment through a holistic consideration of other aspects of the interviewee, including: (1) the interviewee's subjective class status; (2) degree of satisfaction with career and life; (3) other class factors that cannot be reflected in the capitals, for example, the interviewee's house and other aspects of life. Only two cases are adjusted.

given the detailed coding instructions in Chinese. The inter-coder reliability coefficients are: for personal experience, PA [percent agreement]=85 percent, Cohen's *kappa*=0.681; for historical evaluation (recoded into positive, negative, and neutral to increase the number cases in each variation), PA=70 percent, Cohen's *kappa*=0.508). While the inter-coder reliability for personal experience is acceptable, that for historical evaluation is a borderline case. The reason for this relative inconsistency is the complexity of the narrative, which requires coders' ability to understand the historical context, familiarity with the vocabulary, and grasp of nuances in the life stories. All these might not be easy for a young graduate student who does not have much background information about that period of history. Another reason might be the inevitable sampling error.

Hypotheses and Statistical Analysis Results

The main qualitative finding of the personal experience component of the autobiographical memories is stated as the following hypothesis:

Hypothesis 1-1: The higher the zhiqing's present class positions, the more likely they are to hold a positive view of their personal experience in their sent-down years and its impacts on later life.

Because I argue that their political habitus mostly shapes their historical evaluations of the program, which randomly vary on the memory of personal experience, I hypothesize:

Hypothesis 1-2: The variation of the zhiqing's political habitus does not correlate with the variation in the personal experience component of their autobiographical memory.

Both hypotheses are further tested in several logistic regressions, which are to ascertain the effects of class positions on the likelihood that the interviewee has a positive view of their personal sent-down experience, controlling three relevant variables (type of sent-down place, years outside hometown, and sex) (Table A.4).[3]

The results support the hypotheses. Today's class position is a statistically significant variable in *all* the models. In Model 1 (class as a

---

[3] "Type of sent-down place" is chosen because some places like the Heilongjiang Corps required better chushen and gave the zhiqing more upward mobility opportunities. "Years outside of hometown" is chosen because prior studies show that the longer one stayed in the sent-down place, the lower one's class position is (Zhou and Hou 1999).

Table A.4. *Logistic regressions of personal experience on class and related variables*

Variables	Model 1 Continuous class	Model 2 Categorical class	Model 3 Continuous class	Model 4 Categorical class
Class (Categorical)				
Middle to upper class		3.974**	/	5.275**
Class (Continuous)	1.109**		1.247**	/
Habitus				
Faithful red			1.112	1.305
Indifferent red			1.807	1.919
Aspirant			.982	.764
Habitus Change			−3.636	−3.392
Sent-down place				
Chadui	−.733	−.302	−.068	.332
Farm	−3.301	−1.781	−3.165	−2.365
Years outside hometown	−.087	−.058	−.144*	−.103
Sex (Male=1)	2.046*	2.177**	2.277*	2.778**
x^2	62.966	54.060	74.155	65.055
df	5	5	9	9
p	<.001	<.001	<.001	<.001
Nagelkerke R^2	.744	.669	.829	.761
N	87	87	87	87

Note: Coefficients are odds ratios. Omitted categories are working and lower classes (in Categorical class), withdrawer (in Habitus), and corps (in Sent-down place). Habitus change is a dummy variable (Change=1, No Change=0); Sex is a dummy variable (Male=1, Female=0). "Years outside hometown" and "Class (Continuous)" are continuous variables.
* $P<.05$
** $P<.005$.

continuous variable), a one-point increase on the 15-point class scale is associated with the odds of having a positive view of personal experience increasing by 1.109. In Model 3 (class as a continuous variable), in which habitus variables are added, this number is 1.247. Models 2 and 4 (class as a categorical variable) show a similar pattern. In Model 2, other things being equal, those with middle- to upper-class positions in the present are 3.974 times more likely to hold a positive view of their personal experience in their sent-down years. In Model 4, this number is 5.275. In Models 3 and 4, political habitus and habitus change are not statistically significant. In sum, the two hypotheses stated above are supported by the statistical analysis.

Three hypotheses can be formulated from the qualitative findings to explain the historical evaluation part of the generational memory:

Hypothesis 2-1: The zhiqing with habitus of withdrawer and aspirant (based on black to middle chushen) today have more negative evaluations of the send-down program than those with red-chushen-based habitus.

This hypothesis needs some clarification. The aspirant habitus includes two types: those whose habitus remain the same will show no difference than faithful red because of their adherence to the ideology and the active performance (*Hypothesis 2-4*); most of them (18 out of 27) changed their habitus to disbelief and disillusionment and therefore tend to have more negative views (*Hypothesis 2-3*). Because the majority of aspirants changed their habitus, I hypothesize they are more negative about the program than the red-chushenhabitus.

Hypothesis 2-2: Today's class positions of the zhiqing have no impact on their evaluations of the send-down program.

Hypothesis 2-3: The zhiqing's habitus change leads toward a negative view of the send-down program.

Hypothesis 2-4: The aspirants whose habitus remain unchanged tend to have positive evaluations of the send-down program.

To test those hypotheses, I perform ordinal regressions to ascertain the effects of chushen, habitus, habitus change, and social class today (independent variables) on the likelihood that the interviewee has a positive historical evaluation of the send-down program (dependent variable). The results support the hypotheses (Table A.5).

1. Political habitus shapes historical evaluations of the program. Model 1 shows that the ordered logit for "withdrawers" having a positive historical evaluation of the send-down program is 1.436 less than a "faithful red" zhiqing, the "reddest" habitus; for aspirants, it is 1.800 less. The same pattern appears in Models 2 and 3. All these support *Hypothesis 2-1*.

Table A.5. *Ordinal regressions of historical evaluation on habitus and related factors*

Variables	Model 1 Habitus		Model 2 Habitus and no habitus change		Model 3 Habitus without change	
	Coefficient	SE	Coefficient	SE	Coefficient	SE
Habitus					*Only including habitus without changes*	
Withdrawer	−1.436*	.624	−5.057**	.957	−5.450**	1.123
Aspirant	−1.800**	.567	−.797	.687	−.610	.917
Indifferent red	−.580	.634	−3.021**	.849	−3.611**	.985
Change of habitus (No change=0)			6.010**	.948		
Class (Continuous)	.005	.078	.045	.090	−.097	.106
Sent-down place						
Chadui	.373	.833	−.258	.936	−.417	1.053
Farm	−.444	.760	.596	.858	.409	.940
Years outside hometown	.022	.022	.024	.025	.037	.028
Sex (Female=0)	−.018	.492	.326	.556	−.160	.634
x^2	20.187		77.232		48.938	
df	8		9		8	
p	<.01		<.001		<.001	
Nagelkerke R^2	.220		.624		.592	
N	87		87		59	

Note: Coefficients are logits. Omitted categories are black (in chushen), faithful red (in habitus and habitus without change), corps (in Sent-down place), habitus change (in No habitus change), male (in Male). "Years outside hometown" and "Class (Continuous)" are continuous variables.
* $P<.05$
** $P<.005$

2. Habitus change has a negative impact on historical evaluations. In Model 2, those without habitus changes are more likely than those with habitus change (omitted category) to have positive historical evaluations. This supports *Hypothesis 2-3*. Also, in Model 2, the statistical significance of the "aspirant" habitus, which exists in

Model 1, disappears, while the withdrawers' association with the negative view remains strong. This means that aspirants *without* habitus change had similar adherence toward the official ideology in the Mao years and were more likely to have positive evaluations of the program, a result that supports *Hypothesis 2-4*. This is further supported by Model 3, in which I only retain the cases without much habitus change (59): the aspirants do not differ from the faithful red significantly, while withdrawers and the indifferent red are still less likely to have a positive view of the program.

3. Class positions in the present (continuous variable) have no statistically significant relationships with historical evaluations. This supports *Hypothesis 2-2*.

Literary Memory

Table A.6. *Literary works of the zhiqing memory*

Author	Novels		Author	Novellas and short stories	
叶辛 **Ye Xin**	我们这一代年轻人	*Young People of Our Generation*	梁晓声 Liang Xiaosheng	今夜有暴风雪	"A Snowstorm Is Coming Tonight"
	蹉跎岁月	*The Wasted Years*		这是一片神奇的土地	"A Land of Wonder and Mystery"
	孽债	*Karma*			
	客过亭	*The Pavilion of Passersby*			
梁晓声 **Liang Xiaosheng**	雪城	*Snowy City*	阿城 Ah Cheng	棋王	"The King of Chess"
	知青	*Zhiqing*		孩子王	"The King of Children"
	返城年代	*The Years after Returning*			
竹林 **Zhu Lin**	生活的路	*The Road of Life*	张承志 Zhang Chengzhi	骑手为什么歌唱母亲	"Why the Rider Sings about Mother"
	呜咽的澜沧江	*The Weeping Lancang River*		绿夜	"The Green Night"
老鬼 **Lao Gui**	血色黄昏	*The Bloody Sunset*	韩少功 Han Shaogong	西望茅草地	"Looking Westward at Cogon Grass Land"
				飞过蓝天	"Flying in the Blue Sky"
				远方的树	"The Faraway Tree"

Table A.6. (*cont.*)

Author	Novels		Author	Novellas and short stories	
郭小东 **Guo Xiaodong**	中国知青部落 1：1979 知青大逃亡	*The Chinese Zhiqing Tribe 1: 1979 The Exodus of Zhiqing*	史铁生 Shi Tiesheng	插队的故事 我的遥远的清平湾	"The Story of Chadui" "My Remote Qingping Bay"
	中国知青部落 2：青年流放者	*The Chinese Zhiqing Tribe 2: The Young Exiles*	王安忆 Wang Anyi	本次列车终点	"The Final Stop of This Train"
	中国知青部落 3：暗夜舞蹈	*The Chinese Zhiqing Tribe 3: Dancing in the Dark Night*		广阔天地的一角	"A Corner of the Vast Universe"
			孔捷生 Kong Jiesheng	在小河那边	"On the Other Side of the Stream"
				大林莽	"The Big Jungle"
				南方的岸	"The Bank in the South"
陆天明 **Lu Tianming**	桑那高地的太阳	*The Sun over the Sangna Highland*	张抗抗 Zhang Kangkang	白罂粟	"The White Poppy"
				永不忏悔	"Never Confess"
			严歌苓 Yan Geling	天浴	"Celestial Bath"
张抗抗 **Zhang Kangkang**	隐形伴侣	*Invisible Companion*			
王安忆 **Wang Anyi**	69届初中生	*Class 69 of Middle School*			
邓贤 **Deng Xian**	天堂之门	*The Gate to Heaven*			
王小波 **Wang Xiaobo**	黄金时代	*The Golden Times*			
张承志 **Zhang Chengzhi**	金牧场	*The Golden Pasture*			

Exhibits and Museums

I have done research on three exhibits, including "Souls Tied to the Black Soil" in Beijing, "Regretless Youth" in Chengdu, and "Spring Flowers and Autumn Fruits" (*chunhuaqiushi*) in Nanjing, and five museums (Heihe Museum, Heilongjiang Reclamation Museum, Dafeng Shanghai Zhiqing Museum, Shanghai Haiwanyuan, and Nanjing Zhang Xiaoning's Individual Museum). I collected publicly available textual data, such as books, press reports, online discussions, and magazines. I also paid visits to the museums and conducted eight interviews with the administrators, managers, and curators. For the exhibits in the 1990s, I primarily relied on books the organizers published later, which include the main components of the exhibit, visitors' comments, and images (Benshu Bianweihui 1991; Hunxi Heitudi Editorial Committee 1991; Chun 2009). Drawing on the coding system in the analysis of autobiographical memory (Chapters 1 and 2), I coded the exhibits and visitors' comments into two parts: first, their views of the zhiqing as participants; and second, their evaluations of the send-down program as a historical event.

References

Anderson, Don. 1984. "Youth Waiting for Work in China." *The Australian Journal of Chinese Affairs* 12 (July): 167–75.

Assmann, Jan. 1995. "Collective Memory and Cultural Identity." *New German Critique* 65: 125–33.

Baidu, Tieba. 2010. "Heihe bowuguan ruhe lunshu shangshanxiaxiang yiyi." https://tieba.baidu.com/p/744082662?red_tag=2013767597.

Bauman, Zygmunt. 1982. *Memories of Class: The Pre-History and After-Life of Class.* London; Boston: Routledge; Kegan Paul.

Beijing Qingnian Bao. 1983. "Changpian xiaoshuo cuotuosuiyue." *Beijing Qingnian Bao,* November 1, 4.

Beijing Wanbao. 2010. "Zhang Kangkang: Zai zuoping li zuo zai shenghuo li bu zuo." *Beijing Wanbao,* November 7, 12, wenyu xinwen.

Benshu Bianweihui. 1991. *Qingchun wuhui – chengdu zhiqing fudian zhibian ershi zhounian jinianhuodong ziliao huibian* 成都知青赴滇支边二十周年纪念活动资料汇编: Self Published.

Bernstein, Thomas P. 1977. *Up to the Mountains and Down to the Villages: The Transfer of Youth from Urban to Rural China.* New Haven: Yale University Press.

Berntsen, Dorthe, and David C. Rubin, eds. 2012. *Understanding Autobiographical Memory: Theories and Approaches.* New York: Cambridge University Press.

Berry, Michael. 2017. "1985. April. Searching for Roots in Literature and Film." In *A New Literary History of Modern China,* edited by David Der-Wei Wang, 777–82. Cambridge, ᵐᵃ: Belknap Press of Harvard University Press.

Bi, Zili. 1991. "Beidahuang, yushuo dangnian." *Nanfengchuang,* 33–35.

Bianjibu, Beidahuang Fengyu Lu, ed. 1990. *Beidahuang Fengyu Lu.* Beijing: Zhongguo Qingnian Chubanshe.

Bonnin, Michel. 2013. *The Lost Generation: The Rustication of China's Educated Youth (1968–1980).* Hong Kong: Chinese University of Hong Kong Press.

——— 2016. "Restricted, Distorted but Alive: The Memory of the 'Lost Generation' of Chinese Educated Youth." *The China Quarterly* 227 (September): 752–72.

——— 2019. "Popular Memories and Popular History, Indispensable Tools for Understanding Contemporary Chinese History: The Case of the End of the Rustication Movement." In *Popular Memories of the Mao Era: From*

Critical Debate to Reassessing History, edited by Sebastian Veg, 220–34. Hong Kong: Hong Kong University Press.

Bourdieu, Pierre. 1984. *Distinction: A Social Critique of the Judgement of Taste.* Cambridge, MA: Harvard University Press.

———. 1990. *The Logic of Practice.* Stanford: Stanford University Press.

———. 1991. *Language and Symbolic Power.* Cambridge, MA: Harvard University Press.

———. 1993. *The Field of Cultural Production: Essays on Art and Literature.* New York: Columbia University Press.

———. 1994. "Rethinking the State: Genesis and Structure of the Bureaucratic Field." *Sociological Theory* 12 (1): 1–18.

———. 1996. *The Rules of Art: Genesis and Structure of the Literary Field.* Cambridge: Polity Press.

Bourdieu, Pierre, and Jean Claude Passeron. 1977. *Reproduction in Education, Society and Culture.* London: Sage Publications.

Bourdieu, Pierre, and Loic Wacquant. 2013. "Symbolic Capital and Social Classes." *Journal of Classical Sociology* 13 (2): 292–302.

Bourdieu, Pierre, and Loïc J. D. Wacquant. 1992. *An Invitation to Reflexive Sociology.* Chicago: University of Chicago Press.

Brewer, William F. 1986. "What Is Autobiographical Memory?" In *Autobiographical Memory*, edited by David C. Rubin, 25–49. Cambridge: Cambridge University Press.

Buckley, Chris. 2017. "Chinese Village Where Xi Jinping Fled Is Now a Monument to His Power." *The New York Times*, October 8, World, Asia.

Calhoun, Craig J. 1994. *Neither Gods nor Emperors: Students and the Struggle for Democracy in China.* Berkeley: University of California Press.

Cao, Zuoya. 2003. *Out of the Crucible: Literary Works about the Rusticated Youth.* Lanham: Lexington Books.

Chan, Anita. 1985. *Children of Mao: Personality Development and Political Activism in the Red Guard Generation.* Seattle: University of Washington Press.

Chan, Anita, Richard Madsen, and Jonathan Unger. 2009. *Chen Village: Revolution to Globalization.* 3rd ed. Berkeley: University of California Press.

Chan, Anita, Stanley Rosen, and Jonathan Unger. 1980. "Students and Class Warfare: The Social Roots of the Red Guard Conflict in Guangzhou (Canton)." *China Quarterly* 83 (September): 397–446.

Chan, Sylvia. 1988. "Two Steps Forward, One Step Back: Towards a 'Free' Literature." *The Australian Journal of Chinese Affairs* (19/20): 81–126.

Chen, Xiaomei. 2016. "Performing the 'Red Classics': From the East Is Red to the Road to Revival." In *Red Legacies in China: Cultural Afterlives of the Communist Revolution*, edited by Jie Li and Enhua Zhang, 151–83. Cambridge, MA; London: Harvard University Asia Center.

Cheng, Yinghong. 2009. *Creating the "New Man": From Enlightenment Ideals to Socialist Realities, Perspectives on the Global Past.* Honolulu: University of Hawai'i Press.

Chi, Pang-Yuan, and David Der-Wei Wang, eds. 2000. *Chinese Literature in the Second Half of a Modern Century: A Critical Survey.* Bloomington: Indiana University Press.

Childress, C. Clayton, and Noah E. Friedkin. 2012. "Cultural Reception and Production: The Social Construction of Meaning in Book Clubs." *American Sociological Review* 77 (1): 45–68.

Chun, Ming. 2009. *Beidahuang. Hou zhiqing shidai.* Beijing: Zhongguo Qingnian Chubanshe.

Cole, Jennifer. 2001. *Forget Colonialism?: Sacrifice and the Art of Memory in Madagascar.* Berkeley: University of California Press.

Corning, Amy D. 2010. "Emigration, Generation, and Collective Memories." *Social Psychology Quarterly* 73 (3): 223–44.

Corning, Amy, and Howard Schuman. 2015. *Generations and Collective Memory.* Chicago: University of Chicago Press.

Davies, David J. 2005. "Old Zhiqing Photos: Nostalgia and the 'Spirit' of the Cultural Revolution." *China Review* 5 (2): 97–123.

Davis, Fred. 1979. *Yearning for Yesterday: A Sociology of Nostalgia.* New York: Free Press.

DeGloma, Thomas. 2014. *Seeing the Light: The Social Logic of Personal Discovery.* Chicago: University of Chicago Press.

Deng, Xian. 2009. *Zhongguo zhiqing meng.* Beijing: Zuojia Chubanshe.

Denton, Kirk A. 2014. *Exhibiting the Past: Historical Memory and the Politics of Museums in Postsocialist China.* Honolulu: University of Hawai'i Press.

Ding, Yizhuang. 2009. *History of China's Educated Youth: The First Wave (1953–1968).* Beijing: Contemporary China Publishing House.

Dong, Jian, Fan Ding, and Binbin Wang, eds. 2005. *A New Thesis on Contemporary Chinese Literature (Zhongguo Dangdai Wenxueshi Xingao).* Beijing: People's Literature Press.

Durkheim, Emile. 1995 [1912]. *The Elementary Forms of Religious Life.* Translated by Karen E. Fields. New York: Free Press.

Edmunds, June, and Bryan S. Turner. 2002. *Generations, Culture and Society.* Buckingham; Philadelphia: Open University Press.

Eliasoph, Nina, and Paul Lichterman. 2003. "Culture in Interaction." *American Journal of Sociology* 108 (4): 735–94.

Erikson, Robert, John H. Goldthorpe, and Lucienne Portocarero. 1979. "Intergenerational Class Mobility in Three Western European Societies: England, France and Sweden." *The British Journal of Sociology* 30 (4): 415–41.

Erll, Astrid. 2011. *Memory in Culture.* New York: Palgrave Macmillan.

Erll, Astrid, and Ann Rigney. 2006. "Literature and the Production of Cultural Memory: Introduction." *European Journal of English Studies* 10 (2): 111–15.

Eyerman, Ron, and Bryan S. Turner. 1998. "Outline of a Theory of Generations." *European Journal of Social Theory* 1 (1): 91–106.

Fan, Xin. 1998. "Zhiqing wenhua lun – zhongguo zhiqing shangshan xiaxiang sanshi zhounian ji." *Wenyi Pinglun* (6): 51–58.

Fang, Yi. 1991. "Kuaguo heitudi." *Zhongguo Qingnian Yanjiu* (3): 14–15.

Fine, Gary Alan. 1979. "Small Groups and Culture Creation: The Idioculture of Little League Baseball Teams." *American Sociological Review* 44 (5): 733–45.

1991. "On the Macrofoundations of Microsociology: Constraint and the Exterior Reality of Structure." *The Sociological Quarterly* 32 (2): 161–77.

1996. "Reputational Entrepreneurs and the Memory of Incompetence: Melting Supporters, Partisan Warriors, and Images of President Harding." *American Journal of Sociology* 101 (5): 1159–93.

2001. *Difficult Reputations: Collective Memories of the Evil, Inept, and Controversial.* Chicago: University of Chicago Press.

2012. *Tiny Publics: A Theory of Group Action and Culture.* New York: Russell Sage Foundation.

2013. "Sticky Cultures: Memory Publics and Communal Pasts in Competitive Chess." *Cultural Sociology* 7 (4): 395–414.

Gao, Hua. 2004. *Shenfen he chayi: 1949–1965 nian zhongguo shehui de zhenzhi fencheng [Status and Differentiation: The Political Strata in Chinese Society, 1949–1965].* Working Paper for the University Service Center. Hong Kong: Chinese University of Hong Kong.

Garfinkel, Harold. 1967. *Studies in Ethnomethodology.* Englewood Cliffs: Prentice-Hall.

Geertz, Clifford. 1973. *The Interpretation of Cultures: Selected Essays.* New York: Basic Books.

Goffman, Erving. 1959. *The Presentation of Self in Everyday Life.* Doubleday Anchor Books, A174. Garden City: Doubleday.

1983. "The Interaction Order." *American Sociological Review* 48 (1): 1–17.

Gold, Thomas B. 1980. "Back to the City: The Return of Shanghai's Educated Youth." *The China Quarterly* 84 (December): 755–70.

1991. "Youth and the State." *China Quarterly* 127 (September): 594–612.

Goldfarb, Jeffrey C. 2006. *The Politics of Small Things: The Power of the Powerless in Dark Times.* Chicago: The University of Chicago Press.

Griffin, Larry J. 2004. "'Generations and Collective Memory' Revisited: Race, Region, and Memory of Civil Rights." *American Sociological Review* 69 (4): 544–57.

Griffin, Larry J., and Kenneth A. Bollen. 2009. "What Do These Memories Do? Civil Rights Remembrance and Racial Attitudes." *American Sociological Review* 74 (4): 594–614.

Griswold, Wendy. 1987a. "The Fabrication of Meaning: Literary Interpretation in the United States, Great Britain, and the West Indies." *American Journal of Sociology* 92 (5): 1077–117.

1987b. "A Methodological Framework for the Sociology of Culture." *Sociological Methodology* 17: 1–35.

Gu, Hongzhang, ed. 2009a. *Zhongguo zhishi qingnian shangshan xiaxiang shimo.* Beijing: People's Daily Press.

ed. 2009b. *Zhongguo zhishi qingnian shangshan xiaxiang dashiji.* Beijing: renmin ribao chubanshe.

Guan, Shoukang. 1992. "Qingchun wuhui Dong Jiagen." *Nanfengchuang,* 14–15.

Guo, Xiaodong. 1988. *Contemporary Chinese Educated Youths Literature.* Guangzhou: Guangdong Higher Education Press.

2010. *1966 nian de ao.* Nanjing: Jiangsu renmin chubanshe.

2015. "Tiantang meiyou heian." In *Guo Xiaodong Wen Ji,* edited by Xiaodong Guo, 1–8. Guangzhou: Huancheng Chubanshe.

Halbwachs, Maurice. 1980. *The Collective Memory.* 1st ed. New York: Harper & Row.

1992. *On Collective Memory*. Chicago: The University of Chicago Press.

Havlena, William J., and Susan L. Holak. 1991. "'The Good Old Days': Observations on Nostalgia and Its Role in Consumer Behavior." *Advances in Consumer Research* 18 (1): 323–29.

He, Shaojun. 1998. "Raobukai lixiang qingjie de zhiqing xiaoshuo." *Nanfang Wentan* (65): 20–21.

He, Weifang. 2016. "He Weifang: Zhiqing bowuguan: jiang zuie bianchengle weiye." http://hx.cnd.org/?p=131407.

Hershatter, Gail. 2011. *The Gender of Memory: Rural Women and China's Collective Past, Asia Pacific Modern*. Berkeley: University of California Press.

Ho, Denise Y. 2018. *Curating Revolution: Politics on Display in Mao's China*. Cambridge: Cambridge University Press.

Ho, Denise Y., and Jie Li. 2016. "From Landlord Manor to Red Memorabilia: Reincarnations of a Chinese Museum Town." *Modern China* 42 (1): 3–37.

Hobsbawm, Eric. J. 1983. "Mass-Producing Traditions: Europe, 1870–1914." In *The Invention of Tradition*, edited by Eric. J. Hobsbawm and Terence. O. Ranger, 263–307. Cambridge: Cambridge University Press.

Hochschild, Arlie. 2016. *Strangers in Their Own Land: Anger and Mourning on the American Right*. New York; London: The New Press.

Hong, Zicheng. 2007. *A History of Contemporary Chinese Literature (Zhongguo Dangdai Wenxueshi)*. Beijing: Peking University Press.

Honig, Emily. 1992. *Creating Chinese Ethnicity: Subei People in Shanghai, 1850–1980*. New Haven: Yale University Press.

Honig, Emily, and Xiaojian Zhao. 2019. *Across the Great Divide: The Sent-Down Youth Movement in Mao's China, 1968–1980*. Cambridge: Cambridge University Press.

Huang, Xin. 2018. *The Gender Legacy of the Mao Era: Women's Life Stories in Contemporary China*. Albany: SUNY Press.

Hubbert, Jennifer. 2005. "Revolution Is a Dinner Party: Cultural Revolution Restaurants in Contemporary China." *The China Review* 5 (2): 125–50.

2006. "(Re)collecting Mao: Memory and Fetish in Contemporary China." *American Ethnologist* 33 (2): 145–161.

Hung, Eva P. W., and Stephen W. K. Chiu. 2003. "The Lost Generation: Life Course Dynamics and Xiagang in China." *Modern China* 29 (2): 204–36.

Hunxi Heitudi Editorial Committee. 1991. *Hunxi Heitudi*. Nanjing: Jiangsu People's Press.

Hwang, Kwang-kuo. 1987. "Face and Favor: The Chinese Power Game." *American Journal of Sociology* 92 (4): 944–74.

Jennings, M. Kent, and Ning Zhang. 2005. "Generations, Political Status, and Collective Memories in the Chinese Countryside." *The Journal of Politics* 67 (4): 1164–89.

Jepperson, Ronald L., and Ann Swidler. 1994. "What Properties of Culture Should We Measure." *Poetics* 22 (4): 359–71.

Jiang, Jiehong, ed. 2007. *Burden or Legacy: From the Chinese Cultural Revolution to Contemporary Art*. Hong Kong: Hong Kong University Press.

Jiefang Ribao. 2010. "Wo weishemei xie zhiqing xiaoshuo." *Jiefang Ribao*, March 8, 12.

Kertzer, David I. 1983. "Generation as a Sociological Problem." *Annual Review of Sociology* 9 (1): 125–49.

Kong, Jian. 2008. *Han Shaogong pingzhuan*. Zhengzhou: Henan Wenyi Chubashe.

Kong, Jiesheng. 2009. "Shan'ge." www.jintian.net/today/html/41/n-15641.html.

Kraus, Charles Richard. 2017. "Xinjiang's 100,000: State-led Urban-to-Rural Population Resettlement in Socialist China." PhD dissertation, The George Washington University.

Kraus, Richard Curt. 1981. *Class Conflict in Chinese Socialism*. New York: Columbia University Press.

Labov, William. 1972. *Language in the Inner City: Studies in the Black English Vernacular*. Philadelphia: University of Pennsylvania Press.

1997. "Some Further Steps in Narrative Analysis." *Journal of Narrative and Life History* 7 (1–4): 395–415.

Lamont, Michèle. 1992. *Money, Morals, and Manners: The Culture of the French and American Upper-Middle class, Morality and Society*. Chicago: University of Chicago Press.

Lao, Gui. 2010. *Blood and Iron (xue yu tie)*. Beijing: Xinxin Publishing House.

Lao, Yu. 2011. "Lao Gui fangtan: "hongerdai" yanzhong de xuese zhongguo." *Phoenix Weekly* 14: 104–7.

Lee, Ching Kwan. 2000. "The 'Revenge of History': Collective Memories and Labor Protests in North-Eastern China." *Ethnography* 1 (2): 217–37.

2002. "From the Specter of Mao to the Spirit of the Law: Labor Insurgency in China." *Theory and Society* 31 (2): 189–228.

Lee, Ching Kwan, and Guobin Yang, eds. 2007. *Re-envisioning the Chinese Revolution: The Politics and Poetics of Collective Memories in Reform China*. Stanford: Stanford University Press.

Leese, Daniel. 2012. "A Place Where Great Men Rest? The Chairman Mao Memorial Hall." In *Places of Memory in Modern China: History, Politics, and Identity*, edited by Marc Andre Matten, 91–129. Leiden: Brill.

Leung, Laifong. 1994. *Morning Sun: Interviews with Chinese Writers of the Lost Generation, Studies on Contemporary China*. Armonk: M. E. Sharpe.

Li, Jie, and Enhua Zhang, eds. 2016. *Red Legacies in China: Cultural Afterlives of the Communist Revolution*. Cambridge, MA: Harvard University Press:

Li, Rui. 1993. "Cong jiben zhiqing huiyilu xiangdaode." *Wenxue Ziyou Tan*, 46–51.

Li, Weina. 2003. "Lu Tianming: Buba wenxue dangzuo youxi." *Renmin Ribao (Overseas Version)*, December 12.

Li, Xin. 2015. "Bense Wei Junyi." January 4. http://m.aisixiang.com/data/91617 .html.

Li, Zhangjun. 2013. "Haobudongyao jiachi he fazhang zhongguotese shehuizhuyi zai shijiazhong buduan yousuo faxian yousuo chuangzao yousuoqianjing." *Renmin Ribao*, January 6, p. 1, sec. 1.

Liang, Xiaosheng. 1993. *Liang Xiaosheng's Zhiqing Novels*. Xi'an, China: Xi'an Press.

1998. "My View of Zhiqing." *Beijing Literature*, 5–27.

2009a. *Cong Fudan dao Beiying*. Beijing: China Fortune Press.

2009b. *Yige Hongweibing de zibai*. Beijing: Zhongguo Caifu Chubanshe.

Lichterman, Paul. 2006. "Social Capital or Group Style? Rescuing Tocqueville's Insights on Civic Engagement." *Theory and Society* 35 (5–6): 529–63.

Lin, Nan, and Bonnie H. Erickson, eds. 2008. *Social Capital: An International Research Program*. Oxford: Oxford University Press.

Lin, Qianhan. 2013. "Lost in Transformation? The Employment Trajectories of China's Cultural Revolution Cohort." *The Annals of the American Academy of Political and Social Science* 646 (1): 172–93.

Lin, Thunghong, and Xiaogang Wu. 2009. "The Transformation of the Chinese Class Structure, 1978–2005." In *Social Stratification in Chinese Societies: Social Stratification In Chinese Societies*, edited by Kwok-bun Chan, 81–112. Boston: Brill.

Link, Perry. 2000. *The Uses of Literature: Life in the Socialist Chinese Literary System*. Princeton: Princeton University Press.

Liu, Tianshi. 2005. "Zhang Chengzhi: Wo meiyou genzhe chaoliu zou." *Nanfa renwu zhoukan* 6: www.douban.com/event/12931765/discussion/31402882/?author=1

Liu, Xiaomeng. 2009. *History of China's Educated Youth: The Big Wave (1966–1980)*. Beijing: Contemporary China Publishing House.

Lizardo, Omar. 2010. "Culture and Stratification." In *Handbook of Cultural Sociology*, edited by John R. Hall, Laura Grindstaff, and Ming-Cheng Lo, 305–15. New York: Routledge.

Lu, Hanchao. 2019. "More Than Half the Sky: Women and Urban Neighbourhood Workshops in China, 1958–1978." *The China Quarterly* 243 (September): 757–79.

Mannheim, Karl. 1952 [1923]. "The Problem of Generations." In *Essays on the Sociology of Knowledge*, edited by Karl Mannheim, 276–22. London: RKP.

1956. *Essays on the Sociology of Culture*. New York: Oxford University Press.

Mao, Tse-Tung. 1965. *Selected Works of Mao Tse-Tung*. Volume 1. Peking: Foreign Language Press.

1966. *Quotations from Chairman Mao Tse-Tung*. Peking: Foreign Language Press.

Maynes, Mary Jo, Jennifer L. Pierce, and Barbara Laslett. 2008. *Telling Stories: The Use of Personal Narratives in the Social Sciences and History*. Ithaca: Cornell University Press.

McLaren, Anne. 1979. "The Educated Youth Return: The Poster Campaign in Shanghai from November 1978 to March 1979." *The Australian Journal of Chinese Affairs* (2): 1–20.

Mead, George Herbert. 2015. *Mind, Self, and Society. The Definitive Edition*, edited by Charles W. Morris. Chicago: University of Chicago Press.

Meng, Fanhua. 2009. *A General Introduction to Contemporary Chinese Literature*. Shenyang: Liaoning Peoples Press.

Mills, C. Wright. 1959. *The Sociological Imagination*. New York: Oxford University Press.

Misztal, Barbara A. 2003. *Theories of Social Remembering*. Philadelphia: Open University Press.

Mosse, George L. 1990. *Fallen Soldiers: Reshaping the Memory of the World Wars*. New York: Oxford University Press.

Mu, Zi. 1984. "Dongluan niandai de zhuangli qingchun – tan yingpian shengqi de tudi." *Dazhong dianying* (2): 6–7.

Nanfangwang. 2014. "Guo Xiaodong: Women shidai de zhiqing." www.hybsl .cn/beijingcankao/beijingfenxi/2011-09-09/26796.html.

Nguyen, Viet Thanh. 2016. *Nothing Ever Dies: Vietnam and the Memory of War.* Cambridge, MA: Harvard University Press.

Nora, Pierre. 1989. "Between Memory and History: Les Lieux de Memoire." *Representations* 26: 7–24.

O'Brien, Kevin J. 1996. "Rightful Resistance." *World Politics* 49 (1): 31–55.

Olick, Jeffrey K. 1999. "Collective Memory: The Two Cultures." *Sociological Theory* 17 (3): 333–48.

2007. *The Politics of Regret: On Collective Memory and Historical Responsibility.* New York: Routledge.

2010. "From Collective Memory to the Sociology of Mnemonic Practices and Products." In *A Companion to Cultural Memory Studies*, edited by Astrid Erll and Ansgar Nünning, 151–59. Berlin: De Gruyter.

Olick, Jeffrey K., and Joyce Robbins. 1998. "Social Memory Studies: From 'Collective Memory' to the Historical Sociology of Mnemonic Practices." *Annual Review of Sociology* 24: 105–40.

Olick, Jeffrey K., Vered Vinitzky-Seroussi, and Daniel Levy. 2011. *The Collective Memory Reader.* New York: Oxford University Press.

Padgett, John F. 2018. "Faulkner's Assembly of Memories into History: Narrative Networks in Multiple Times." *American Journal of Sociology* 124 (2): 406–78.

Palmberger, Monika. 2016. *How Generations Remember: Conflicting Histories and Shared Memories in Post-War Bosnia and Herzegovina, Global Diversities.* London: Palgrave Macmillan.

Pan, Yihong. 2002. *Tempered in the Revolutionary Furnace: China's Youth in the Rustication Movement.* Lanham: Lexington Books.

Peterson, Richard A., and N. Anand. 2004. "The Production of Culture Perspective." *Annual Review of Sociology* 30: 311–24.

Platform, Heilongjiang Cultural Industry 2017. "Heihe Beidahuang zhiqing wenhua caiye yuanqu." www.hljcci.cn/pages/5909ca2a12c15be36ef15c03.

Portelli, Alessandro. 1991. *The Death of Luigi Trastulli, and Other Stories: Form and Meaning in Oral History.* Albany: SUNY Press.

Qian, Zhenchao, and Randy Hodson. 2011. "'Sent Down' in China: Stratification Challenged but Not Denied." *Research in Social Stratification and Mobility* 29: 205–19.

Rene, Helena K. 2013. *China's Sent-Down Generation: Public Administration and the Legacies of Mao's Rustication Program.* Washington, DC: Georgetown University Press.

Riessman, Catherine Kohler. 2008. *Narrative Methods for the Human Sciences.* Los Angeles: Sage Publications.

Roseman, Mark. 1999. "Surviving Memory: Truth and Inaccuracy in Holocaust Testimony." *The Journal of Holocaust Education* 8 (1): 1–20.

Rosen, Stanley. 1981. *The Role of Sent-Down Youth in the Chinese Cultural Revolution: The Case of Guangzhou.* Berkeley: Institute of East Asian Studies, University of California, Berkeley.

Rubin, David C., ed. 1986. *Autobiographical Memory*. Cambridge: Cambridge University Press.

Samuel, Raphael, ed. 1981. *People's History and Socialist Theory*. London: Routledge & Kegan Paul.

Schuman, Howard, and Amy Corning. 2014. "Collective Memory and Autobiographical Memory: Similar but Not the Same." *Memory Studies* 7 (2): 146–60.

Schuman, Howard, and Amy D. Corning. 2000. "Collective Knowledge of Public Events: The Soviet Era from the Great Purge to Glasnost." *American Journal of Sociology* 105 (4): 913–56.

Schuman, Howard, and Cheryl Rieger. 1992. "Historical Analogies, Generational Effects, and Attitudes toward War." *American Sociological Review* 57 (3): 315–26.

Schuman, Howard, and Willard L. Rodgers. 2004. "Cohorts, Chronology, and Collective Memories." *Public Opinion Quarterly* 68 (2): 217–54.

Schuman, Howard, and Jacqueline Scott. 1989. "Generations and Collective Memories." *American Sociological Review* 54 (3): 359–81.

Schutz, Alfred, and Thomas Luckmann. 1973. *The Structures of the Life-World*. 2 vols. Evanston: Northwestern University Press.

Scruggs, Bert M. 2014. "Landscapes and Sublime Memories: Revisiting Liang Xiaosheng's 'A Land of Wonder and Mystery.'" *Frontiers of Literary Studies in China* 8 (4): 513–31.

Shi, Huige. 2014. *Zhu Lin wenxue chuangzuo lun*. Zhenjiang: Jiangsu daxue chubanshe.

Shi, Tiesheng. 2006. *Bingxi suibi*. Xi'an: Shaanxi Shida Chubanshe.
    2010. *Jiyi yu yinxiang*. Changsha: Hunan wenyi chubanshe.

Shi, Zhanjun. 1998. "Kunan de kongwu: Remarks on 'zhiqing wenxue.'" *Nanfang Wentan* 66 (5): 16–17.

Shi, Zhi. 2012. *Winter Sun: Poems*. Translated by Jonathan Stalling. Norman: University of Oklahoma Press.

Shirk, Susan L. 1982. *Competitive Comrades: Career Incentives and Student Strategies in China*. Berkeley: University of California Press.

Simko, Christina. 2015. *The Politics of Consolation: Memory and the Meaning of September 11*. Oxford: Oxford University Press.

Siu, Helen F., and Zelda Stern, eds. 1983. *Mao's Harvest: Voces from China's New Generation*. Oxford: Oxford University Press.

Small, Mario Luis. 2009. "'How Many Cases Do I Need?' Skirting Common Pitfalls in Pursuit of Scientific Fieldwork." *Ethnography* 10 (1): 5–38.

Steidl, Christina R. 2013. "Remembering May 4, 1970: Integrating the Commemorative Field at Kent State." *American Sociological Review* 78 (5): 749–72.

Steinmetz, George. 1992. "Reflections on the Role of Social Narratives in Working-Class Formation: Narrative Theory in the Social Sciences." *Social Science History* 16 (3): 489–516.

Sturken, Marita. 1997. *Tangled Memories: The Vietnam War, the AIDS Epidemic, and the Politics of Remembering*. Berkeley: University of California Press.

Swartz, David. 2013. *Symbolic Power, Politics, and Intellectuals: The Political Sociology of Pierre Bourdieu*. Chicago: University of Chicago Press.

Swedberg, Richard. 2012. "Theorizing in Sociology and Social Science: Turning to the Context of Discovery." *Theory and Society* 41 (1): 1–40.

———. 2014. *The Art of Social Theory*. Princeton: Princeton University Press.

Tao, Dongfeng, and Lei He. 2008. *Chinese Literature since Reform and Opening Up (1978–2008)*. Beijing: Chinese Social Science Press.

Tavory, Iddo, and Stefan Timmermans. 2014. *Abductive Analysis: Theorizing Qualitative Research*. Chicago: University of Chicago Press.

Trouillot, Michel-Rolph. 1995. *Silencing the Past: Power and the Production of History*. Boston: Beacon Press.

Tu, An, ed. 2016. *Chaonei 116 hao jiyi*. Beijing: Renmin Wenxue Chubanshe.

Tuchman, Gaye, and Nina E. Fortin. 1984. "Fame and Misfortune: Edging Women out of the Great Literary Tradition." *American Journal of Sociology* 90: 72–96.

Tumblety, Joan, ed. 2013. *Memory and History: Understanding Memory as Source and Subject*. London: Routledge.

Turner, Victor Witter. 1969. *The Ritual Process: Structure and Anti-Structure, The Lewis Henry Morgan Lectures, 1966*. Chicago: Aldine Pub. Co.

Unger, Jonathan. 1982. *Education under Mao: Class and Competition in Canton Schools, 1960–1980*. New York: Columbia University Press.

Unger, Jonathan, ed. 2008. *Associations and the Chinese State: Contested Spaces*. Armonk: M.E. Sharpe.

van Maanen, John. 2011. *Tales of the Field: On Writing Ethnography*. Chicago: University of Chicago Press.

Veg, Sebastian. 2014. "Testimony, History and Ethics: From the Memory of Jiabiangou Prison Camp to a Reappraisal of the Anti-Rightist Movement in Present-Day China." *The China Quarterly* 218 (June): 514–39.

Veg, Sebastian, ed. 2019. *Popular Memories of the Mao Era: From Critical Debate to Reassessing History*. Hong Kong: Hong Kong University Press.

Vinitzky-Seroussi, Vered. 1998. *After Pomp and Circumstance: High School Reunion as an Autobiographical Occasion*. Chicago: University of Chicago Press.

Vinitzky-Seroussi, Vered, and Chana Teeger. 2010. "Unpacking the Unspoken: Silence in Collective Memory and Forgetting." *Social Forces* 88 (3): 1103–22.

Wagner-Pacifici, Robin, and Barry Schwartz. 1991. "The Vietnam Veterans Memorial: Commemorating a Difficult Past." *American Journal of Sociology* 97 (2): 376–420.

Walder, Andrew. 2004. "The Transformation of Contemporary China Studies, 1977–2002." In *The Politics of Knowledge: Area Studies and the Disciplines*, edited by David L. Szanton, ix, 314–40. Berkeley: University of California Press.

Wang, Anyi. 2014. "Wang Anyi huiyi zhiqing suiyue: qingchun de fengrao he pingji." http://culture.ifeng.com/redian/detail_2014_03/23/35053205_0.shtml.

Wang, Ning. 2017. *Banished to the Great Northern Wilderness: Political Exile and Re-education in Mao's China*. Vancouver: University of British Columbia Press.

Wang, Zhen. 1990. "Wang Zhen fuzhuxi zai quanguo nongken nonggongshang zuotanhui shang de jianghua June 25, 1990." *Nongken Jingji Yanjiu*, 91–92.

Weber, Max. 1946. *From Max Weber: Essays in Sociology*. Oxford: Oxford University Press.

Weigelin-Schwiedrzik, Susanne, and Cui Jinke. 2016. "Whodunnit? Memory and Politics before the 50th Anniversary of the Cultural Revolution." *The China Quarterly* 227 (September): 734–51.

Wenxue Bao. 1983. "Fuye wenxue qingnian shi lingdao tongzhi yingjing de yiwu." *Wenxue Bao*, April 28, Duzhe Zhisheng.

——— 2012. "Zhongguo wenxue ji dongya wenxue de kenenxing." *Wenxue Bao*, April 19, p. 5, sec. 5.

Whyte, Martin King. 1975. "Inequality and Stratification in China." *The China Quarterly* 64 (December): 684–711.

Winter, J. M. 1995. *Sites of Memory, Sites of Mourning: The Great War in European Cultural History*. Cambridge: Cambridge University Press.

Winter, Jay M. 2006. *Remembering War: The Great War between Memory and History in the Twentieth Century*. New Haven: Yale University Press.

Wright, Erik Olin. 2005. *Approaches to Class Analysis*. Cambridge: Cambridge University Press.

Xi, Jinping. 2012. "Woshi huangtudi de erzi." *Xibu Dakaifa*, 109–12.

——— 2015. "Zai Huashendun zhou dangdi zhengfu he meiguo youhao tuanti lianhe huanying yanhui shang de yanjiang." www.xinhuanet.com/world/2015-09/23/c_1116656143.htm.

Xia, Yu 夏榆. 2014. "《陆犯焉识》：阅读严歌苓，而非观看." New York Times website, Chinese version. https://cn.nytimes.com/books/20140505/tc05yangeling/.

Xiao, Lijun. 1983. "Shengqi tudi shangde yinxiong ernv." *Wenhui Bao*, March 24, 3.

Xie, Yong. 1998. "Youpai zuojia qun he zhiqing zuojia qun de lishi juxian." *Dangdai Zuojia Pinglun* (5): 51–54, 65.

Xu, Bin. 2019. "Intra-Generational Variations in Autobiographic Memory: China's 'Sent-Down' Generation." *Social Psychology Quarterly* 82 (2): 134–57.

——— 2021. "Historically Remaining Issues: The Shanghai–Xinjiang Zhiqing Migration Program and the Tangled Legacies of the Mao Era in China, 1980–2017." *Modern China*, (April, 2021). Online first: https://doi.org/10.1177/00977004211003280

Xu, Tian. 2014. "Hunxi heitudi: Zai gemin bowuguan li zhi qingchun." *Zhongguo Xinwen Zhoukan*, 80–83.

Xu, Ye. 2015. "Zhiqing guan niaochao fuzeren huiying Beida jiaoshou zhiyi: Youderen bieyouyongxin." http://news.ifeng.com/a/20150708/44128567_0.shtml.

Xu, Zidong. 2011. *Xu Zidong jianggao: Chongdu wenge*. Beijing: Renmin Wenxue Chubanshe.

Yang, Bin. 2009. "'We want to go home!': The Great Petition of the Zhiqing, Xishangbanna, Yunnan, 1978–1979." *The China Quarterly* 198 (June): 401–21.

Yang, Guobin. 2003. "China's Zhiqing Generation: Nostalgia, Identity, and Cultural Resistance in the 1990s." *Modern China* 29 (3): 267–96.

2016. *The Red Guard Generation and Political Activism in China*. New York: Columbia University Press.

Yang, Haidi. 2011. "Han Shaogong Yang Haidi fangtan lu." http://wxs.hi2net.com/home/blog_read.asp?id=4086&blogid=58089.

Yang, Jian. 2002. *A History of Chinese Educated Youths Literature*. Beijing: Workers' Press.

Yang, Jing. 2009. "Lu Tianming: Wo yuanyi bei chenwei you zerengan de zuojia." *Liaoning Ribao*, March 24, 2009, sec. wenhua zhoukan.

Ye, Weili, and Xiaodong Ma. 2005. *Growing up in the People's Republic: Conversations between Two Daughters of China's Revolution*. 1st ed. Palgrave Studies in Oral History. New York: Palgrave Macmillan.

Ye, Xin. 1999. *Ye Xin tan chuangzuo*. Shanghai: Xuelin Chuban She.

Yi, Haitao. 2018. "Initial Explorations on the Allowance of Shanghai Educated Youth Arrangement at the Xinjiang Production and Construction Corps During 1963–1966." *Contemporary China History Studies* 25 (6): 86–96.

Yin, Hongwei. 2004. "Zhiqing: Meiyou zhongjie de zhongjiezhe – zhuanfang zhiqing zuojia Deng Xian." *Nanfengchuang*, 80–84.

Young, James Edward. 1993. *The Texture of Memory: Holocaust Memorials and Meaning*. New Haven: Yale University Press.

Yu, Jie. 2015. "Laoji, dan juebu gesong – guanyu niaochao zhiqing zhan yu pengyou de duihua." http://zqjy.dbw.cn/system/2015/07/20/000996751.shtml.

Zhang, Everett Y. 2013. "Grieving at Chongqing's Red Guard Graveyard: In the Name of Life Itself." *China Journal* (70): 24–47.

Zhang, Faju. 2014. "Fujian zhiqing hunqianmengying de qingchun xuange." *Dongnan Kuaibao*, April 28, B3.

Zhang, Hong. 2010. "Deng Xian: Cong yuanzui de beifuzhe dao zhiqing yidai de daiyanren." *Zhonghua Dushu Bao*, May 26, p. 7, sec. 7.

Zhang, Kangkang. 1998a. *Dahuang binghe*. Changchun: Jilin Renmin Chubanshe.

———. 1998b. "Wufa fuwei de suiyue." *Wenhui Bao*, April 13, p. 12, sec. Bihui.

Zhang, Qinghua. 1991. "Hunxi heitudi – Beidahuan zhiqing huiguzhan ceji." *Funv Zhiyou*, 6–18.

Zhang, Yiwen. 1998. "Xuzhao minyun de qihedian – houlaizhe tan zhiqing yidai." *Beijing Literature* (6): 33–38.

Zhong, Qiyuan, and Xun Yao. 1997. "Huishou rensheng qingchun wuhui – caifang Xing Yanzi." *Dangshi Wenhui*, 15–17.

Zhong, Xueping, Zheng Wang, and Di Bai, eds. 2001. *Some of Us: Chinese Women Growing Up in the Mao Era*. New Brunswick: Rutgers University Press.

Zhou, Xueguang, and Liren Hou. 1999. "Children of the Cultural Revolution: The State and the Life Course in the People's Republic of China." *American Sociological Review* 64 (1): 12–36.

Zussman, Robert. 2000. "Autobiographical Occasions: Introduction to the Special Issue." *Qualitative Sociology* 23 (1): 5–8.

Index

Ah Cheng, 124, 127, 134
aspirants (habitus), 28, 59, 79, 230
  class of, 89
  double ascending stories of, 60
  double descending stories of, 60
  habitus change of, 79, 89
  idealism of, 114–16, 185
  identification with Xi Jinping, 61
  ideology of, 215, 221–22
  literary works of, 114–17, 128, 154
  as losers, 82
  malleability of, 66
  political awakening of, 67, 70
  political performance of, 53, 82, 89, 99
  send-down program, view of, 60–61, 89, 252
  as winners, 71, 82
Association of Zhiqing Academic Research and Culture, 194–95, 211
  and "people but not the event," 197
  public vs. private views in, 196–98, 200
autobiographical memory, 26, 28, 32, 42, 53, 62, 101, 185, 231, 237, 243
  and class, 46, 62, 128
  and group memory, 234
  and habitus, 109
  and historical evaluation, 28, 99
  and literary works, 104
  and personal experience, 27, 47, 99
autobiographical occasions, 29, 187

Beidahuang, spirit of, 144, 148–51, 164, 172
Big Jungle, The (novel), 121
Big Tree Is Still Small, The (novel), 137
Blood and Iron (autobiography), 114
Bloody Sunset, The (novel), 114, 134
Bourdieu, Pierre, 23, 25, 28–29, 46–48, 97–98, 223, 237, 242

capital, cultural, 47, 87, 99, 138, 227
capital, economic, 47

capital, political, 48
capital, social, 47–48
capital, symbolic, 25–26, 30, 35, 47, 127, 130, 223
"Celestial Bath" (short story), 122
chadui, 9–10, 65, 76, 92, 156, 192
Chairman Mao's children. *See* zhiqing
Chinese Zhiqing Tribe, The (novel), 117
chuanlian ("link-up", "exchanging revolutionary experience"), 201–3, 212
chushen (family class background), 3
  bad, 40–41, 51, 59–60, 90, 209
  black, 28, 50, 71, 111
  middle, 28
  ordinary, 50
  and political performance, 49–51, 110
  red, 11, 28, 50, 59, 61–62, 74, 90, 180
class
  and autobiographical memory, 28
  and capital, 47, 58
  and habitus, 28, 79, 84, 92
  historical specificity of, 28
  and memory, 231, 236
  and personal experience, 47
  and political habitus, 51
  send-down program, view of, 48, 79, 100
  in sociology, 236–37
Class 69 of Middle School (novel), 124
class in the past, 46, 100, 231, 246
class in the present, 47, 53, 231, 246
class, operationalization of, 247–48
class, political, 4, 8, 28, 49–51, 66, 70, 97, 100, 235
collective memory, 23, 242
communicative memory, 23, 176
Confessions of A Red Guard (novel), 110
critical-years hypothesis, 21, 28, 48, 242
cultural production, 27, 32, 104, 146, 224, 237
Cultural Revolution, 5–6, 8, 10, 13, 15, 40, 90, 209

CPSIA information can be obtained
at www.ICGtesting.com
Printed in the USA
LVHW082201091221
705816LV00002B/60